S0-BBV-150

Making Public Policy

MAKING
PUBLIC POLICY

A Hopeful View of
American Government

STEVEN KELMAN

BASIC SERIES IN AMERICAN GOVERNMENT

James Q. Wilson, EDITOR

WITHDRAWN

BASIC BOOKS, INC., PUBLISHERS

NEW YORK

Library of Congress Cataloging-in-Publication Data

Kelman, Steven.
  Making public policy.

  (Basic series in American government)
  References: p. 297
  Includes index.
  1. United States—Politics and government. I. Title.
II. Series.
JK271.K33 1987   320.973   85–73886
ISBN 0–465–04334–8

For Shelley and Jody

It is . . . possible to visualize a kind of social science that would be very different from the one most of us have been practicing: a moral-social science where moral considerations are not repressed or kept apart, but are systematically commingled with analytic argument, without guilt feelings over any lack of integration; where the transition from preaching to proving and back again is performed frequently and with ease; and where moral considerations need no longer be smuggled in surreptitiously, nor expressed unconsciously, but are displayed openly and disarmingly. Such would be, in part, my dream for a "social science for our grandchildren."

—ALBERT O. HIRSCHMAN
"Morality and the Social Sciences"
in *Essays in Trespassing*

CONTENTS

ACKNOWLEDGMENTS

Support for writing this manuscript was provided as part of a grant by the Alfred S. Sloan Foundation to the Kennedy School of Government, Harvard University, for research in issues of public management. Additional support was also provided by the Blum-Kovler Foundation and the Ethel and Philip Klutznick Charitable Trusts.

Many of the ideas expressed in this book have come out of a collaborative enterprise in teaching and researching issues of public policy at the Kennedy School. I want to express particular thanks to my colleagues Mark Moore and Robert Reich for many useful discussions. They read and commented on significant parts of this manuscript, as did Richard E. Neustadt, Jim Verdier, and Kurt and Sylvia Kelman.

The idea for this book was James Q. Wilson's. As editor of a series of books being published by Basic Books, he was an invaluable critic and colleague. His advice, like that of Martin Kessler of Basic Books, made this book a much better one than it otherwise would have been.

Responsibility for factual errors and normative excesses is my own.

—STEVEN KELMAN
Cambridge, Massachusetts

Making Public Policy

1

Introduction

Americans are of two minds about our governmental institutions. Although our democracy has been, and continues to be, a source of pride, there has always coexisted a cynical view that holds politicians to be corrupt and government programs to be mismanaged.

Ever since the founding of the Republic, our pride has been nourished by the vision of America as a democratic experiment in a world just emerging from absolute rule. In the late 1950s, the authors of *The Civic Culture,* Gabriel Almond and Sidney Verba, asked Americans, together with citizens in four other countries, what things about their country were they most proud of.

Eighty-five percent of the American respondents cited some feature of the American government or political tradition—the Constitution, political freedom, democracy, and the like—as compared with 46 percent for the British, 7 percent for the Germans, 3 percent for the Italians, and 30 percent for the Mexicans.[1]

The authors found that features of our political system were far more frequently cited as a source of pride than any other aspect of American society, such as our economic system, religious values, or position in world affairs. And these views persist. In a 1976 survey Americans were asked whether they agreed more with the statement, "I am proud of many things about our form of government" or the one, "I can't find much in our form of government to be proud of." Seventy-six percent of respondents said they were proud of our government.[2]

But a cynical view of government, just like a reverential one, also has deep roots in our history, because people often came to the United States to escape overweening government power. In the late 1800s, Mark Twain quipped about politicians being America's only native criminal class. In the 1930s, when somebody wanted to complain about people working too slowly, the line frequently used was, "What is this, a WPA project?", referring to the Depression-era public works program.

High government positions have traditionally enjoyed great prestige. A study published in 1931 showed that "politician or statesman" ranked as the sixth most-respected occupation among a sample of eighteen-year-old boys, behind doctors, bankers, or ministers, but ahead of college professors, civil engineers, inventors, or businessmen.[3] In 1943 a report on occupational prestige ranked Supreme Court justices, cabinet secretaries, U.S. Senators, and state governors above any other of the listed occupations, including large-city bankers.[4] Measures of support for government institutions increased between the 1930s and the early 1960s. From 1943 to 1965, the proportion of people stating they would like to see their child go into politics as a career increased from 18 percent to 36 percent.[5] Comparing a study they did in Detroit in 1954 with one that had been done in Chicago in 1929, Morris Janowitz and Deil Wright found a marked improvement in the prestige of government employment.[6] A 1960 survey of public attitudes toward high-level appointed federal officials in the executive branch showed an overwhelming predominance of favorable attitudes. On average, respondents rated top federal appointees at about eight, on a scale of one to ten, on characteristics such as honesty, ability, and interest in serving the public.[7]

Since the late 1960s, public attitudes toward government institutions have become more cynical. The percentage of Americans asserting that the government could not be trusted to "do what is right" most of the time increased from 23 percent to 73 percent from 1958 to 1980. This shift ranks among the most dramatic recorded in the history of survey research. The percentage believing "people in Washington waste a lot of money we pay in taxes" increased during the same period from 43 percent to 78 percent.[8]

At the same time the view of government among academics studying the policy-making process grew equally dour. (Let nobody think that academics, off in ivory towers, stand blithely aloof from currents of opinion that swirl around them, any more than other citizens.) School textbooks changed, and even children were affected. Textbooks written in the late 1960s began featuring the "underside" of American history to a much greater extent. One textbook, reports the journalist Frances FitzGerald, "quotes a soldier on the use of torture in the American campaign to pacify the Philippines at the beginning of the century."[9] Comparing a 1962 study of elementary school children with one he did in 1973, F. Christopher Arterton discovered dramatic declines in positive attitudes of children toward governmental institutions. In answer to the question, "Is the president your favorite?" 50 percent of the fifth-grade respondents in 1962 replied that the president was "my favorite of all" or "almost my favorite of all." In 1973 a mere 5 percent of respondents thought so.[10]

This is a book about the policy-making process in the United States. The way this process functions must provide a key to why Americans feel both admiration and distrust for their government. Government goes about the process of making policy in certain ways. That process can be a source of pride or disgust. And out of the policy-making process come substantive government actions (or inactions). These results, too, can encourage or disturb people.

The policy-making process starts with ideas citizens have about actions they want the government to undertake. These ideas are churned around within the processes of government. The result is a set of governmental actions (or inactions) that have effects on people's lives, positive or negative.

The following sequence is a simple roadmap of the policy-making process, comprising a set of stages that starts with proposals and ends with government actions that affect people's lives.

1. *Policy idea:* Policy ideas are the raw material for the policy-making process. A policy idea is a proposal for some change in government action. Policy ideas may be very vague ("the government should set up a job-training program for the unemployed," or "the government should reduce expenditures on food stamps"). These ideas may be more specific about features the program should have ("only the long-term unemployed should be eligible," or "nobody with an income above the poverty line should get food aid").

2. *Political choice:* People with policy ideas seek to achieve commitments from government to put their ideas into practice. When government undertakes such a commitment, it has the authority to do something individuals cannot do: it may legitimately coerce citizens, if necessary, to contribute to the realization of or to act consistently with the commitments it has made. In a democratic society, the price that those with policy ideas must pay for this is to submit their proposals to others for approval. In such a process, it is likely that different participants will disagree about what government should do. Choices are political when (1) they formally commit the authority of government to the achievement of certain actions (or formally reject any such commitment); (2) they are made collectively; and (3) people disagree about what government should do.

A political decision may be made to set up a job-training program, and other political decisions may follow to give the program certain specific features. Political decisions frequently find expression in laws (as when Congress passed the Comprehensive Employment and Training Act of 1973). Bureaucracies may also make political decisions (as when the Department of Labor issues regulations specifying features of local job-training programs eligible for government support), and they may be made by the courts as well (through, for example, a ruling that job-training programs must meet certain affirmative action requirements).

3. *Production:* Once political choices have been made, policies must be carried out; this is generally the responsibility of large government organizations. Production is part of the policy-making process because, just as political choices specify and modify policy ideas, so too does the production process specify and modify political choices that have been made. We might assume that if a question is important, it would be the subject of political controversy and that only minor features of a policy would get established during the production stage. However, many small features of a policy, and sometimes some fairly large ones, get set only when a program is being produced. For a job-training program, for example, these features may include the types of applicants accepted, the nature of the instruction, or the placement efforts after instruction is completed.

4. *Final government actions:* The political and production processes result in a set of government actions. It is these actions that citizens experience, to use Michael Lipsky's phrase, at the "street level."[11] Job-training programs offer training to specific people in specific skills; they offer out-placement services that are excellent or poor; they cost taxpayers a certain number of dollars. Depending on the results of the political and production processes, final government actions may resemble or differ from the concept of the originators of the policy idea.

5. *Real-world outcomes:* The final actions that emerge from earlier stages of the policy-making process are government's last shot at affecting what goes on in the real lives of citizens. However, people's lives are not affected solely by what government does. How well people learn skills in a job-training program depends not only on how those skills are taught but on how individuals react to the instruction. The success of job-training candidates in the labor market will depend partly on employer attitudes and the unemployment rate. The connection between government policies and a set of real-world outcomes is always a

hypothesis by policy makers about the effect of certain actions on those at the receiving end. A rehabilitation policy for prisoners is expected to reduce recidivism. An environmental protection policy may be based on the hypothesis that reductions in air pollution will save lives or reduce illness. Development of a new defense weapons system may be based on the hypothesis that its deterrent effect will lower the possibility of war. Such theories may be correct. Then again, they may be mistaken.

A great deal, therefore, occurs between the development of a policy idea and the outcomes of government's involvement (or noninvolvement) in the lives of people. As we trace the development of policy ideas to the final actions of government, policies develop more specific features than they had when they first began. When we follow the progress of final government actions to their real-world outcomes, still other factors become involved.

Note how the sequence I have described differs from the common division of governmental processes into legislative, executive, and judicial—where Congress "makes" the law, the executive branch "executes" them, and the courts "interpret" them. This common division will not be used in this book because it misleadingly suggests that the political process occurs only in Congress, leaving relatively minor and technical policy-making functions to the other branches of government. In fact, presidents, government agencies, and courts are all involved in politics. Including them all in a discussion of the political process underlines, correctly I believe, the similarities among them rather than the differences.

The distinction between political and production processes may remind us of one of the classic distinctions in public administration between "policy" and "administration." The idea of such a distinction, introduced by scholars such as Frank Goodnow and Woodrow Wilson, was that elected officials should make policy, while the bureaucracy should keep out of the policy-making process and stick to administering policy decisions competently.[12]

In reality, this separation of responsibility is not maintained for two reasons. First, in contemporary societies government agencies are very much involved in making political choices. Second, what occurs during the production process within government organizations greatly affects the content of policy as citizens experience it. This happens partly because important decisions are made after the political shouting has stopped. These range from decisions by police officers about how to handle family quarrels, to decisions by welfare caseworkers about whether to counsel applicants on how to increase their chances of getting benefits, to decisions by government antitrust lawyers about whether to persist with a tough ten-year case against IBM or to request transfer to other work. And production is also part of policy making because organizations are not always capable of doing what they are asked to do. For these reasons, the final government actions that emerge from the production process fill in many gaps and may look quite different from what had been decided politically.

This book is organized around the processes of politics and production. I examine the institutions at the federal level where these processes occur. I also lay out some generic features of these processes that apply, I believe, not only to the policy-making process at the national level in the United States but also to the process anywhere in the Western democratic world. I hope that the discussions both of policy making in specific institutions and of generic features of the process will be useful to people who want to understand better how government works.

This book has a point of view. I undertake to evaluate how well the policy-making process works in the United States. Like any evaluation, mine is based both on normative standards for judgment and empirical observations about how well the system performs according to those standards.

I evaluate the policy-making process against two standards— the ability to produce good public policy and the less tangible effects of the process itself on promoting our dignity as people and molding our character. I argue that for the policy-making process to work well, high levels of public spirit on the part of participants in the process are necessary. By "public spirit," I mean an inclination to make an honest effort to achieve good public policy. This contrasts with the behavior of self-interested participants in the process, who do not ask what policy would be right overall but, rather, simply what policy would be best for themselves. I realize the expression "public spirit" sounds somewhat archaic, and I am using it on purpose to recapture an approach to thinking about the policy-making process that has tragically suffered a precipitous decline in recent decades. (Indeed I toyed with using the expression "civic virtue" for the same reason.)

My conclusion is unfashionable: that public spirit is widespread enough so that the role the government plays in our lives is more worthy of admiration and faith than of dislike and cynicism.

Advocating this view, however, does not relieve me of the responsibility to try to understand what it is about the policy-making process that produces negative emotions. I believe the discussion of how the process actually works can provide clues.

Finally, I also confess a special intention and special hope, perhaps not typical in works of this sort, that this book also provide practical guidance to people who have decided to *participate* in the policy-making process. And, here too, it is my hope that an exposition of how the process works can assist the practitioner in locating pitfalls and potentials.

This book thus mixes description and evaluation. Parts of it will be detached and other parts engaged. That mixture is a perilous enterprise. The German poet Hoelderlin once wrote (in a passage cited by Albert Hirschman):

If you have brains and a heart, show only one or the other, You will not get credit for either should you show both at once.[13]

I ask the reader's indulgence in displaying a willingness to prove Hoelderlin mistaken.

PART I

HOW DOES THE POLICY-MAKING PROCESS WORK?

2

Politics:
A Framework for
Analysis

Political decisions are the collective choices of people who disagree; behind these decisions stands the coercive power of government. Political decisions take place in institutional settings. In the United States federal government the major institutional settings are Congress, the presidency, the bureaucracy, and the federal courts. Each of these institutions is the subject of a chapter of this book. Choices about the design of these institutions establish rules for who may participate in the process and what procedures will be used to make decisions. Into these institutional settings flock citizens who wish to take part in the political process. They have different views about what government should (or should not) do. Some participants are driven by public spirit, others by self-interest. Some are determined advocates of a particular set of views, others are unsure or undecided. Participants in the process have widely varying sorts and degrees of power. Out of this amalgam of institutions and people come the results of the political process. These results include the substantive content of the policies that have been decided. The results of the process also include the consequences of the process itself for us as human beings, for our feelings of dignity, and for our character.

This chapter presents a framework for analyzing the political process. It is organized around the institutions and the people that constitute the process. The chapter is designed to provide some guidance for the chapters that follow on the operation of the political process in Congress, the White House, the bureaucracy, and the courts. It is also designed to provide some guidance for the evaluation of how well the political process works that appears in chapter 11.

The "feel" of this chapter may strike some readers familiar with works of this genre as at least a bit idiosyncratic. I linger to an unusual extent on the question of how choices about institutional design affect the political process. I discuss strategies that participants in the political process use to a degree that will strike some political scientists as vaguely sweaty and unseemly. I take up the question of how issues get on the political agenda toward the end of the chapter, in the context of political strategies, rather than at the beginning of the chapter, where it normally goes in discussions of this sort. And some readers will doubtless experience other idiosyncracies as well. For each of these eccentricities I have an explanation. I cannot exclude, however, sheer orneriness.

Institutions

Institutions are themselves products of choice. Sometimes the choices may constitute fundamental features of our political system. Our political institutions grant all adult citizens the right to vote. Our institutions divide up formal authority among many different parts of the government. Political parties are relatively weak, interest groups have a relatively easy time gaining access to the system, and the staffs of members of Congress and of the president are relatively numerous and strong. Some rules have their origin in the Constitution. The Constitution itself establishes that the president is elected separately from Congress rather than being chosen by the legislature as in a parliamentary system. It allows the president to appoint justices to the Supreme Court and the Senate to reject those selections. Other basic choices about the design of our political institutions are venerable even though they are not laid down in the Constitution. The authority of the Supreme Court to declare laws unconstitutional was established in 1803. Congress began giving significant authority to its committees during the Jeffersonian years. Sometimes features of our institutions are the result of historical evolution rather than conscious choice, as with the relative weakness of our political parties. Other features have grown out of prior choices about institutional design, such as the way Congressional independence in considering legislation has in turn produced powerful committees and their staffs.

Beyond these kinds of fundamental choices are a myriad of small choices, often not nearly grandiose enough to be labeled questions of institutional design, that are made all the time. These range from choices about which committee in Congress gets to consider a bill, to whether agency officials get to argue their cases in the presence of the president.

Rules may be informal as well as formal. Jury members are instructed to examine evidence impartially, but nobody arrests them if they do not. And at some point rules fade into norms. In the Senate of the 1950s it was not written anywhere that freshmen members should not speak on the floor, but few did. Informal lobbying of Supreme Court justices is not forbidden, but it is essentially unknown.

The chapters that follow this one focus significantly on how the decision-making structures of our various political institutions have evolved, constitutionally and otherwise. The skeptic will ask if it is of the slightest import for the policy-making process whether the chief executive is chosen by a popularly elected legislature or by the people directly, whether committees in Congress are strong or weak, whether the White House is large or small, or whether freshmen Senators distinguish themselves by thundering oration or thundering silence. Such skepticism is awakened by dim memories of dreary high-school civics courses, with their mechanical accounts of the separation of powers and how a bill becomes a law. It is nourished by the natural tendency to regard the human drama of politics as vivid and alive—the stuff for Washington novels—while seeing the rules and procedures as musty and drab—material with all the fascination of *Robert's Rules of Order*. The scholar can rationalize a lack of interest in institutional design via contempt for the political science of an earlier epoch, which was preoccupied with elaboration of formal procedures used for decision making in various places and times, while generally devoting only scant effort to the demonstration of what differences institutional choices might make.

If I convey a single message in this chapter, I would like it to be that choices about institutional design do matter, and matter a great deal. They matter for the substantive results of the political process. And they matter for the effects of the political process on us as people. We cannot afford not to be interested in them.

Choices about institutional design have an impact on what substantive policies are selected, first of all, because different rules give relative advantages and disadvantages to different participants in the process. How do choices about institutional design distribute these advantages and disadvantages? They do so first by establishing who is granted formal authority to make political choices. Those with formal authority are empowered to commit the resources of government, including its coercive resources, to some course of action. To be given formal authority to make a decision is quite a prize. Those who lack such authority are reduced to the status of supplicants. And grants of formal authority—decisions that bestow important power upon individuals over the results of the political process—result from choices about institutional design.

The way our institutions have been designed, a majority of the members of the House and Senate has the formal authority, acting together, to pass laws. The president, for example, is not granted even a single vote, although he does have the formal authority to veto legislation of which he does not approve. Statutes frequently grant the assistant secretary of a government agency the formal authority to issue regulations pursuant to a law. A majority of justices on the Supreme Court has the formal authority to declare a law unconstitutional. In our political system, formal authority is frequently shared, so that no decision can be made without approval at all of several clearance points. Congress makes decisions on agency budgets, but agencies may not send budget proposals to Congress until the president has first approved them. The president signs treaties, and appoints Supreme Court justices and assistant secretaries, but these actions must be ratified by the Senate before they can take effect. Bills may generally not be considered by the full Congress before at least one committee has approved them.

The more that formal authority is shared, the harder it is to get a decision made, because more concurrences are needed. If it often seems hard to get political decisions made in our system, this is because our institutions were purposefully designed that way. At the same time, the decentralization of formal authority provides our system with many access points for outside advocates. If one door is closed, other doors are usually available. The more that formal authority is centralized, the harder it is for outsiders to have an impact on the process.

Second, choices about institutional design distribute advantages and disadvantages by determining what procedures must be followed before those with formal authority may make a decision. Government agencies are required to listen to various kinds of input from the public and must answer the major arguments of critics before making decisions. Members of Congress, by contrast, need give no public justification of their votes. The procedures that must be followed before decisions are made can make it easier or harder for those with formal authority to make decisions without taking into consideration the views of others.

Finally, choices about institutional design distribute advantages and disadvantages in influencing the results of the process by establishing whether (and how) people may try to influence those with formal authority. Democratic institutions allow certain forms of participation to every citizen. Every citizen may vote, write a letter to a public official, join a peaceful demonstration, and so forth. Beyond that, though, specific rules establish ways that people may participate in the process. Congress permits individuals and organizations to contribute money to congressional candidates. Congressional committees may seek to influence decisions in the bureaucracy by holding oversight hearings to examine an agency's behavior. To authorize people to vote for their leaders empowers them. Conversely, to prohibit some form of influence can severely limit the ability to affect the results of the process. If it were legal to offer bribes to legislators, the influence of those with money over decisions made in the Congress might dramatically rise. Often, rules for how it is permissible (or impermissible) to influence those with formal authority are informal rather than formal. Such is the case for the influence of congressional staff and the inability of interested parties to lobby Supreme Court justices.

Rules, formal or informal, can also establish the order in which people seek to influence those with formal authority. Why does this matter? Anyone who has ever been asked to comment on the first draft of a speech or on a paper that has been written by somebody else knows that the person who places the initial proposal on the table is likely to have disproportionate influence over what finally emerges. The same is the case for the last person to get a foot in the door. In both cases, this is because it is easier from those positions to emphasize the aspects of an issue that are most favorable to the policy one is promoting.[1]

Decision-making procedures can even influence the agenda of issues to be discussed in the political system. The establishment of a separate budget process in Congress in 1974 made the size of the budget as a whole—and, in the 1980s, the size of the deficit—an issue that would be discussed each year in a way it was harder to do previously. The switch to annual program authorizations in Congress during recent years has provided a recurring opportunity for people interested in a program to bring up proposed changes in the program in ways that were more difficult earlier, when there was no regularly established Congressional forum for doing so.

The advantages and disadvantages that different institutional arrangements confer on the various participants in the political process have an impact on substantive political decisions only when the people who are advantaged by the arrangements have political views that differ from the views of those who are disadvantaged. If there are no systematic differences in political opinions among those whom the institutional arrangements help and those whom they hurt, then institutional design will make no difference. Courts have an important role in civil liberties cases. This makes a difference, because judges as a group have different views on such questions from a cross-section of the public. If judges on the whole had views on civil liberties issues that were identical to those of law enforcement officers, then it would make no difference whether questions about the civil liberties of criminal suspects were left to judges or to police officers. Because they do not, it does. Congressional committees play an important role in the decision-making procedures for passing laws. This can make a difference when members of a committee do not represent a random sample of the membership of Congress. The Constitution allows the Senate, but not the House, to vote on treaties with foreign nations. This can make a difference if the House on the whole is more isolationist than the Senate.

The first important statement about choices on the design of institutions is that they make a difference. The second is that they are not made in heaven. They are themselves the process of choice. The choices could have come out differently, and they may come out differently in the future. As we shall abundantly see in the chapters to come, such choices may vary over time and across countries. The design of American political institutions differs considerably in many respects from the design of similar institutions in many other democratic countries. Our political institutions today look very different from the way they looked fifty—or even twenty—years ago. A law passed in 1921 required government agencies to submit their budget proposals for presidential approval before they could be sent to Congress. Prior to that, such approval was not required, and agencies submitted budgets directly. It was not until an executive order was issued in 1981 that regulatory agencies needed to get approval from the Office of Management and Budget, an organization responsive to the president, before they could begin to develop new regulations. And vague statutes, which grant significant formal authority to the bureaucracy, are largely a product of the twentieth century. Similarly, courts in few other countries are able to declare laws unconstitutional, and legislative committees in few other countries can prevent proposed bills from coming to the floor for a vote of the body as a whole.

Note an implication of the foregoing: if choices about rules make a difference for substantive results, and if those choices are not preordained or cast in stone, then it should not be surprising that one strategy advocates frequently follow is to seek to make the rules as favorable to their views as possible. If one believes, for example, that the current rules for assigning members of Congress to committees leads to a bias in favor of programs under each committee's jurisdiction, this could be changed by altering the rules for committee assignment to, say, random selection. On a much grander scale, the movement in nineteenth-century Europe to extend the suffrage to the working class, and the twentieth-century movements in the United States for voting rights for women and blacks, represent efforts to change the results of the political process by changing the rules for how decisions are made.

The preceding discussion may offend the sense of fairness of many readers. Shouldn't institutions be designed to be fair to everyone and not to give advantages to some and disadvantages to others? That is an appropriate concern. The basic answer is that *any* rules help some and hurt others compared to alternative rules that could have been chosen. Leaving aside the uncertainties about what constitutes fair rules in the first place, we can state that fair rules put at a disadvantage people who would have benefited by unfair ones.

People will disagree about what rules are, indeed, fair. Is it ever fair to allow a minority, for example, to delay or block the views of the majority? Is it fair to allow people to participate in the political process with money or with their time as well as with their votes? Nonetheless, the norm that the design of institutions be fair does influence the terms of debates about institutional design and also puts a brake on the ability of advocates to change decision-making procedures simply to give them advantages in the process.

While existing institutional choices are not cast in stone, there is generally a presumption in their favor. People often focus on the change being sought and assume, perhaps incorrectly, that the procedures in place are neutral. Thus, a frequent reaction to proposals to change procedures is that, having lost out on the issue "fair and square," advocates of change are now trying to manipulate the rules to obtain unfair advantage. The image evoked is of a small boy who loses at marbles and then demands that the rules be changed. Hence, changes in established procedures often require approval by more stringent criteria than do substantive political choices. A body that normally makes decisions by majority vote, for example, might require a two-thirds vote for decisions to change procedures. In some cases, such as institutional features established in the Constitution, an extraordinarily complex process is required to change them.

The argument up to now has been that choices about the design of political institutions affect the substantive results of the political process by distributing advantages and disadvantages to some participants rather than others. Institutional choices also have an impact on the substantive results of the process in a second way. If the design of our institutions promotes public spirit, that may well have an impact on the views that participants in the political process advocate, and hence the content of political decisions.

There are, indeed, ways that our political institutions work to encourage public spirit. There is the elementary fact that political decisions apply to an entire community. That they do so encourages people to think about others when taking a stand. This is in contrast to making personal decisions, when people think mainly of themselves.

Furthermore, our political institutions are democratic. The standard view emphasizes the impact of democratic institutions on the results of the political process through the way they allow a wide range of people to articulate their views and get them considered when decisions are made—in other words, through the impact these institutions have on the distribution of advantages and disadvantages in the political process. I wish, however, to emphasize the impact of democratic institutions on public spirit. When political decisions are made democratically, they require the participation and consent of others. The requirement for cooperation among like-minded individuals to get political demands realized reminds us of the importance of others in achieving our goals. The need to gain the consent of others means that political arguments inevitably must be formulated in terms broader than the self-interest of the individual or the group making the claim, because there is no reason for anyone to support a claim based simply on another's self-interest. When a poor person demands increased welfare payments, or a journalist, freedom of the press, or a farmer, price supports, the claims must become formulated in terms of general ethical arguments about rights, justice, or the public interest, or at least in terms of the interest of some other groups, to stand any chance of being convincing to others.[2]

The difficulty and complexity of getting political choices made has the unintended consequence of promoting public spirit among such full-time participants in the political process as members of Congress, agency officials, or leaders of organized groups. If self-advancement, or the accumulation of money, is the only goal, there are many easier ways to accomplish it in the private sector. This tends to select out the self-interested from work in government—as anyone who observes students in business schools and schools of public policy can attest.[3]

Democratic institutions encourage public spirit in one final way. That we grant every citizen the opportunity to participate in the political process is a powerful statement about the worth and dignity of each citizen, from the highest to the lowliest. And what is the basis of public spirit but the recognition that every person has human worth and hence that public policy decisions require that attention be paid to everyone's situation? Democratic institutions signal to each of us that the circumstances of others deserve to be acknowledged when we make political choices.

To be sure, the force of all this should not be exaggerated. When we present arguments in ethical terms, it does not mean that we genuinely think that way; the presentation may be purely hypocritical. In addition, not all political participants seek to persuade others of their views. Self-interested participants may, for example, cast their votes based on self-interest, never having to defend their actions as long as they do not try to persuade others to follow them.

The specific institutions of government may also be designed to promote public spirit. Think of two alternate ways of determining the guilt or innocence of a criminal defendant—a mass meeting featuring torches and impassioned pleas by criminal victims, or a decision made by twelve people deliberating in private after having been instructed by a robed figure about their solemn obligation to consider all evidence impartially. Or think of the difference between rules that require a government agency or a court to explain its decisions and rules that simply allow decisions to be announced without explanation. Often, the features of an institution that encourage the individual who works within it to be public spirited are matters of norms and of trappings, rather than formal rules. For example, the president lives and works in a White House filled with inspiring portraits of illustrious predecessors and of heroic moments in the history of the Republic.

Formal authority to make decisions tends to promote public spirit. When we talk about people growing in office—or about the transformation that occurs when a person who has been a lawyer becomes a judge—we are acknowledging the impact of the grant of formal authority on individual behavior. In particular, people with formal authority are expected to be more open to persuasion and to the possibility of changing their minds than advocates who do not themselves have formal authority to make decisions. One way, then, to increase public spirit and open-mindedness is to expand the circle of people sharing formal decision-making authority.

Participants: Deciding What Policy to Support

As noted earlier, political processes involve both institutions and the people participating in them. The people who take part in the process affect its substantive results in several ways. First, they have different views about what the government should do. The range and distribution of those views are crucial in determining the results of the process. Second, those involved in the political process have power resources available to attempt to affect decisions. Third, participants employ various strategies to increase their chances of favorable decisions. This section considers how people develop their policy views; the next two sections examine power and political strategies.

How does a person decide what position to take on a policy issue when any stand has bad as well as good features? Developing a new missile system may decrease the chances of Soviet aggression, but it costs a lot of money. Tightening fraud detection of welfare recipients may keep some dishonest people off the relief rolls, but it also may prevent some eligible ones from receiving aid. What is so exasperating is that such tradeoffs are *necessarily* the case. Any policy uses up resources. Usually these resources include money and effort; at a minimum, they include time. When time is spent on one endeavor, it is necessarily unavailable for another. Thus, any policy, even if it seems to have only good features, has at a minimum one bad feature: it makes it impossible to use the time spent on it for some other attractive venture. Hence we can never get all we want.

The model of *rational maximization* provides one account of how people make decisions when faced with choices that have bad as well as good features. The process of rational maximization involves a conscious acceptance of, and a willingness to make tradeoffs among, different values by calculating the empirical consequences of the various alternatives in terms of one's different values and selecting the alternative that achieves the greatest net attainment of those values. One choice is made over another because that choice provides us with more than any other choice, even though it means giving up some things we like.[4]

How would rational maximization determine what policy alternative to support? Let us suppose there are various alternative levels of protection a proposed environmental regulation could mandate. Assume that alternatives vary in how many lives they will save, the good feature of the alternatives, and in how much they cost, the bad feature. Rational maximizers would determine how much they valued saving a life and how much they wanted to avoid spending money. They would calculate the consequences of the different policy alternatives in terms of numbers of lives saved and of cost. Finally, they would support the policy alternative that maximized the net sum of attainment of their values. This would likely be neither the alternative that saves the largest possible number of lives—

because its cost in dollars would be too great—nor the one that cost the least money—because its cost in lives would be too large.

The theory of rational maximization has been subjected to considerable attack as a description of how individuals actually make choices. Some criticisms have centered on the information requirements for rational choice; critics have noted the impossible burden of determining the consequences of numerous alternative policies and of establishing the precise weight of each of the values at stake. Another line of criticism is psychological. Not only is it *difficult* to make tradeoffs among values, it can also be extremely *unpleasant* to do so. Linus, in the *Peanuts* comic strip, expresses the trauma that can accompany a difficult choice when he opines, "No problem is so big or so complicated that it cannot be run away from." Determining how many apples we are willing to sacrifice for an orange is an amusing parlor exercise. Answering for ourselves how many lives we are willing to sacrifice to save some dollars is a nightmare.[5]

A more realistic view is that most participants in the political process do not look at the consequences of various alternative policies in light of a large number of values. Instead, most people evaluate different policy alternatives in light of only *one* value (or a very small number). Doing so allows people to avoid difficult calculations and painful tradeoffs. Whatever policy alternative looks best in light of that one value will be the policy alternative they support.

If this is the case—and there is a good deal of psychological evidence that it frequently is—then the crucial battle for individuals' political allegiance will occur over the question of which among the many values that people *could* consider when they think about a policy issue they *will* in fact consider. Which policy alternative people favor will depend, to use Richard Neustadt's evocative description, on which "face of the issue" they see when they choose what policy alternative to support.

The basic insight here is simple, but powerful. Say that environmental regulation has implications in terms of two values, saving lives and spending money. When individuals choose what stand to take on an environmental issue, if they are thinking about emphysema and lung cancer, they will favor strict regulation. If, instead, they are thinking about dollars, they will oppose strict regulation. People's minds can therefore be up for grabs. This means that their views are up for grabs. That implies in turn that the results of the political process are up for grabs.

To be sure, there are participants in the political process who consider more than one aspect of an issue. This is particularly the case among those charged with formal authority for making decisions. Some participants even act more or less according to the rational maximization mode. (Not infrequently, they are people who have studied it in graduate programs in economics or public policy and who work in organizational units, such as divisions for policy analysis, whose job it is to think this way.) Nonetheless, most people do considerably simplify making political choices by looking at only one face of a policy issue. Grasping this fact is crucial to understanding what determines the views of participants in the political process.

The tendency to see only one face of an issue can operate on people who are self-interested, public spirited, or anything in between. Self-interested participants in the political process need evaluate policy alternatives only in light of what will help them most personally, ignoring any other possible bad features of policies. We might think that public-spirited individuals always try conscientiously to see the many considerations at stake in choosing a policy, but one need not have a Ph.D. in public policy to display public spirit. People motivated by public spirit frequently use the same techniques to simplify the process of making political choice as other participants do.

Much political debate and rhetoric represent efforts by advocates to persuade people to fix on the face of the issue favorable to the policy the advocate supports. Thus, advocates of budget cuts for social welfare programs talk about how the high taxes to support such programs shackle the nation's productive capability. Opponents focus on the sufferings of the unfortunate. Advocates of strict environmental regulations address the horrors of pollution. Critics bemoan the burdens regulation imposes. Advocates may try to get people to fix on a certain value itself—the value of life, for example—or on facts that act in support of the value—the number of people who might die if a certain chemical is not regulated.

It is noteworthy how infrequently political advocacy addresses tradeoffs among conflicting values. Left to their own devices most advocates would probably avoid talking about conflicting values at stake. Political consultants generally encourage advocates to present their own case rather than to spend much time answering the arguments of others. Advocates want people to believe that the policy alternative they support has no bad features, or at least that the bad features are dramatically exaggerated by the other side. Thus, advocates of budget cuts for social welfare programs deny that these cuts will hurt the disadvantaged: they argue that the "truly needy" will still be protected or that welfare hurts the poor in the long run by making them dependent. Advocates seldom argue something like, "I realize that the proposed budget cuts will hurt the poor, but I think they are necessary to save the economy."

Sometimes, the face of an issue that people see is set in stone. In particular, it might be hard to budge those who decide what policy to support simply on the basis of self-interest, unless they can be persuaded that a certain policy is actually in their self-interest in ways they did not suspect. For example, advocates of ending government farm price supports might try to persuade farmers that they will actually fare better without such supports.

Often, though, the face of the issue that people see—and hence the policy alternative they support—is up for grabs. This may be the case especially for those with formal authority to make decisions, because there is a norm that they listen to the arguments before deciding.

Much of political debate and deliberation concerns a battle for preferences that are not fixed in advance in people's minds. Political debate and discussion are about *influencing* values. By contrast, the problem economics addresses is how people can obtain as much satisfaction as possible, *given* certain fixed preferences. This is one reason economists have difficulty understanding the political process: for example, in Anthony Downs's "economic theory of democracy," the only role of political leadership is to give people information about how the consequences of certain policies will best help them attain the set of fixed values that they already hold.[6]

When people's views are up for grabs, the face of the issue that they come to see depends in significant measure on the persuasive skill of advocates. Rhetorical skill is important in politics because dramatic images and arresting anecdotes can influence the way people focus on an issue. President Reagan has demonstrated this ability very often. One of the reasons the media are so influential in politics is that newspaper stories, and especially pictures, can do the same thing. Newspaper exposés about $400 hammers threaten defense budgets because they get people to stop thinking about Soviet aggression. Film footage of Ethiopian children with distended bellies sets famine relief campaigns in motion.

Events also influence the face of an issue people perceive. It is no coincidence that mine safety legislation is frequently passed right after a mining disaster or that defense budgets increase after an incident of Soviet military aggression. When there are dead miners, people are unlikely to think about what safety regulations might cost down the road.

The factors influencing how an issue is perceived might appear to exist quite independently of how the institutions of government are designed. In fact, though, decisions about institutional design do affect the ability to influence the way people see an issue and hence the relative level of support for different policy alternatives.

Decisions about institutional design affect the ability of

participants to present their cases. The institutional evolution of the presidency into the focal point of the American political system, for example, has enhanced the ability of the president to use the office as a "bully pulpit" from which to seek to influence the public: the president can get attention whenever he chooses to do so. Institutional arrangements that allow certain participants to write the first draft or to be the last in the door increase the influence that those participants have over the political process by increasing their ability to impart an attractive face to the issue at hand. John Steinbruner's account of the choices made by President Kennedy regarding allied defense posture vis-à-vis the Soviet Union shows the president paradoxically making decisions at different times that reflected conflicting, inconsistent approaches to the issue. A closer examination indicates that when the procedures allowed State Department advocates to write the first draft or to be the last ones in the door (as when the president was to speak to a foreign parliament), presidential decisions reflected the views of State Department advocates. When the procedures gave the same advantage to Defense Department advocates (as with a speech to defense ministers), decisions favored them.[7] In his memoirs, Jimmy Carter expressed surprise at the different stands that President Giscard d'Estaing of France took on the 1979 Soviet invasion of Afghanistan. He wrote in his diary:

They've had at least five different public positions: first saying that this was no threat to Western Europe; then a . . . public statement by Valery condemning the Soviets and saying this was a threat to detente; then Giscard's visit to India, where he issued a noncommittal statement with Mrs. Gandhi; then his meeting with Helmut [Schmidt] and a very strong communique they issued.[8]

Had President Carter realized the impact that different settings can have on the ability to affect the face of the issue people see, and hence to influence political choices, he would not have had to be so surprised.

Participants: Power

To have political power is to have the ability to affect the content of political choices, to change the course of government decisions from what it otherwise would have been.[9] Political power can include the power, as theorists of "nondecisions" have reminded us, to block decisions or even to prevent discussion of issues. It is also alleged, although this is a far more debatable proposition, that power can somehow be exerted successfully to discourage consideration of policy alternatives, such as the proposition that industry should be nationalized or the income tax should be abolished.[10]

When the analysis turns to political power, outside observers of the political process often think that they have "finally" come to what the political process is all about. "Clout" is the stuff of political journalism and of Washington novels. People who style themselves "political junkies" typically pursue the latest on who is powerful and who is not. Yet the Washington journalist's or the political junkie's approach to the role of power in the political process is confused and misleading on several counts. First, it tends to obscure the substantive issues over which politics is fought, focusing attention on the game itself to the exclusion of what the game is about. Second, it tends to exaggerate the importance of the crudest resources, such as money or threats, compared with other, more subtle resources. Third, it suggests that power is something that advocates import into the political process from the society outside, rather than being, as it in fact so frequently is, the result of institutional choices made within the political system itself.

People are able to exert power because they have various resources at their disposal. The following resources serve as sources of power:

1. formal authority to make decisions
2. contingent inducements to influence other participants

    3. persuasiveness
    4. deference from other participants
    5. strategic skills

First, the formal authority to make decisions is obviously a crucial resource. As noted earlier, decisions about formal authority are decisions of institutional design, made within the political system itself, and thus serve as examples of political power that originates within the system itself rather than simply being imported into the political system from the larger society. Decisions about institutional design create power.

A second resource is the ability to offer inducements—to say, "If you follow my views on this issue, I will give you . . ." or, "If you don't follow my views, I will take away from you . . ."). Inducements may be classified along two dimensions: (1) as normative, economic, or coercive and (2) as reward or punishment. Normative inducements are those involving "esteem, prestige, and ritualistic symbols" and "acceptance and positive response." Economic inducements involve material goods. Coercive inducements involve "infliction of pain, deformity or death" and "restriction of movement."[11]

Typically, people lacking formal authority offer inducements to those who have it. Interest groups give campaign contributions to legislators, not the other way around. When a group shares formal authority, such as in Congress, those sharing formal authority may seek to offer inducements to each other. Frequently, in such circumstances, the inducement is to furnish support on some other decision in exchange for support on the decision at hand: "I'll vote with you on budget cuts for Amtrak if you vote with me on keeping the budget for children's nutrition." Colleagues sharing formal authority can also grant or withhold praise and regard from each other.

The person being induced is the one who decides whether an inducement is worth enough to bring about a change in behavior. A man not afraid to die will be unresponsive to another who threatens to kill him unless he behaves a certain way. R. H.

Tawney captured this point when he wrote that the power of those controlling a large stock of inducements is "both awful and fragile, and can dominate a continent, only in the end to be blown down by a whisper. To destroy it, nothing more is required than to be indifferent to its threats, and to prefer other goods to those which it promises."[12]

The size or weight of an inducement obviously has an impact on its effectiveness. If 50,000 angry voters threaten to abandon a congressman if he votes a certain way, it is likely to have more impact than if 50 do so; a scathing attack by the pope means more than one by Lyndon LaRouche. This is why it makes sense to organize interest groups, which can pool individual resources and offer them as a large lump sum. Inducements, ranging from campaign contributions to direct organization of voters, are thus a stock-in-trade of organized groups.

Because popular accounts concentrate so heavily on the cruder coin of muscle and money, it is important to emphasize the importance of normative inducements in the political process. Most people care what others think of them; few are indifferent to being shunned or despised. The scarlet letter was a terrible punishment, and an Olympic medal is worth far more than the gold on which it is stamped. People who go into public life have chosen to work in an arena where they are visible to others, and it is frequently suggested that people in public life choose to do so because the regard and esteem of others is particularly important to them.

The importance of normative inducements in politics is illustrated perhaps most dramatically by the power of the media. In the whole well-worn debate within political science over power in American society, the media are hardly mentioned. Yet a 1976 survey of American leadership groups shows that virtually every group surveyed regarded the media as the *most powerful* actor in the political process, more influential either than business or labor.[13] This is amazing, because the resources the media have at their disposal are almost exclusively normative ones: they can hand out roses for good behavior and brickbats for bad. The perceived power of the media is an indication of the importance of normative inducements in politics.

Decisions about the design of political institutions affect the ability to use various inducements and the impact that different inducements will have on those they are intended to affect. Laws about campaign financing or bribery affect the extent to which advocates may employ monetary inducements. A congressional rule that makes committee chairmanships a function of seniority reduces the inducements available to congressional leadership, or to the membership of Congress as a whole, to influence committee chairmen. More broadly, the more that our decision-making institutions are designed to be open rather than secret, the easier it is to influence the behavior of those with formal authority through inducements, because it is easier to determine what their behavior was and hence whether it deserves reward or punishment. This can apply to whether a member of Congress voted the right way on a particular bill. It can also apply to conformance to general political norms such as public spirit.

Informal norms are crucial here as well. The expectation that people should use substantive arguments and not simply offer contingent inducements unrelated to the substance makes it more difficult to use such inducements. The pejorative usage of the word "politics" refers to the norm against attempts at influence based on inducements rather than persuasion. "He made a political decision, not one based on the merits" is an invidious statement that has an impact on the ability to exercise power through using inducements. Hence lobbyists seldom go to a congressman and say, "Vote with me on this bill or you won't get any campaign contributions." Lobbyists generally start off by presenting a substantive argument. Talk of inducements, if it is at all explicit, generally comes somewhat later in the process, and may even be introduced with some embarrassment.

A third resource that participants can use is persuasiveness. Perhaps the most unfortunate product of the Washington journalist's perspective on power is that persuasiveness is the most underrated resource in politics. Political scientists hesitated to acknowledge the importance of persuasiveness until Richard Neustadt, in 1960, announced in *Presidential Power* that "presidential power is the power to persuade."[14] Yet even lobbyists, generally seen as masters of "pressure," testify to the importance of persuasiveness. A survey of representatives of a diverse set of organized groups in Washington, conducted by Kay Schlozman and John Tierney, showed that organizational representatives saw "a reputation for being credible and trustworthy" as by far the most important resource at their disposal. By contrast, "a large budget" was rated, by far, the least important resource.[15] "Lobbyists are unequivocal," writes Jeffrey Berry in a book on interest groups, "about what makes for effective 'messages'—the more factual the better. In memos, handouts, reports, formal comments on regulations, and in conversations, the only content that counts is the specific fact."[16]

Repeated success at exerting influence through persuasiveness or through using inducements shades gradually over to a fourth resource, deference. Somebody who defers to another changes behavior without any need for persuasiveness in the individual instance or for any actual offer of inducements. A congressman who takes cues from a trusted committee member does not require persuasion on each issue. Somebody may listen to a "recognized expert" on weapons systems without demanding that the expert persuade him on a particular weapons system.

The fifth resource of power is strategic skills. The ability to develop skillful political strategies clearly affects the capacity to achieve political choices more in line with an advocate's views. Political strategies and their role in the political process are discussed separately in the next section of this chapter.

It is important to keep in mind when thinking about political power that professional political participants do not simply take part in one political decision and then vanish. Elected officials, public managers, and interest group representatives participate constantly in the process. Therefore, individual political decisions should not be regarded as discrete, unconnected events. What underlies logrolling is that people who share power may agree to make a trade whereby one participant uses his or her power to support another on one issue in exchange for a similar commitment by the other participant on a different issue. That requires some ongoing political life. Furthermore, people develop reputations over time: their persuasiveness and their ability to use normative inducements depend on how they are perceived by others. A good reputation increases their power in future situations. Success (and failure as well) builds upon itself. A person who is initially relatively powerless can gradually build up power through a succession of victories.

A fascinating element of the phenomenon of power is what Sidney Verba and Garry Orren have dubbed "power denial."[17] Verba and Orren asked members of different leadership groups in the United States to rate the power of their own and of several other groups. They found that business leaders rated their own power as less than that of organized labor, whereas labor leaders rated the power of business as greater than its own.

Power denial is visible in a wide variety of contexts. We tend to see the Soviets as "ten feet tall" while deprecating our own strength. The Soviets apparently have the opposite perception. In the late 1960s student protesters against the war in Vietnam regarded themselves as powerless outcasts unable to influence the Establishment. At the same time, we now know from histories of the Nixon presidency, the president of the United States was obsessed by the danger the protesters posed to his ability to conduct foreign policy.

One explanation for power denial might be false modesty or even the conscious decision to be coy about the immense power one knows one really has. Such an interpretation would be a mistake. I am convinced that power denial is not only genuine but constantly present in politics. The interesting question is why it occurs so pervasively. My own view is that it reflects the fact that virtually everyone in politics loses frequently, and that people tend to remember their defeats more vividly than their victories. Furthermore, because people know more about their own situation, and that of their allies, than they do about others, they are more likely to recognize their own flaws as well as their strengths. There is, finally, a tendency to attribute defeats to the superior power of one's opponents, rather than to see the role that bad luck or simple inertia often plays.

While those with power use certain resources for its maintenance, are there other resources available to relatively powerless participants in the political process? Because they often deal with only one issue, the relatively powerless have "time on their hands." They can singlemindedly devote themselves to that issue, while the powerful, by contrast, have less time to spend on each matter.

Persuasiveness, broadly understood, is also available to the powerless. "When all else fails, try the substance," expresses in a cynical way the insight that powerless people may have little going for them but the substance of their ideas. Furthermore, there is probably less inequality in the distribution of substantive knowledge about policy issues than in the distribution of resources such as money: individuals can hang up a shingle in Washington and come to be accepted as participants in political debates over a policy issue if they succeed in generating research and arguments relevant to that issue.

Finally, the media are a resource for the powerless. Because journalists frequently regard themselves as representatives of the unrepresented and unorganized, one's very powerlessness can increase the ability to garner media attention.

Participants: Strategies

A political strategy is a plan to maximize one's chances of success, given a set of institutional arrangements and resources. People differ dramatically in their strategic skills, and such differences are an important source of differences in the power

they have. Any account of the political successes of President
Reagan during the early months of his presidency that fails to
mention the administration's strategic flair will simply miss an
important part of what was going on. Reagan was smart enough
to take immediate advantage of events (the economic disarray
and his own electoral margin) with a specific program of actions
he wanted adopted, and to concentrate his energies in a few
areas (budget and tax changes) rather than dissipating them
over a large agenda. He made use of a new decision-making
procedure that was favorable to the results he wanted—the new
binding "reconciliation" process for congressional budgeting,
which allowed numerous spending reduction directives based
on a single congressional vote. He knew how to present a face
to the issue that was most favorable to his views—the idea that
the country would collapse economically if his changes were
not adopted. His success is evidence that the greater the political achievement, the more important a role strategic skill generally plays in bringing it about.

The earlier discussion in this chapter suggests a number of
strategies that skillful advocates can follow. Thus, advocates
who see that the decision-making procedure is unfavorable to
their cause can attempt to change the rules to make them more
favorable. Advocates who realize that they are unlikely to
be successful as long as most participants in the process
see a certain face of the issue can work toward changing that
perception.

Advocates need to develop an ability to move issues onto the
political agenda and then to be ready when an issue's time
becomes ripe. The question of how, from among all the social
facts around us, a certain small sample become subjects for
public political attention, is both fascinating intellectually and
crucial to a political advocate. If an issue cannot get on the
political agenda, it certainly will be lost.

For a social fact to have any prospect of making it onto the
political agenda, it must generally involve an unsatisfactory
state of affairs affecting a significant number of people, about
which a case can be made that a change in government will

improve things. Typically a long period of incubation precedes an issue's ripeness.[18] During this time, advocates frequently try to soften up the system, presenting their ideas in whatever forums are available, ranging from academic conferences to congressional hearings. Partly, this allows testing and modification of the ideas in the light of suggestions and criticism. Partly, this allows application of what I have called the "diminishing astonishment principle," according to which an idea that initially appears outlandish comes to seem less so simply by virtue of repetition.[19]

Much of what happens during the incubation period takes place in what John Kingdon calls "the policy stream," the professional community inside and outside government who make it their business to think seriously about policy problems in a substantive area. Out of debates in the policy stream can gradually emerge "solutions waiting for problems to be attached to." These are policy ideas that many people within the policy stream consider to be good ones, but which do not have any particular substantive urgency or political momentum behind them. Years of discussion and a host of academic publications during the 1960s and early 1970s created a near-consensus among academic students of transportation policy that the price regulation of airlines and trucking increased prices to consumers. During the 1970s the view spread among economists that existing tax and welfare policies hindered economic growth. But little happened with these issues immediately.

For an issue to ripen some sort of precipitating event must usually occur. Often such events occur in what Kingdon calls "the problem stream." Advocates work to attach preexisting solutions to newly perceived problems. Issues have good potential for moving onto the political agenda when there are signs that a problem is getting worse—either because of the deterioration of some statistical indicator (the number of homeless people, the unemployment rate, or medical care costs) or because of some crisis, real or perceived. Problems focus the attention of many people on a certain face of an issue.

There are countless examples, some quite dramatic, of the

ability of events to provide opportunities for those seeking new policies. The Depression of the 1930s permitted a dramatic expansion of the role of government in the economy and in taking responsibility for the poor, policies that some had been advocating unsuccessfully for decades. After having failed to get anywhere for years, a voting rights bill was passed in a matter of weeks after violence occurred in Selma, Alabama, against peaceful black demonstrators.

The precipitating event may also take place in the political sphere. Public opinion about an issue may change, providing an opportunity for advocates. When a new president is elected, or when the president is to deliver a State of the Union message, advocates will seek to take advantage of those political events to get their issues onto the agenda. The same may occur when the chairmanship of a congressional committee, the composition of the Supreme Court, or the head of an agency changes. Advocates may also use regularly occurring political events such as the annual budget cycle, statutory reauthorization in Congress, or election campaigns as events that provide opportunities to get issues on the agenda.

There are a number of lessons here for political strategy. Events may simply be seen as lucky breaks, and success in the aftermath of such events a bit of luck that has blown one's way. That is an incomplete account. The existence of problems may be hidden in some arcane collection of data or in poorly reported stories that advocates often need to dig out. The fact that traffic fatalities and occupational accidents were increasing in the 1960s would probably have gone unnoticed had not advocates of auto and occupational safety legislation highlighted these facts and used them as an argument for legislation. Furthermore, it requires skill to attach a particular issue to a generally perceived problem. Advocates of airline and trucking deregulation, after laboring in obscurity for decades, succeeded in getting their issue on the agenda by presenting it as a solution for national concerns with inflation and with big government. Finally, a skillful advocate can convince people that a crisis exists. Most people agreed that the American economy was in serious shape when President Reagan took office in 1981. But his budget director, David Stockman, attempted to make people see the situation as an immediate crisis by foreseeing an "economic Dunkirk" of industrial collapse and hyperinflation unless dramatic budget cuts were instituted immediately.[20]

Favorable events provide an opportunity, but the opportunity is only a window. Good political advocates are brokers of problems with solutions; their role is matchmaking. Advocates must be prepared for events. Good advocates will act quickly and seize the moment by having proposals to present. Thus, gun control advocates quickly emerge after political assassinations with specific proposals for restricting access to guns. Bureaucrats in the Civil Rights Division of the Department of Justice had over a long period of time developed proposals for legislative reforms to make the right to vote for blacks in the South a reality. Thus, after the violence at Selma, they were quickly able to develop new legislation while the level of indignation was high. As soon as it was revealed that General Motors was investigating his personal life, Ralph Nader took advantage of GM's embarrassment by flooding the media with a series of other accusations about the safety of other products. Success may appear to be a matter of simply riding a lucky break. But, like many feats, in fact it's harder than it looks. It is a matter of skillful strategy.

The previous work in the policy stream is important because it allows advocates to be ready with solutions as soon as a problem strikes. If a specific idea is not quickly available, the window may close. With things back to normal, the advocate is back at the beginning.

The ability to devise ingenious strategies is a resource available to relatively powerless as well as powerful participants in the political process. With time on their hands, the powerless can develop strategies and persistently keep trying if their first strategy fails. The reader of *The Dance of Legislation,* Eric Redman's youthfully enthusiastic account of how he, as a twenty-one-year-old temporary staff assistant to Senator Warren Magnuson, succeeded in shepherding through Congress a bill for sending Public Health Service doctors to serve in medically underserved parts of the country, cannot fail but be impressed by Redman's persistence. Like a rat exploring a maze or an indefatigable door-to-door salesman, Redman simply kept on looking for alternative paths whenever he bumped against a brick wall.[21] Strategic skill as a resource serves to equalize the impact of differences in other kinds of resources. Indeed, 900-pound gorillas don't need strategies. They can frequently get their way through less subtle means.

Just as choices about institutional design influence the ability to use other resources in the political process, so too do they influence the ability to use different kinds of strategies. Rules may make it harder or easier to succeed at a strategy of changing decision-making procedures to increase the chances of getting favorable results. Norms are important as well. Just as norms about politics inhibit the use of inducements in the process, so do norms about manipulation inhibit excessive strategic cleverness. At the same time, the way our system has been designed to make action difficult by spreading formal authority encourages the development of "policy entrepreneurs" who, like entrepreneurs in a hard marketplace, must be strategically skilled if they ever are to succeed.

Combining the Pieces Into Political Choice

The dominant image of the political process presented in this chapter is one of jousting among advocates. We should, however, keep in mind another image as well, partly because it is normatively attractive and partly because it in fact describes something of how the process actually works that is missed by the imagery of jousting. The image is one of deliberation where all participants, advocates as well as the undecided, are open to possibilities for political learning and of—actually!—changing their minds. This image is normatively appealing because if political choices are about what ideas make the most sense for public policy, then it seems natural to conclude that the issue is less who has a larger stock of inducements at his disposal than who has better ideas. Additionally, though, jousting imagery may be incomplete as a description of the process. Anyone who has, for example, observed liberals in recent years adapting their views of what government programs are appropriate or of the importance of economic growth can hardly help but believe that people, including advocates, *can* change over time, that learning does take place in the political process. When politics is conceived as deliberation more than confrontation, we are led to regard those with different views less as obstacles in our way and more as resources in a common problem-solving venture.

The design of political institutions can make it easier or harder for the participants in the process to learn from each other. When political institutions are designed to encourage people to talk with each other—as opposed to talking *at* each other or, worse, not talking at all—greater political learning is likely to occur.

Every political encounter is different. The political world involves human beings whose behavior is very imperfectly predictable and rules that are indeterminate enough to leave lots of wiggle room. It involves ideas about right and wrong in a world where the discernment of ethical truth is a difficult and frustrating task. This makes politics a human drama, and a drama of the clash of ideas. These are the sources of its fascination.

3

Institutional Settings for Politics: Congress

"Congress," begins Randall Ripley's textbook on the subject, "is at the heart of public policy-making."[1] This statement is not a trivial one. Indeed, it cannot be made about the legislatures of even most democratic countries. In parliamentary systems the legislature ostensibly reigns supreme, because the prime minister is dependent on support from a parliamentary majority to remain in office. But in parliamentary systems with high levels of party discipline, a dynamic occurs to eradicate the apparent supremacy of parliaments. The prime minister and cabinet, selected by parliament, become representatives and leaders of the parliamentary majority. Having been elected by a parliamentary majority, prime ministers are then assured a legislative majority for proposals they present. Prime minister and cabinet take responsibility for developing policy proposals and use the prodigious resources of government ministries to do so. Parliament becomes a rubber stamp. Its functions become reduced to certifying election results by choosing the prime minister—something like an electoral college—and to serving as a forum for public debate between government and opposition.[2] Parliamentary power increases as fewer votes are made into votes of confidence, over which a government can fail. When a vote is not a vote of confidence, individual members of parliament have greater room to vote independently without threatening the continuation of "their" government. The parliamentary system in Germany works somewhat along these lines.[3]

The paradox of congressional power in the United States is that appearances might suggest that Congress should have less power than a parliament, for it does not participate in choosing the head of the executive branch. Instead, our institutions have been designed to divide up formal authority, with the president elected separately from Congress. Moreover, the Constitution proscribes legislators from holding positions in the executive branch—officials of the president's cabinet, for example, may not be members of Congress while they serve in the cabinet. This inhibits the development of informal ties between the two branches.[4]

Congress does not gain the apparent ascendency over the executive that comes from selecting its head. But it keeps the real power that comes from uncertainty about whether it will pass legislation. When the president belongs to one party and the congressional majority to the other, the automatic approval common in parliamentary countries would be impossible even if there were high party discipline in Congress. Even when the president and the congressional majority are of the same party, the imperfection of party discipline in Congress still rules out automatic majorities.

There have been surges and declines in the relative strength of the president and Congress during American history. The power of the presidency grew from the 1930s through the 1960s. Congress reasserted itself during the 1970s. As in European parliamentary systems, much of our legislation is now prepared within the executive branch and introduced by the president. But, if the president proposes, Congress, to cite an oft-repeated adage, still disposes.

Many features of the political process in Congress flow from these basic elements of institutional design. These include most prominently the decentralization of power *within* Congress and the immense time pressures on members.

Consequences of Institutional Design: Decentralization of Power

Power in Congress must become decentralized if Congress is to give genuine consideration to legislation and not simply rubber-stamp proposals emanating from elsewhere. To be able genuinely to deliberate, Congress needs to develop expertise about the issues involved in proposals that come before it. Members, however, can hardly be experts on everything; they must specialize. As Adam Smith was perhaps the first to note, specialization increases the productivity with which complex tasks are performed. Hence the decentralization of congressional power to committees. Committees allow individuals to divide up the task of considering legislation and to have each member specialize in a few policy areas.

Committees began to become important during the Jeffersonian years of the new Republic as Congress, following Jeffersonian doctrine, refused to rely on the executive for preparing legislation.[5] The idea for legislative committees actually came from the British Parliament, but in England committees atrophied with the growth of cabinet government.[6]

Once committees have been established to allow more expert consideration of proposals, it is easy to see why Congress will show a reasonable degree of deference toward committee decisions. If you don't want to listen to experts, don't consult them in the first place. Hence the congressional rules that make it hard for the body as a whole even to consider a bill unless it has first been voted out by the committee to which it has been assigned. Hence the proclivity of most members, most of the time, to support committee bills that come to the floor, especially if there has been considerable agreement on the bill within committee. These two facts are the basis of committee power.

In a system where committees are important, the procedures by which committees function are themselves important. During the period, before 1910, of strong leadership within Congress, the most senior member of a committee was selected chairman only about half the time.[7] Seniority became entrenched for selection of committee chairmen only after the revolt against "Czar rule" in 1910. Since it operated automatically and took discretion away from the leaders of Congress, the seniority system reduced the power of congressional leaders over members. Indeed, where chairmanships are based strictly on seniority, outsiders of all stripes (lobbyists as well as leaders of Congress) are less able to influence the behavior of chairmen, since chairmen owe their appointments not to any leader but simply to the impersonal passage of time. Since the 1970s there has been a move away from automatic reliance on seniority, dramatized by occasional, albeit still unusual, instances of junior members being elected as chairmen over more senior colleagues. This increases the ability of others to influence the behavior of committee chairmen.[8]

In a world where committees are powerful, not only are the procedures for selecting committee chairmen important, so are the procedures for selecting people to serve as committee members. The crucial point here is that members themselves have considerable, though certainly not unlimited, ability to control their own committee assignments. Generally, members get on the Agriculture or Public Works or Interstate Commerce committees because they request to be on them. This means that committee membership risks being unrepresentative of the body as a whole, attracting people who are unusually interested in the programs under the committee's jurisdiction. Most often this means unusually supportive, although it can also mean unusually opposed. Self-selection applies less to the more important committees such as Ways and Means (Finance in the Senate) or Budget. There, members must often campaign for slots.

If committees are crucial in determining the fate of legislation, then the selection of which committee will consider a bill can also determine its fate. Take legislation regarding access for the handicapped to public transportation. The welfare committees tend to look at such questions more from the point of view of the handicapped, the transportation committees more from the point of view of the burdens on transit systems. Decisions about jurisdiction will thus strongly influence legislative results.[9] Bills are frequently drafted so as to gain referral to one or another committee, and the impact of a bill's specific provisions on jurisdiction decisions will often influence provisions placed in the bill. Environmentalists, for example, have been hesitant to promote proposals for the use of pollution fees rather than regulatory standards in environmental policy lest this change result in a shift of jurisdiction for environmental legislation from the proenvironment committees where they currently go to the antienvironment tax-writing committees. In 1977 President Carter chose to make changes in energy *taxes* a centerpiece of the national energy plan he submitted to Congress. This got the proposals routed to the Senate Finance Committee, whose chairman was an inveterate opponent of Carter's views on energy. Carter's failure to consider the impact of the bill's provisions on decisions about committee jurisdiction helped doom the entire national energy program when it went to the Senate.[10] Frequently, in recent years, bills have been referred to several committees simultaneously. In such situations, it is decided on a case-by-case basis whether all committees must approve a bill before it goes to the floor or whether approval by only one of the committees suffices. The decision on that question of procedure can determine whether a bill ends up on the President's desk or in a dustbin.

Two final examples of the impact of rules on how committees work may be cited: Congressional rules require that every government program be both authorized to operate, under certain statutory provisions, and have money appropriated for operations. Funds have always been appropriated annually. Traditionally, though, programs were authorized on a permanent basis. During the 1970s the practice of requiring annual (or at least more frequent) authorizations grew. This has provided a new window for advocates to seek statutory changes in programs. Opponents of the consumer protection regulatory activism of the Federal Trade Commission, for example, were able to use the occasion of the agency's reauthorization to win statutory limitations on the agency's activities in such areas as the regulation of children's television advertising and of funeral-home practices that would have been harder to achieve had not congressional procedures required the agency to come up for reauthorization. Likewise, the creation during the 1970s of the new Budget Committee to establish overall budget targets provided a single place where advocates of budget restraint could go, because previously there had existed no committee responsible for the size of the budget as a whole.

Significant power in Congress is decentralized to the level of the individual member. The relative weakness of party discipline in Congress increases the independent power of each member, for the same reason that the inability of the president to count on a majority in Congress increases the power of Congress as a whole compared to European parliaments. Congressional rules allow any individual member to introduce a bill, and this helps decentralize power in Congress to the level of the individual member. By contrast, in parliamentary countries bills are normally introduced by the prime minister.[11]

The extent of the decentralization of power within Congress

has varied during our history. During the heyday of strong congressional leadership, around the turn of the century, for example, the Speaker of the House appointed committee members and chairmen, served himself as chairman of the Rules Committee (which scheduled bills for floor consideration), and had considerable discretion about whom to recognize to speak on the floor.[12] After 1910 the rules were altered. The Speaker was yanked from the Rules Committee and deprived of the power to appoint committee members and chairmen. This inaugurated a period, lasting more or less to the present, when congressional leadership has been relatively weak.

From the 1940s to the 1960s power, to a significant measure, was in the hands of committee chairmen. These chairmen were relatively independent of the leaders of Congress (such as the Speaker), because they owed their jobs to seniority alone. The rules also gave chairmen significant power over the selection of subcommittee membership and leadership in their committees, times for committees to meet, and other elements of their committee's operations. This was the period of widespread complaint about conservative committee chairmen blocking liberal proposals from consideration by the whole body.

In recent years decentralization to the committee level has come more and more to turn into decentralization to the level of the subcommittee and the individual member.[13] The same logic that impels decentralization to the committee level has impelled it further to the subcommittee level as demands on Congress for expertise have grown with the further increases in the complexity and scope of government policy.

The growth of the importance of subcommittees in Congress was also spurred by changes in House rules in 1971 and 1973 that increased the independence of subcommittee chairmen and members from committee chairmen. The rules were changed to authorize committee membership as a whole, rather than the committee chairman, to select subcommittee chairmen. The committee as a whole was also given authority to decide on subcommittee jurisdictions and budgets. Members were also limited to chairing one subcommittee, which meant that assignments would be spread among a larger number of individuals. Power devolved not only from committee chairmen to subcommittees but also to individual members. Indeed, one of the thrusts behind the rules changes that increased the number of subcommittee chairmen and the independence of subcommittees was a demand by younger members for a bigger individual share of the action. And a number of changes in the political system outside Congress—involving party organization, voter attitudes, and the role of the media—have encouraged members to "go into business for themselves," acting as independent entrepreneurs rather than as members of a larger organization. The weakening of party organization has made members of Congress more dependent on their own efforts for securing election. So is the decline of presidential "coattails" (the proclivity of voters to vote for a congressman of the same party as the presidential candidate they select). When the Republicans won the presidency in 1952, fewer than 20 percent of all districts elected a congressman of a party different from the one that won the majority of votes for president in the district. When the Republicans won in 1980 this figure had increased to almost 35 percent.[14] By contrast, in British parliamentary elections, the swing from election to election is similar in all districts, suggesting that voters are responding to nationwide forces.[15] The lessened dependence on party organization and on presidential coattails to secure election makes members of Congress more independent of those forces when they do get elected.

A second change in the political system that has tended to decentralize congressional power to the level of the individual member is that the growth of media coverage of Congress enables members to gain rewards from favorable coverage, independent of those that can be granted by one's own colleagues. Since wallflowers rarely get media attention, the possibility of favorable media coverage encourages members of Congress to be independent, even flamboyant.

What would have been defined as errant or maverick behavior in the past—challenging a committee's recommendations or expertise with amendments on the floor, criticizing the leadership or Congress itself, challenging the motives of other legislators—is no longer grounds for chastisement or even murmurs of disapproval. It may even bring two minutes of television exposure on the evening news, which would elicit widespread envy among colleagues.[16]

In a series of off-the-record discussions among new congressmen, a freshman Republican noted that

the two most effective Republicans in recent years, in terms of coming out of nowhere and achieving something, have been Henry Hyde and Jack Kemp. . . . And they have both done it by being very stubborn, by getting outside their zones. Kemp is not on Ways and Means, yet he is the dominant tax figure in our party.[17]

Decentralization increases the number of access points that outside advocates have into Congress. Thus, for example, when Ralph Nader first tried to promote interest in auto safety legislation during the 1960s, there was no interest in the Commerce Committee, which normally would have been the venue to consider such proposals. However, Abraham Ribicoff, a freshman Senator, was interested in the issue from his earlier days as governor of Connecticut. Ribicoff did not sit on Commerce, but he did sit on Governmental Affairs. So he conducted hearings on "how the government is organized to deal with auto safety."[18]

Decentralization is also crucial to the ability of Congress to "soften up" or to act as a political "incubator" for new policy ideas.[19] Parliaments rarely consider proposals that are too new, too vague, or have too little political support to become law. The fact that Congress considers many proposals that do not become law establishes an environment favorable to presenting new ideas, whether by introducing a bill or holding hearings and seeing the reaction. For example, the various liberal ideas that eventually were to be adopted during the Great Society spurt of the mid-1960s incubated in Congress. They lacked presidential support or congressional majorities, but they could be discussed, and support could be built for them.[20] Congressman Jack Kemp began promoting the idea of broad-based tax cuts to encourage economic growth at a time when the idea had little serious backing. After several years of incubation in Congress, the idea was adopted by presidential candidate Ronald Reagan and then enacted into law in 1981. Kemp (along with Senator Bill Bradley) accomplished something similar with the idea of tax simplification. In a parliamentary system, by contrast, ideas must frequently incubate within the executive branch, for only fully developed concepts come to parliament. This is a darker, more closed, and less hospitable environment for them.

Consequences of Institutional Design: Time Pressure on Members

In addition to decentralization, a second result of the institutional design of Congress is to produce, in an era of an increased role for government, enormous time pressures on members of Congress. As the tasks government undertakes grow, the burdens put on an institution that aspires to put its stamp on the content of public policy increase proportionately. But the number of members of Congress remains the same, despite the increased burdens.

One way members cope with these increased demands is simply to labor longer and harder. The number of hours a year that Congress is in session increased from under 1,000 in the mid-1950s to almost 2,000 at the beginning of the 1980s. The number of committee and subcommittee meetings increased from just over 3,000 to 7,500 during the same period.[21] Roger Davidson and Walter Oleszek quote a description of the typical

day of a member of the House in the 1950s that reports atten-
dance at one committee meeting during the morning and an
afternoon spent on the floor listening to debate. As Davidson
and Oleszek comment, those days "have gone the way of the
Edsel and the Hula-hoop." Now they write, "conflicting committee sessions and snatches of floor deliberation are . . . the
order of the day."[22]

The increased work load gives legislators less time to contemplate the content of proposals on which they must vote. One
study comparing the workday of congressmen in 1965 and 1977
shows that the time members spent doing research and reading
about legislation plunged from one *day* a week to about one *hour*
a week.[23] Beyond the obvious effect of this change on the
quality of voting decisions, time pressures are likely to have
other impacts on the individual member's decision-making
process as well. When people must decide quickly, they are
more likely to use decision-making shortcuts. A common such
shortcut in Congress has been for members to take cues from
colleagues who sit on the committee in the policy area in which
a vote is taking place (and hence are more expert) and who share
the member's own values.[24] Increasing time pressures thus tend
to increase further the power of committee members over bills
in their policy areas (or, if there are countervailing tendencies
in the other direction, to prevent that power from eroding
more). And former congressman Abner Mikva and legislative
aide Patti Sarris note that astute congressmen have taken advantage of the installation of a large electronic board on the
floor of the House that displays how members are voting while
votes are taking place. By casting their votes early and getting
them on the board, they assure that those who might take cues
from them will see how they have voted.[25]

A second response to time pressures on legislators has been
the growth of congressional staff. European parliamentary
staffs are generally quite modest, for these bodies do not attempt to consider legislation and hence do not generate the
same time pressures on their members. The French and German

parliaments have about one-tenth as many staffers as does Congress, the British parliament about one-twentieth.[26] According to one survey, members did not even have secretaries in 42 percent of foreign parliaments, and in 46 percent they had no office space. In the British Parliament, "Not long ago very few backbench MP's were officially provided with private working spaces of any kind. . . . [Now] about 190 MP's are provided with whole rooms for their exclusive use, and the remaining 400 or so must share offices with other members."[27]

Until the 1890s members of Congress had no personal staff at all.[28] Congressional staff then grew from around 2,000 in 1945 to about 16,000 in 1980. Much of this growth occurred during the 1970s. "Individual members of both houses have become, in effect, managers of 'enterprises,'" Randall Ripley notes, employing anywhere from 20 to 125 staffers *each* (the latter for Senators from large states).[29] Committees each have extensive staffs of their own, and during the 1970s Congress also created new staff support offices such as the Congressional Budget Office and the Office of Technology Assessment.

Staff are often different kinds of people from members. They tend to be younger, frequently more specialized in a single policy area, and on the whole more highly educated. And they do not have to run for reelection.

The role of staff as well as its size has changed over the years. As late as the mid-1960s, staff spent most of its time handling requests and complaints from constituents.[30] A fair proportion of staff resources still go to such activities, but with the increased congressional work load, staff has become more and more involved in the process of political choice.

Staff do much of the work of selling new policy ideas to members. They often work together with other staff on framing specific provisions of proposed legislation. And they frequently advise members how to vote.

Increased work loads make legislators more harried and increase the role of staff. A final result of increased work loads is the now almost-universal use of vague language in legislation.

During the nineteenth century, at a time when government didn't do much,

individual positions and their salaries were itemized in law; post roads were plotted by Congress; tariff schedules were enacted for hundreds of imported goods; pensions were voted for designated soldiers and their survivors.[31]

The Smoot-Hawley Tariff Act of 1930, which legislated specific tariff rates, was 170 pages long. The Reciprocal Trade Agreements Act was enacted only four years later. But its enactment occurred after the beginning of the dramatic expansion of the role of government in the New Deal. In stark contrast to the tariff legislation passed only a short time before, it simply authorized the president to negotiate tariff reductions—and was *two* pages in length.[32] Now statutes that establish programs typically set only vague standards for the specific content of political choices. The Occupational Safety and Health Act of 1970, for example, merely states that the standards set for worker exposure to chemicals "assure to the extent feasible . . . that no employee will suffer material impairment of health or functional capacity."[33] The statute leaves the Occupational Safety and Health Administration with the formal authority to determine specifically how much lead, cadmium, or asbestos a worker may inhale. The result is that a good deal of the formal authority to make controversial, and hence political, choices has left Congress and gone to the bureaucracy.

There are certainly other reasons besides time pressures for vague statutory language, such as the desire to be able to say one is doing something about a problem without making the tough decision about what, exactly, to do. And Congress certainly can make exceptions to its general practice when it so chooses, as when it enacted specific standards for permissible automobile emissions in clean air legislation during the 1970s. Such exceptions, though, can only be made so long as Congress does not make a habit of it. Time pressures place a cap on the ability of Congress to get specific when it legislates. It is this brute fact that has led Congress to give up some of its power to make political choices, not the usurpations of other rapacious participants. "Every transaction embodying a shift of power and influence" from Congress to the president or the bureaucracy, James Sundquist notes, "was one of mutual consent, for the shifts were made pursuant to the law, and the Congress wrote and passed the laws."[34]

Congress, of course, has means available to exert influence over the bureaucracy to which it delegates formal authority. For starters, Congress passes the laws that grant (and delimit) an agency's authority. Presidents sometimes suggest that agencies are part of an executive branch that stands under presidential control. When they do so, members of Congress are quick to point out that agencies are created by laws that give them certain responsibilities independent of what the president in power happens to want. Thus, for example, if the Clean Air Act states that air pollution regulations should be established at a level that protects the health of sensitive people, that statute should continue to guide the behavior of the Environmental Protection Agency, even though the president then in power believes that setting regulations at such a level makes no economic sense. The only way to change that situation should be to change the statute.

Congress has available other ways to influence the bureaucracy. The Senate must confirm presidential appointees to executive branch positions. (Periodically from the early years of the Republic through the second half of the nineteenth century, in fact, the president's authority to fire presidential appointees without congressional approval was controversial.)[35] Agency budgets must be approved by Congress. And committees may conduct oversight of an agency's activities. During the nineteenth century, oversight generally centered around individual inquiries to agencies from members (usually about particular cases rather than legislation) and around the annual reports that agencies had to file with Congress.[36] Now oversight takes place mainly through public hearings, investigations by committee staff, and informal contacts with agency leaders. Oversight committees have a stick available through their influence over proposed changes in an agency's formal authority. Neither oversight nor appointment approval has any real counterpart outside the United States, although parliamentary question periods do allow deputies to ask ministers questions about what is going on in government organizations.

We have been discussing the effects of increased work-load pressure on members. These also have an impact on the behavior of advocates trying to influence Congress. To the extent that increased use of cueing makes the influence of committee members greater than it otherwise would be, lobbyists will be more likely to concentrate their efforts on committee members rather than on members in general. Second, work-load pressures make staff a crucial point of access for advocates trying to influence Congress. Lobbyists frequently deal with staff more than with members, especially in the Senate. In particular, staff typically is a point of entry for academics and others in the policy stream trying to get ideas on the agenda.[37] Michael Malbin, who has written a study of congressional staff, notes that many members instruct staff to "read the leading academic journals in their fields."[38] Staff act as middlemen between people with policy ideas and members.[39] Finally, increased work loads raise the value of an asset that relatively powerless advocates have, namely, time on their hands that they can singlemindedly devote to the issue in which they are interested.[40]

Congress and Public Spirit

Among the institutions involved in the political process, Congress, according to the common view, is the one least likely to examine policy alternatives in terms of what would be good for the nation as a whole. Congressmen, it is noted, represent constituencies considerably smaller than the entire country. The exigencies of getting reelected, it is argued, drive them to ask which policy would be in the interests of their constituents, not which would be best for the nation as a whole. (Some would defend this as a matter of conscious institutional design, intended to provide a localistic component in the political process.) A local orientation may be strengthened further because jobs that foster such an orientation attract people who already find it congenial: Samuel Huntington presents interesting statistics showing that the proportion of congressional leaders still living in their hometown is much higher than that of executive branch leaders or corporate executives.[41] Furthermore, the devolution of so much formal authority to committees means that disproportionate power over the results of the process goes to an often unrepresentative subset of the membership as a whole, since members may seek the committee assignments that allow them to shape programs to help their districts. (Members representing rice-growing districts are likely to try to get onto the agriculture subcommittee dealing with price supports for rice.) This also discourages examination of bills from a wider range of considerations. Lack of party discipline may be seen as contributing to the same result, because the process of developing a single position for an entire party encourages a similar broader examination.

More recently a different fear has been expressed, by journalists more than scholars, of the consequence of the need to return so often to the voters. This is the fear of the effect of campaign contributions and of political action committees on the inclination of representatives to do the right thing. The fear is that political action committees are giving us "the best Congress money can buy," with members beholden to the interest groups that give them contributions and hence not inclined to examine issues on their merits.

Certainly there is something to all this. Members of Congress naturally care about getting reelected. If nothing else, a natural

selection process works to weed out those who do not. To the
extent that voters themselves care only about what is best for
themselves personally, there will be pressure on congressmen to
share that preoccupation. For example, when an issue has a
direct effect on a large number of jobs in the district, members
can be counted on to vote their constituency rather than to
think about what good public policy would be. Antidefense
congressmen support weapons systems being built in their districts; free-market congressmen from farm districts support
subsidies for the farmers. And the forces that have caused congressmen to rely more on their own efforts for obtaining electoral success increase the tendency of members to seek benefits
for their districts or campaign contributions from interest
groups.

Anyone who wished to make even a perfunctory examination could easily find many examples where some or even most
members of Congress looked no further than the' interest of
their district or the demands of some campaign contributors in
deciding what stand to take on an issue. Thus it is understandable that Congress can be perceived as dominated by "special
interests" or peopled by members who look no further than
getting reelected.

Nonetheless, many congressmen frequently display public
spirit when deciding how to act. A growing body of empirical
evidence argues that, when important national issues are at
stake, many members vote their ideology—their general conceptions of what kinds of public policies are right—over the
interests of their districts.[42] Economist Joseph Kalt, for example, found that the ability to predict a Senator's votes on oil
price regulations was significantly improved if one looked at the
Senator's overall rating on the liberalism scale of the Americans
for Democratic Action in addition to whether the Senator came
from an oil-producing or oil-consuming state. For votes on
legislation on the environmental regulation of strip mining,
overall ideology did a significantly better job in explaining a
congressman's vote than did measures of whether the state

would gain or lose economically from such legislation. In fact, votes on issues such as child pornography and the neutron bomb, questions totally unrelated to strip mining but tapping an underlying dimension of liberal ideology, did a much better job of predicting votes on strip mining than did the economic interests of the Senator's constituents on the issue.[43]

Evidence of a different sort on public spirit comes from the account of two journalists who spent significant time following Senators Edmund Muskie and John Culver in the late 1970s to observe what the life of a Senator was like.[44] What is especially significant about their accounts is that journalists normally are inclined to expect sleaziness, and yet both these accounts found mostly substance. (Bernard Ashball, who wrote the book on Muskie, was apparently surprised enough by what he saw to title his book, *The Senate Nobody Knows.*) Both volumes are filled with accounts of Senators, mostly in committee settings and hence on issues about which they are knowledgeable, seriously debating the merits of proposed legislation. The accounts of committee mark-up sessions (where committee members craft actual legislative language) on Clean Air Act Amendments, which take up much of the space in Ashball's account, include surprisingly sophisticated arguments about philosophical and practical questions involved in the design of environmental policy.

Those who argue that congressmen pay attention mostly to the particular interests of their constituents or to campaign contributors point to features of Congress as an institution that encourage such behavior. However, there are other features of Congress that promote public spirit.

First, the view that there is a conflict between voting the district and looking at a broader range of concerns assumes that the voters want their representatives to do only the former and will punish them electorally if they do not. Yet if this were so, why would candidates running for election stress so often their independence and their desire to stand up to do what is right? In fact, Americans are split on the question of whether congressmen should vote their own best judgment or the opinion of the majority in the district. Results of the few surveys where citizens have been asked how they believed congressmen should behave in instances of such a conflict show that, depending on the wording, anywhere from one-third to somewhat more than half of the population believes that in such cases representatives should vote their own judgment.[45] These answers suggest that many voters do not necessarily prefer that their representative simply vote the district.

A second feature that encourages public spirit is the growing importance of staff. Staff people tend to be interested in issues and in making an impact on policy. Not having to face election themselves, they are not as concerned as are members of Congress with the district or with campaign contributions (although obviously no wise staffer ignores the concerns of the boss). Like journalists for national media, they tend to regard themselves as representatives for poorly organized groups and as people trying to do the right thing.

Third, as Arthur Maass emphasizes in his book, *Congress and the Common Good,* committee members do not enjoy the unconditional deference of the body as a whole. They must pay attention to whether proposals they are considering are acceptable to the wider range of congressional concerns. Deference to committee proposals can be withdrawn if committees exploit this presumption to advance narrow concerns.[46] Furthermore, the growing practice of multiple committee referral reduces the danger that bills will be considered at the committee stage from only a single, narrow point of view.

Fourth, constituency interests and the interests of campaign contributors may pull in opposite directions. Certainly, lobbyists do attempt to show members how their district would be affected by legislation in which the lobbyists are interested. But the demonstration of commonality between constituency interest and the interests of campaign contributors is frequently difficult or impossible. Competing pressures of this sort can create room for members to exercise independent judgment.

Finally, members of Congress are under the eye not only of their own constituents or of political action committees, but of their colleagues and of the media. Members of Congress spend a great deal of time together and thus can be expected to care about the regard of other congressmen. Furthermore, the more their colleagues respect them, the more influence they are likely to have over floor votes and over the results of legislation. Concern about the regard of their colleagues encourages members to behave so as to gain respect. And the evidence suggests that members tend to respect colleagues who are well informed and able to argue on the merits. The books about both Muskie and Culver emphasize how important the ability to make a credible and convincing argument is as a political asset in Congress. "Real power" in the Senate, Muskie is quoted as saying, "comes from doing your work and knowing what you're talking about. . . . The most important thing in the Senate is credibility."[47] "When a Senator makes a speech," writes Elizabeth Drew in her book on Culver, "he is far more likely to command the attention and respect of his colleagues if he seems to know actually what he is talking about."[48] Along similar lines, a group of freshmen congressmen, discussing their experiences for political scientists, "made frequent allusions to the importance of knowledge and expertise" in determining "who wielded real power in committee and in the House."[49]

By contrast, it is hard to imagine that ability to advance the interest of a congressman's own constituents would engender much respect among colleagues who do not share the same constituents, except for the kind of respect generally referred to as "grudging." The same is the case for the member who shows special devotion to the interests of some favored lobby or lobbies. And the national media are likely to regard devotion to the mere interests of one's own constituency or of political action committees as a craven bow to "special interests." Since the 1970s there has been an increase in the extent to which the various features of the political process in Congress are public. Previously closed committee mark-up sessions are now public.

The number of recorded floor votes has increased. This makes the behavior of members of Congress more accessible to constituents (and, perhaps, especially to lobbyists). But it also makes it more accessible to the media.

Where does this leave us in terms of thinking about the importance of public spirit in animating the behavior of members of Congress? We have adduced features of Congress as an institution that promote attention only to a congressman's constituents or to campaign contributors, and other features that encourage attention to a broader range of considerations. These features, of course, balance differently in the minds of different members. Richard Fenno noted this prosaic truth when he pointed out in his study, *Congressmen in Committees,* that members have different primary goals. Some mainly seek assured reelection; others mainly seek influence within Congress; still others mainly seek to formulate good public policy.[50] Also, these considerations balance out differently for different issues. Although few members vote against their constituency on matters of overriding concern to the district, such bills constitute only a small proportion of those before Congress. Similarly, congressmen try to get discretionary government funds for public works and government buildings in their districts, but this makes up only a modest proportion of the federal budget. "The question of where a few thousand office workers will be located is usually secondary," notes R. Douglas Arnold, "to the issue of exactly what they will do."[51] And lobbyists tend to be most effective on technical, low-visibility issues—although I am sensitive to the observation that the distinction between important issues and technical ones may be similar to the one in the story about the family where one spouse made the "important" decisions about whether we should give aid to Nicaragua and the other the "unimportant" ones about what the family should eat for dinner.

A study that measured the significance of "the district" in explaining the votes of Congressmen has found a long-term decline in the influence of constituency interests on voting behavior beginning around the time of the New Deal.[52] It is important to note that the big increases in government spending since the 1950s have not been in federal grants to localities, which provide visible constituency benefits, but rather in various general transfer programs that do not allow members to demonstrate that they have gotten something special for the district.[53] In addition, the tendency since the beginning of the 1970s has been to decrease dramatically the use of categorical grants to localities and to increase the use of formula ones. As R. Douglas Arnold points out, this is exactly the opposite of the prediction that would be generated by a view that members singlemindedly seek reelection by bringing goodies to their districts for which they can claim credit. Localities must *apply* for categorical grants, and members can therefore take credit for helping their districts get them. Formula grants, by contrast, are allocated automatically. They are generally not even tied to specific projects, where congressmen can be present at the opening ceremonies and cut a ribbon. Yet it is the formula grants that are increasing, not the categorical ones. This shift is the result of a debate on the merits of federal versus local control.[54]

A similarly interesting phenomenon has been the occasions in recent years when Congress has voted to *deprive* itself of the opportunity to provide visible constituency benefits, by granting formal authority to the executive branch or by legislating automatic formulas. In trade policy, Congress has given up the opportunity to save constituents in trouble from foreign imports by forswearing tariff power to the executive branch. And when Congress indexed social security benefits in 1972 it denied itself the chance each year to vote politically visible benefit increases. In the Gramm-Rudman budget balancing legislation of 1986 Congress deprived itself of the opportunity to save politically popular programs by requiring certain budget cuts. Each of these three situations shares something in common. If Congress legislated in these areas, there would be intense constituency pressures to act a certain way—to protect threatened industries, to legislate large social security increases, to save popular programs. Yet in each case the policies that would result from such pressures would go against what most congressmen believe to be good public policy—free trade, moderate benefit increases, a balanced budget. So, like the psychopathic murderer who pleads, "Stop me before I kill again," members of Congress have voted to deprive themselves of some things that many commentators believe they seek above all—power and the chance to provide visible constituency benefits—so as to bring about good public policy.

One interesting piece of evidence on the relative significance of constituency versus broader considerations in the minds of members is that the most sought-after committees in Congress are not those that dispense benefits to constituents, such as Public Works, or those that help members procure a stable of eager campaign workers, such as Post Office and Civil Service. They are, rather, the committees that deal with broad issues of national policy.[55] Furthermore, in a 1977 survey of members of the House, the most common problem members cited about their work-load pressures was that "constituent demands detract from other functions."[56] The view among congressmen appears to be that they should look after their constituency to make sure to be around to do the important thing—participating in making public policy. Public spirit, even in Congress, lives.

4

Institutional Settings for Politics: The Presidency

The president stands as the focus of political attention in the United States. One scholar, in a fit of enumeration mania, has calculated that the president was the object of about three-quarters of all national news coverage during the first half of the 1970s.[1] Partly, this focus is an emotional one. As Michael Nelson notes:

Studies of school children indicate that they first come into political awareness by learning of, and feeling fondly toward, the president. As adults, they "rally" to the president's support, both when they inaugurate a new one and in times of crisis. Popular nationalistic emotions, which in constitutional monarchies are directed toward the king or queen, are deflected in American society onto the presidency.[2]

Nelson notes that surveys taken shortly after the assassination of President Kennedy "found Americans to be displaying symptoms of grief that otherwise appear only at the death of a close friend or relative." Forty-three percent did not feel like eating, 68 percent were "nervous and tense," 57 percent "dazed and numb."[3]

Partly, the focus on the president results from the unique vantage point of the office. The president is our only nationally elected leader. And as Graham Allison and Peter Szanton have written, the president

> is the single point in the American system of government at which "civil" and "military," "foreign" and "domestic," "legislative" and "executive," "administrative" and "political" merge. He is the sole official elected by the whole nation, the only figure whose authority can effect those merges.[4]

Partly, the focus on the president results from the apparent awesomeness of the power of the office. Presidents have their fingers on the nuclear button, and we read about the anonymous man with an attache case who accompanies the president wherever he goes, in case a quick decision must be reached about unleashing Armageddon. The Watergate revelations painted a picture of a president able by his orders or those of his staff to get tax returns audited, television licenses challenged, and offices burglarized.

Given all this, it is hardly surprising that the untutored citizen believes the president "runs" the government. That impression, however, is not even nearly correct. The Constitution designed the presidency so that the president does not, in fact, run the government. The major responsibility of the president according to the Constitution is simply to "take care that the laws be faithfully executed"; the president is also designated commander-in-chief of the armed forces and given the authority, subject to approval by the Senate, to make treaties and appoint Supreme Court justices as well as some executive branch officials. Unlike either Congress or the bureaucracy, the president—except, importantly, in the area of foreign affairs—

has seldom been given formal authority to make political choices. The president makes neither laws nor regulations. Congress does one and the bureaucracy the other. The role of the president is generally limited to seeking to influence decisions that others with formal authority are empowered to make. Different institutional choices—such as establishment of a parliamentary system—would have come much closer to producing a situation where the head of the government runs the government.

The impression that the president runs the government is emphatically not shared by presidents themselves. After acceding to the presidency, President Kennedy, who had been in Congress prior to election as president, noted that "Congress looks more powerful sitting here than it did when I was there in the Congress."[5] And Lyndon Johnson gave the following advice to President Nixon when the latter was entering the White House:

Before you get to be president, you think you can do anything. You think you're the most powerful leader since God. But when you get into that tall chair . . . you'll find your hands tied. . . . The office is kinda like the little country boy found the hoochie-koochie show at the carnival, once he'd paid his dime and got inside the tent: "It ain't exactly as it was advertised."[6]

"Let's stay with it," President Kennedy once remarked about an architectural renovation project that the White House was following in LaFayette Square, across the street from the White House. "Hell, this may be the only thing I'll ever really get done."[7]

Some of this may simply be a particularly dramatic example of the phenomenon of power denial.[8] However, it is not only presidents who are impressed by the limits of their office; so are scholars of the presidency. Referring to his classic work on the subject, Richard Neustadt has written, "Presidential weakness was the underlying theme of *Presidential Power.*"[9] Ex-White

House staffer Stephen Hess, in his book on organizing the presidency, warns the reader at the very beginning that "often in the following pages the President will seem a hapless giant, surrounded by enemies, hemmed in by competing power centers, responding to events that he did not create and cannot control."[10] The title of another recent collection—*The Illusion of Presidential Government*—is self-explanatory.[11]

The Development of Presidential Power Vis-à-Vis Congress

For much of our history the role of the president in the political process was as minimal as a literal reading of the Constitution would suggest. Presidents, for example, sought to exert little or no influence on Congress, presenting only a limited number of proposals of their own to Congress and doing little (if anything) to get them adopted. And with little administrative rule making, there were not many political choices within governmental organizations the president might try to influence.

The exception, from early in American history, was foreign affairs.[12] As early as 1793 President Washington declared American neutrality in the conflict between Britain and revolutionary France. This was an action that might have been seen as presidential lawmaking, and, indeed, the action was criticized as unconstitutional by contemporaries no less weighty than James Madison.[13] Constitutional arguments aside, the fact remains that from Washington on presidents have enjoyed the formal authority to make many political choices involving foreign affairs. Thus, in foreign affairs, other political participants, such as Congress, have often been limited to seeking to influence presidential choices from the outside.

Twentieth-century presidents, unlike most of their predecessors, have sought to influence political choices in Congress.

Only members of Congress can actually introduce bills. This is unlike the situation in parliamentary countries, where the prime minister's government does so. The Constitution does, however, provide a basis for a presidential role in influencing the content of legislation through the provision that the president "shall from time to time give to the Congress information on the state of the Union, and recommend to their consideration such measures as he shall judge necessary and expedient." Presidents did little to try to influence legislation, however, until President Woodrow Wilson reinstituted the custom of oral delivery of the State of the Union message and used the occasion to proclaim a legislative program for Congress to consider. Wilson also reinstituted efforts, dormant since Jefferson, to influence congressmen to support his program. He frequently used the office space provided the president in the Capitol to lobby members personally. Wilson even had a telephone line installed between the White House and the Senate.[14]

Since Wilson, Congress has come to expect the president to set its agenda with a legislative program and budget proposal to which it can then react. By the end of the Truman administration, congressional Republicans criticized the president for *not* presenting draft legislation to deal with problems the president had identified. When President Eisenhower failed to present any legislative program to Congress, he was told, "That's not the way we do things here. You draft the bills and we work them over."[15]

It is easy to see why Congress has grown comfortable with this arrangement. Congress lacks any institutional features or informal arrangements (such as strong parties) that could serve as internal agenda-setting mechanisms. And Congress can comfort itself with the observation that the president only proposes, while Congress disposes. Nonetheless, the role of the president in setting the congressional agenda is an important source of influence over the results of the political process in Congress. It is obviously not insignificant to be able to play such an important role in determining which among the many issues

Congress could discuss it actually does seriously consider. Beyond that, the president gains the advantages of preparing a first draft.

Since the most important role of the president in the legislative process involves the design of legislative proposals, advocates will often concentrate their efforts on trying to get items on the president's agenda. This occurs especially in connection with the beginning of a new administration and with annual State of the Union messages.[16]

Once legislation has been introduced, the president has a number of assets to influence the votes of congressmen. For all the images of arm-twisting, and the occasional tales of presidents who vow to locate federal buildings in a member's district in exchange for a vote, a president's assets basically come down to a conviction by congressmen that the president has popular support for what he wants to do—to the president's ability to persuade.[17] Sounding very contemporary, Woodrow Wilson argued as early as 1908 that if Congress allows itself to be influenced by the president, it can be "only because the President has the nation behind him, and Congress has not." The president "has no means of compelling Congress except through public opinion."[18] Members of Congress who defer to a popular president may do so to help their chances at reelection, or they may do so out of a conviction that a democratic respect for the views of citizens requires it. The success of President Reagan in using his popularity to influence Congress, in an era of declining presidential coattails, suggests that the role of democratic norms should not be disregarded.

Simply by being president, any president enjoys some baseline standing with the public and hence some ability to move public opinion in his direction. Survey data suggest that merely by describing a proposal as the president's, support for it increases. For example, a 1981 poll of Utah residents showed two-thirds opposed to stationing MX missiles in that state; however, only one-third remained opposed when this was stated to be President Reagan's policy. A similar dramatic switch occurred when citizens were asked, in 1970, whether they supported the American incursion into Cambodia and whether they supported *President Nixon's decision* to send troops into Cambodia.[19]

Beyond that baseline, variations in a president's standing with the public will depend partly on events, some of which the president has little ability to control. It will also depend partly on the president's ability to use what Theodore Roosevelt described, innumerable repetitions ago, as the "bully pulpit" the office provides him as the only leader elected by the people as a whole. Efforts by the president to improve his standing with the public will of course aid his ability to achieve reelection. But the growth in presidential use of the bully pulpit should be seen mainly in the context of presidential efforts to influence political participants who have the formal authority the president lacks. Historically, the expansion of presidential interest in media relations and speech making occurred during the presidency of Franklin Roosevelt, when there was a dramatic expansion in attempted presidential influence over Congress. In parliamentary systems, where the interest in reelection is presumably as great but where persuading the public is not as important in getting bills through the legislature, speeches to the nation by prime ministers are still relatively uncommon events. The interest of President Reagan in displaying his talents as a great communicator have hardly diminished during his second term, when he need not think about reelection.

Contemporary presidents make assiduous attempts, to put it mildly, to persuade. Anyone who believes that speeches are "only words" will be surprised to discover the careful attention presidents give them. William Safire's account of President Nixon's first term, in his book *Before The Fall,* is filled with stories of careful and continuous presidential scrutiny of the themes, contents, and even choice of words in speeches. *Before The Fall* presents a picture of a president for whom the content of his addresses was of obsessive importance.[20] It is tempting to discount Safire's account since it was, after all, written by a speechwriter. Yet John Hersey presents a similar picture in the portrait of Harry Truman he wrote based on direct observation of Truman in the White House. One chapter in Hersey's book records a conversation in the Oval Office where the president was going over a draft of a speech on the war in Korea with his advisors. Hersey provides a vivid report of the degree of concern for each syllable the president was to utter. At one point, for example, Secretary of State Dean Acheson raised an objection to a draft sentence that read: "We will continue to work —and where necessary to fight—for the principles of the United Nations." What was the problem? Hersey recorded the following dialogue, starting with Acheson:

"I think we ought to be very careful . . . to make it clear that it is the other fellow who is inclined to start fights—not we. Could we say 'We will continue to work for—and if necessary to defend with arms—the principles of the United Nations?' " "That's good, Dean," the President said. Lloyd [of the president's speechwriting staff] said, "It ought to be 'where necessary,' rather than 'if necessary.' We are already fighting for those principles in one locality."[21]

In a fascinating essay on President Carter's national energy plan of 1977, Michael Malbin exposes Carter's failure to use the presidency to persuade.[22] Carter made his energy plan the centerpiece of the first year of his administration. But he had failed to discuss the need for a conservation crusade during the 1976 election campaign. His plan was thus sprung on the public in 1977 almost by surprise. Furthermore, Carter remained publicly silent at crucial moments of the congressional debate, even passing up tailor-made opportunities (such as the installation of the new secretary of energy) to rally citizens. And what presidential rhetoric there was lost its effectiveness by its inconsistency. Early on Carter emphasized the need for sacrifice to meet a stupendous challenge, but he soon began to suggest that his plan would be largely painless. All this stands in stark contrast to President Reagan's 1981 achievement on behalf of his economic program. Certainly Reagan was a more effective public speaker than Carter, and that made it easier for him to communicate with the public. Beyond that, though, he fought for a budget and tax reduction plan that was already the core of his election campaign. He timed his key public appeals to important congressional action. And he was consistent and unwavering in his rhetoric.

The Development of Presidential Power Vis-à-Vis the Bureaucracy

The constitutional basis for a presidential role in influencing the content of decisions made in the bureaucracy grows from the general provision that the president "shall take care that the laws be faithfully executed." Since 1921 agency budgets must be approved by the Office of Management and Budget, subject to appeal to the president, before they can be sent to Congress. Furthermore, unlike the situation in most European countries, the president appoints not only cabinet secretaries, but also assistant secretaries in charge of various specific government programs. (In most European countries, the counterparts of assistant secretaries are civil servants.) And assistant secretaries in turn may make their own appointments to some senior positions. The result is that the senior ranks of the bureaucracy are far more subject to presidential control than in most European countries. Almost one-third of the senior positions in American agencies are designated as political, while in Britain only about 2 percent of such positions are.[23] Presidential appointees serve at the pleasure of the president and may be dismissed for any reason, including dissatisfaction with decisions these individuals make.

Still, probably the most important way a president influences the bureaucracy is the same way he sways Congress, through his standing with the public. Such popular standing, however, cannot help bureaucrats with something they need not seek anyway, namely, reelection. Also, political choices in the bureaucracy seldom have the visibility that major decisions in Congress do. So the ability of the president to apply public pressure on specific issues handled by the bureaucracy is less than with Congress.

Institutional Design and the Effectiveness of the President

The institutional design of the American presidency makes it difficult to translate voter choices into governmental choices, compared with parliamentary systems. The election for the presidency is our only national referendum on the course we wish to choose for public policy. But the person we choose in that referendum does not in our system run the country. At the same time, as the discussion of Congress made clear, the fact that the president does not run the country opens up a larger number of access points than in a parliamentary system, where political choices are made, de facto, by a much smaller, more centralized group.

How good are presidents likely to be at exerting influence over Congress and the bureaucracy? The record shows that presidential skill in this regard varies very widely. However, if one looks at the baseline provided by the design of the institution, and not at the perturbations around that baseline that differences among individuals produce, it may be noted that American presidents are more likely, compared with prime ministers in parliamentary countries, to be relatively unskilled as political leaders. In parliamentary systems, candidates for prime minister are chosen as leaders by their parliamentary colleagues. This arrangement tends to favor people with experience (for the same reasons that the U.S. Congress usually chooses its own leaders among senior members) and those whom colleagues regard as skilled at the political profession to which they all belong.

The average British prime minister installed since 1945, for example, had *twenty-eight years* of parliamentary experience before assuming office. Only one British prime minister in the twentieth century had not served in the cabinet before acceding to the prime ministership.[24] Since presidents are not selected as leaders of a group of legislators, there are fewer pressures to select for experience and insider political skills in the United States. Nominating conventions, even when they were gatherings mostly of party professionals, were never like parliamentary caucuses, for they did not consist of a group of colleagues who worked on a continuing basis with the person they were contemplating selecting as leader. And the spread of presidential primaries has moved the presidential selection process even further away from the influence of those for whom experience and skill at politics have significant importance. Indeed, the primary marathon now gives advantages to candidates who hold no political office at all when they are running for the nomination, so they can devote full time to campaigning. That presidents tend to be politically relatively inexperienced reduces their ability to influence the results of the political process, because it makes them less skilled players than they might otherwise be.

In an important sense, Congress and the bureaucracy are lucky. Having much of the formal authority to make decisions, they can sit back and affect the results of the political process without trying hard. The presidency is, by contrast, more what its occupant makes of it. Except for foreign policy, the president largely seeks to influence choices made by others. As is the case for anyone lacking formal authority, success depends in significant measure on political skill.

What is perhaps most noteworthy about a president's potential ability to influence Congress or the bureaucracy is its wide scope. President's can regularly seek to exert influence over decisions in areas as diverse as requirements for cleaning sulfur dioxide out of the stacks of power plants and the level of price supports for sorghum. Few other participants in the political system would dare venture so widely. The ability of members of Congress to become significantly involved in an issue of their choice is constrained by their committee assignments; for interest group representatives, choice is constrained by the group's issue areas. But presidential latitude can be a curse as well as a blessing. Presidents, to be successful, must take what Paul Quirk calls a "strategic view" of the presidency. They must avoid the temptation to get involved in everything. They must concentrate on a small list of major efforts.[25] Presidents Carter and Reagan can be dramatically contrasted in this regard. Carter began his administration by sending a colossal number of major proposals to Congress, addressing a hodgepodge of areas spanning the range from energy to taxes to administrative reorganization. Reagan, by contrast, focused on an agenda of budget and tax cuts around the unified theme of "economic recovery." He shunted aside such issues as abortion and school prayer. Reagan succeeded. Carter failed.

This assessment of the assets of the president provides fodder for almost any sort of discontent. Those who support the things a president is trying to do are likely to be frustrated by the fact that the president does not, in fact, run the government. Those who oppose what the president seeks to do are likely to find evidence that the office has become imperial. The great hopes we have for our presidents have, more often than not over the past decades, bred great disappointments, with the president blamed for every problem the country faces.

Finally, in terms of the nature of the political stands it leads presidents to take, our institutions produce presidents with both the defects and virtues of leaders who often have not come up through the ranks. Their judgments may be less seasoned, but they may also be less hidebound. The system tends to generate greater surprises compared with more predictable parliamentary systems where leaders almost invariably tramp a

long march through the system before finally reaching the end
of the path.

Organizing Policy Development in the White House

The presidency has evolved to the point where the president
will wish to take a stand on many policy issues the government
faces. In foreign affairs, the president may have formal authority to make decisions himself. In domestic affairs, the president
must determine what to propose to Congress. He must decide
whether and how to try to influence political choices that the
bureaucracy is authorized to make. And the president must
decide how to react to the initiatives of others.

Through what institutional mechanisms should these decisions get made? One approach would be to reach collegial judgments in the cabinet. Thus, in parliamentary systems, not only
the prime minister but the cabinet as a whole are closely involved in major decisions. In the United States, however, the
Constitution put executive powers in the hands of the president
alone rather than a council as had been the arrangement in a
number of the American states.[26] "Seven nays and one aye, the
ayes have it," Abraham Lincoln (in an oft-cited remark) is said
to have announced after a cabinet vote went against him.[27] In
our system, cabinet secretaries lack the independent standing
that comes in parliamentary countries from the fact that they,
like the prime minister, are legislative leaders. The cabinet thus
has rarely been much of a forum for determining presidential
inputs into the political process.

A second approach would be simply to ratify what individual
executive branch departments propose in a given policy area.
Thus, the president would support foreign policies developed
by the State Department. He would send to Congress proposals

for job-training programs developed by the Labor Department. He would simply let the bureaucracy make choices they are formally authorized to make. There are arguments for going this route. The departments have many experts in the areas under their jurisdictions. And cabinet secretaries, appointed by the president, are certainly not unsympathetic to presidential values.

Nonetheless, modern presidents have been uniformly disinclined to this approach. For one thing, it appears extremely passive. It conflicts with a view that presidents like to hold of themselves (and that, as noted, citizens may hold of the presidency as well) that executive branch decisions should emanate hierarchically from the White House and flow downward to the departments. Second, presidents worry that the departments, dominated by civil servants whose tenure is much longer than a president's, will be inclined toward cautious investigation rather than toward the expeditious decisions needed if a president is to make his mark. Beyond that, presidents tend to worry—and worries often grow to obsessions the longer the president serves —about the policy stands that departments would take if left to their own devices. For although the departments are full of experts, presidents do not trust career civil servants to share the president's values. In particular, presidents worry that civil servants are likely to be too committed to the existing programs of their organizations and to a world view that has become typical for the agency.[28] "It is difficult to overestimate," Thomas Cronin writes, "the degree of frustration and resentment that White House aides develop about the seeming indifference of the permanent government toward presidential policy."[29]

It is not just the presidential will that moves initiatives out of the departments and up to the White House. In new proposals to be sent to Congress, or in foreign policy decisions, issues are frequently interdepartmental. Most foreign policy issues, for example, have both diplomatic and defense aspects. It is thus often uncertain in exactly whose bailiwick an issue would land if the dictum "leave it to the department" were followed.[30] And as the role of government in society increases, the extent to which programs run by one department impinge on values dear to other departments increases. In such cases, one department may seek to get issues bucked up to the White House level, hoping to achieve a different decision from the one the other department would make. Thus, for example, the Department of Energy might try to get political choices by the Environmental Protection Agency that have an impact on energy consumption moved out of that agency and into the White House. "It is," Hugh Heclo notes, "simply very useful to the agencies to have someone at the end of the line who, after otherwise interminable wrangling across bureaucratic boundaries, can at least make a decision."[31]

Presidents, then, are drawn to establish mechanisms for policy development in the White House itself. And once cut off from reliance on the prodigious staff resources of the departments, time pressures grow on the president as they grow on Congress. In an era before presidents tried so actively to influence political choices in Congress or the bureaucracy, the job of a president was almost leisurely. Grover Cleveland answered the White House telephone himself; Woodrow Wilson typed many of his own speeches; Calvin Coolidge slept eleven hours a day.[32] The president bumps up against the same kind of problem Congress does, but even more dramatically. There are hundreds of members of Congress; the number of presidents serving at any given time is immutably fixed at one. As with Congress, a main response to time pressures has been an increased reliance on staff, which Congress, with its larger membership, initiated seriously only in the 1960s. Until 1857 the president had no personal staff at all. Up through the Roosevelt years, presidents made do with a very modest retinue. But the 1937 report of the Roosevelt-appointed Brownlow Commission on Administrative Management exclaimed, "The President needs help." Between the beginning of Roosevelt's first term and the 1970s, the size of the White House staff increased from 37 to over 500. The growth of the Office of Management and Budget over the same period was even greater.[33]

Today the scope of the institutionalized presidency is stupendous. It consists not only of the White House staff itself, but also the Office of Management and Budget, which prepares the president's budget, clears departmentally prepared legislative proposals before they can be sent to Congress, and is now involved in oversight and approval of regulatory proposals being considered by the bureaucracy.

The growth of the institutionalized presidency has made the design of institutions for policy development in the White House an important question.[34] There are a number of recurring issues in the design of these institutions. Should White House staffers act as "honest brokers," making sure that departmental views are represented to the president? Or should they filter any departmental input through the lenses of a presidential perspective? Should efforts be made to get departmental representatives to work things out among themselves, with the White House adopting more or less the role of mediator? Or should decisions be bucked up to the presidential level?

There have been wide variations in the institutional mechanisms used, depending on the president and, even for a given president, on the policy area at issue. Presidents have chosen institutional configurations to fit their personal (or even personality) styles. This contrasts with Congress, where procedures are more fixed. In Congress, formal authority is shared among a large number of people, and procedures are needed to regulate the interactions. In the White House, one person is in charge, and systems get established with which that person feels comfortable.

The greater the independent role of White House staff in the determination of presidential stands, the more important it becomes to look at the distinctive features of presidential advisors and staff. Top presidential advisors have traditionally been close and long-time personal friends of the president, or at least people who have been with him through the presidential campaign. This is still the case more frequently than for congressional staff. Increasingly, however, especially below the level of the most senior positions, presidential staff looks demographically and culturally like congressional staff—young, well-educated, and interested both in general ideas and in wielding considerable power at a tender age. The increase in education began under President Kennedy; the drop in age began under President Nixon. The average age of the Domestic Policy Council staff in the Nixon White House was 35, compared with an average of 45 for staffers during the previous four administrations. One-third of Nixon staffers had Ph.D. degrees (compared with 14 percent of Kennedy and 7 percent of Johnson staffers), and most of the rest held law degrees.[35]

Critics argue that this staffing pattern produces people who are too slow to question the president's judgment. This occurs both because of the youth and the close past political association of staffers with the president. The tags "more royalist than the King" and "more Catholic than the Pope" have been applied to White House staff in all modern administrations. To insulate the president from criticism, the argument continues, is to increase the chances that the president will make bad decisions. "There is much to recommend having potential presidential aides step down, rather than up, to White House service," argues Stephen Hess.[36] Since group decision making in Congress inevitably exposes members to many views, these dangers are less of a worry for congressional staff. The more the White House is organized to give genuine consideration to the views of people from departments, the less these problems of White House staff matter.

The Presidency and Public Spirit

The conventional wisdom is that, just as the election of congressmen by district tends to make them more responsive to the interests of their specific districts, so the election of the president by the nation as a whole makes him more responsive to the interests of the nation. The view that the president is more likely than Congress to take a broad range of considerations into account lies at the center of the support for an expansion of presidential power—what Michael Nelson calls the "savior" view of the presidency.[37]

Activist presidents—hardly surprisingly—endorse this view. "No-one else represents the people as a whole," wrote Woodrow Wilson of the presidency. "He is the representative of no constituency, but of the whole people. When he speaks in his true character, he speaks for no special interest."[38] "The office of the Presidency is the only office in this land of all the people," stated Lyndon Johnson.[39]

I have no quarrel with this basic analysis.[40] I do believe, however, that the argument needs to be made more subtle. Responsiveness to a nationwide constituency is not sufficient to encourage public spirit. For in some situations, good policy requires overriding the interests of the majority for the sake of a minority whose interests are more intense or whose rights are at stake. Responsiveness to a nationwide constituency by itself only encourages attention to what the majority wants, not necessarily public spirit.

There are, however, aspects of the presidency other than its electoral basis that encourage presidents to display public spirit. I think especially of the norm that the president is the representative of, or (with excessive grandiosity) even the embodiment of the nation, and should behave accordingly. This norm is somewhat different from the simple observation that the president is elected by the whole nation. The latter view merely informs the president who his constituents are; the former suggests something of his obligation. "The buck stops here" was not the only saying in President Truman's office. Framed behind his desk was also a quotation from Mark Twain: "Always do right—this will gratify some and astonish the rest."[41]

Such a lofty view of the presidency is impressed on modern presidents by our focus on the presidency as repository of national hopes and concerns. It is also impressed on them by the trappings of history and tradition in which they are surrounded in the White House—trappings that, if one is to believe statements modern presidents have made, produce a constant impact on them as they go about their business. Presidents can certainly be sleazy even in those surroundings; the White House tapes of President Nixon assure us of this. But one suspects that the Harry Truman described by John Hersey is more typical:

President Truman seemed to think of himself sometimes in the first person and sometimes in the third—the latter when he had in mind a personage he still seemed to regard, after nearly four years in office, as an astonishing tenant in his own body: the President of the United States. Toward himself, first-personally, he was at times mischievous and disrespectful, but he revered this other man, his tenant, as a noble, history-defined figure. He was a separation of powers within a single psyche.[42]

There is much talk of the tendency of the American political system to produce political leaders who are pragmatic to the point of lacking all conviction. For all that talk, most modern presidents—our politicians who have come furthest—have been, if anything, overly stern in their public spirit and too slow to compromise with others. Presidents Truman and Ford vetoed bills with regularity. President Carter's stiff-neckedness brought down an entire administration. In 1985 Ronald Reagan, flush from a landslide election victory and needing every ounce of his political prestige to get difficult budget and tax cuts through Congress, was willing to take it on the chin, for essentially no domestic political reward, to honor a commitment to the chancellor of West Germany to visit a German war cemetery where, it turned out, SS troops were buried.

Take the cases of Johnson, regarded during his congressional career as a master of compromise and accommodation, and of Nixon, criticized for ignoring the distinction between his own personal advancement and that of the nation. Yet with regard to Vietnam—the most important issue of their administrations —each behaved less like convictionless pragmatists and more like a profile in courage. Late in his administration Johnson stated:

In this job, a man must set a standard to which he's working. In my case, it is what my grandchildren think when I'm buried out there under the tree on the ranch. I think they will be proud of two things. What I did for the Negro and seeing it through in Viet Nam for all of Asia. The Negro cost me 15 points in the polls and Viet Nam cost me 20.[43]

(And, one might add, eventually his job.) When President Nixon announced the American move into Cambodia in 1970, he stated to the nation:

I have noted . . . that a Republican Senator has said that this action I have taken means that my party has lost all chance of winning the November elections, and others are saying that this move . . . will make me a one-term President. . . . I would rather be a one-term President at the cost of seeing America become a second-rate power than to see this nation accept the first defeat in its proud 190-year history.[44]

(His party did do badly in November.)

Furthermore, the connection between the president's own electoral interest and the presidential display of public spirit is not quite as direct as is suggested by the observation that the president is elected by the population as a whole and therefore needs to satisfy a majority to get reelected. That account of the connection suggests that while each voter wants the president to advance the voter's personal interest, the president must advance the personal interests of the majority to craft a winning coalition. However, less ambiguously than with popular views of the proper behavior of members of Congress, many citizens instead want the president to do what he thinks is right, whether or not it is popular. A 1979 survey of expectations for presidential leadership showed that the two characteristics Americans thought were most important for a president were "placing the country's interest ahead of politics" and "taking a firm stand on the issues." "Saying what one believes, even if unpopular" came in the top third of the list of attributes. By contrast, "flexibility, willingness to compromise" and "political savvy, know-how" were characteristics that came in the bottom third of the list.[45]

Similarly, presidential concentration on foreign policy results not only from the president's greater formal authority in that area. It also results from the fact that in the conduct of foreign affairs the president can act more as representative of the nation and less as partisan.[46] Preoccupation with foreign policy also tends to distinguish European leaders, despite the lack of any special constitutional status for foreign affairs in those countries and despite the lesser importance of foreign affairs for those nations. As Ezra Suleiman comments regarding the interest in foreign issues on the part of modern French presidents, "It creates a more prestigious presidential image than do other roles that he assumes. Here the President represents France, and not merely a political party."[47] Fred Greenstein, in his interesting account of Eisenhower's "hidden-hand presidency," notes that every president faces a tension between his role as partisan leader and leader of the nation. Eisenhower, he argues, dealt with this conflict by showing the public the leader of the nation side and acting in a partisan manner only privately.[48] Thus, he, unlike many of the presidents since him, managed to maintain a high level of popularity throughout two terms in office.

The suggestion, then, is that it may well be the conception of the office that many voters have, as much as the simple fact that a president's constituency is the entire nation, that encourages presidents, in their own political interest, to try to do what is right. For if voters expect the president to be a lofty leader of the nation, he will be punished electorally if he is not.

The danger for the presidency is thus different from that for Congress. The danger in Congress is that public spirit will collapse under the onslaught of simple attention to local concerns or to the interests of campaign contributors. The danger for the presidency is of a public spirit that is stiff-necked and hence unable to change or compromise, or fanatic and hence capable of going to any lengths to realize what is believed to be right.

5

Institutional Settings for Politics: The Bureaucracy

Nobody would ever guess it from reading the Constitution, but the bureaucracy is very much a part of the political process. This is so for two reasons. One is that Congress frequently delegates government agencies the formal authority to make choices that have the force of law. Thus, in passing the Clean Air Act, Congress did not establish exactly what concentrations of harmful substances (such as sulfur dioxide, benzene, or hydrocarbons) are permissible in the air. Instead, it delegated to the Environmental Protection Agency the formal authority to make those determinations. Likewise, in passing the Trade Adjustment Assistance Act, Congress authorized the Department of Labor to determine when workers in industries affected by foreign competition are eligible for benefits. Although they frequently have a large technical component, nonetheless the decisions so delegated to the bureaucracy are often highly political because they involve values and people disagree deeply about their outcome. The question of whether lowering workplace exposure to benzene will save 1,000 lives a year or one life a year—and whether it will cost $50 million or $5 billion—are technical questions. The decision about where exposure levels to benzene should be set, given those facts, is a political one.

A second reason the bureaucracy is part of the political process is that government agencies are often an important source of the information about policy problems that other participants in the political process use. This was the case as early as the Jeffersonian period in American history. "Substantially all major legislation and much minor legislation," writes administrative historian Leonard White, "was based on administrative reports, giving facts and opinions for the guidance of Congress."[1] During the Age of Jackson, "at almost any point of legislative business, whether technical or not, the executive agencies were likely to be called on for information."[2] Indeed, government agencies often bring to the attention of Congress and the White House problems that need examination and provide specific proposals for dealing with them, even proposing statutory language.

There are several explanations why legislatures give government agencies such discretion. Some believe that legislators seek to avoid having to make difficult political choices—they pass legislation expressing the general sense that a problem exists and leave the actual tough decisions for the bureaucracy. However, there is a simpler explanation. Hundreds, probably thousands, of discrete, often highly technical decisions have to be made in arriving at political choices in a given policy area. As a practical matter, it is impossible for any significant number of decisions to be made directly by a legislature that has many complex issues to deal with. Legislators can, of course, pick a few highly visible areas and make specific rules themselves. Thus Congress has set emissions control and fuel economy standards for automobiles. Also, some laws give greater guidance to administrative agencies by establishing relatively specific performance or cost criteria. However, the ability of the legislature to guide agency behavior through specific criteria in legislation is limited by the frequent difficulty of applying such criteria to specific cases, and by the fact that the huge number of issues legislatures must deal with limits their ability to get enough information to establish such criteria. A large degree of delegation of formal authority is inevitable.

The bureaucracy thus provides a capacity for surges or peak loads within the political process. The number of Congressmen and presidents cannot be increased. There are practical limits to the ability to expand the size of the staffs working for these elected officials. Government agencies, more flexible in size, are thus given more tasks as elected officials become unable to deal with them. For this reason, the role of the bureaucracy in the political process grows disproportionately as the activities of government increase.

For similar reasons the bureaucracy has become involved in developing suggestions on policy problems to be used by the White House and Congress. Generally, no part of government has more expertise about a policy area than the government organization involved in the area. The bureaucracy employs people who work full-time on a problem, unlike elected officials and their staffs whose time is divided among many issues. Agency officials are also closer to the situation. They get more ongoing feedback from the world outside government. Because of their experience they understand the political constellation surrounding an issue better than short-term participants such as White House staff. The bureaucracy is also a unique source of information on whether production capabilities exist or can be created with regard to various policy alternatives. For these reasons, elected officials and their staffs need the participation of the bureaucracy in the early stages of the political process.

Interestingly, for many years the dominant assumption among sociologists and among political scientists who study the policy-making process in general and not bureaucracy in partic-

ular has been that decisions made within government organizations are simple epiphenomena: bureaucrats merely register a
balance of social forces without having any independent influence over choices made. Sociologist Theda Skocpol, in her work
on "bringing the state back in," and Eric Nordlinger, in his book
On the Autonomy of the Democratic State, have recently presented
what they appear to regard as the epochal and paradigm-shat-
tering insight that the views of bureaucrats exert an independent impact on the results of the process.[3] Thus, concludes
Nordlinger, presenting what he apparently sees as a revelation,

it seems most improbable that the modern democratic state—the individuals who populate this large, weighty, resource-laden, institutionalized, highly prized ensemble of authoritative offices—is consistently unwilling and unable to act on its preferences when these
diverge from society's.[4]

These expressions of astonishment would doubtless occasion
a chuckle among those who study government organizations—
and among those who work in them. That the values of agency
officials exert influence over political choice is taken as a matter
of course by students of government organizations and participants in the political process.

The serious question probably is not whether government
officials lack the ability to exert independent influence but
whether their ability to do so is too great.

The bureaucracy is the institutional participant in the political process that everybody loves to hate. (Indeed, the very word
used to name the institution is an epithet.) Yet, although Congress and the Supreme Court play an unusually important role
in America compared with other democratic political systems,
this is not the case for the bureaucracy. Instead, the role of the
bureaucracy in the political process in the United States is probably somewhat smaller, and is certainly far more controversial,
than in most other countries. When formal authority to make
political choices is delegated to the bureaucracy in other coun-

tries, that authority is not fenced in with nearly as many protections against the abuse of power as in the United States. Furthermore, in many countries agency officials have considerably more influence over the content of legislation than they do in this country. Outside the United States, career civil servants hold jobs that in the United States are filled by people appointed by elected officials—for example, the people who actually have line responsibility for running most government programs, the equivalent of our assistant secretaries, are career bureaucrats in most countries outside the United States.

The roots of these differences are historical. In most countries, a strong bureaucracy predated the development of democracy. Bureaucrats were initially servants of the king and benefited from the awe that attached to royalty in an age of divine right. In many countries, bureaucratic office was held mostly by the nobility; indeed, the primary occupation of the nobility was that of government official.[5] These historical traditions leave their traces today: significant bureaucratic participation in the political process is a matter of long-standing custom.

In the United States, by contrast, the development of democracy predated the development of a strong bureaucracy. The tendency to keep high positions in government organizations subject to appointment by elected officials rather than having them in the career civil service is the result. This has produced two impulses in American history. One is the concern, dating back to the Age of Jackson, with the democratization of the bureaucracy. Bureaucrats in the United States failed to gain the advantage of the pride Americans feel in our democratic institutions, becoming, instead, objects of distrust because they were nondemocratic. The other impulse has been the hesitancy to admit the bureaucracy into influential positions in the political process. The degradation of the technical abilities of the civil service, produced by the Jacksonian spoils system, undermined any willingness to trust the bureaucracy with a role in the political process. Reality, of course, intervened. There has been a steady growth of bureaucratic participation in politics, but the hesitancy has remained. The first issue examined in most American administrative law textbooks is the legitimacy of the delegation of powers. By contrast, the standard Swedish textbook on the subject, for example, has no discussion of this issue at all.[6]

The Bureaucracy and the Political Process: Rule Making

A result of our hesitancy to admit unelected officials into participation in political choice has been the establishment of very specific procedures that must be followed before the bureaucracy can make decisions that have the force of law. These procedures have been established in the individual statutes creating agencies, in the Administrative Procedures Act of 1946, and by various court rulings. They are designed to make agency rule making as open as possible to participation from outside the agency and to reduce the scope for arbitrary decision by requiring that decisions be justified and susceptible to extensive court challenge.[7] Establishment of these procedures represented a victory for the bureaucracy, since with these safeguards in place the way was left free for an expansion of bureaucratic formal authority. However, the fact that establishment of these procedural safeguards was needed reflects the relative weakness of the bureaucracy in the American political system.

Before it can issue a rule, an agency must fulfill many requirements. The simplest, most bareboned procedures require that agencies publish all proposed actions in the *Federal Register* and allow at least thirty days after publication for submission of written comments. The *Federal Register* is arguably the most excruciatingly boring periodical published in this country and is, of course, hardly breakfast-table reading in homes across the land. But it is read carefully by interest groups. Thus notices in the *Federal Register* do not pass unnoticed. Furthermore, organizations inform members about proposed regulations affecting them so they can send in comments themselves. Generally, as well, agencies now also publish an Advance Notice of Proposed Rulemaking and solicit written comments.

For important regulatory proposals, there are almost always public hearings. These are generally held in Washington, although sometimes hearings are also held elsewhere so more people can participate. At public hearings, interested organizations and individuals present testimony before an administrative law judge. Witnesses at hearings on occupational safety and health regulations, for example, have included businessmen operating the processes being regulated and individual workers exposed to the hazards, fingerless machine operators and cancer victims who have had parts of lungs, throats, or other organs removed.[8] Agency officials who testify at public hearings do so as witnesses seeking to justify a point of view.

The audience at public hearings is filled with lawyers for the parties. At occupational safety and health rule-making hearings, occasional local delegations of unionists or construction contractors have appeared in the audience. There have been instances of demonstrations, complete with chants and placards. Reporters from weekly newsletters dealing with occupational safety and health are generally present to record what witnesses say. In some cases, television klieg lights emblazon the hearing room. Verbatim transcripts of public hearings are made.

Following testimony, witnesses are cross-examined by government lawyers and by anyone else who wishes; cross-examination privileges are not limited to the lawyers. Since there is no limit to the number of individuals who cross-examine witnesses, it is not unusual for an important witness to be examined for several hours, or even a few days, by a succession of questioners. Hearings may last for a month or more.

Witnesses present both opinions and data. Frequently, lengthy research reports and other material not suitable for oral presentation are entered into the hearing record. The record of the rule-making proceedings of the Occupational Safety and Health Administration on the chemical vinyl chloride, preserved for posterity in a special room at the agency's headquarters, includes a plastic shoe.

After the public hearing, additional time is made available for submitting post-hearing comments. Frequently, lawyers submit full-blown legal briefs. The agency project manager must go through the entire record. The record is usually so extensive that it is impossible for a more superior official to look at anything but the highlights. When a final rule is published in the *Federal Register,* it must be accompanied by a "statement of reasons" explaining why each provision was adopted and answering arguments against it. The reasons must be related to evidence and arguments in the rule-making record. Statements of reasons are themselves frequently of considerable length, sometimes taking up twenty-five pages or more of tightly packed space in the *Federal Register.*

This process takes a long time to complete. It is easy to see how citizens who wish to see government act quickly could become upset at what they may well perceive as a grinding—or spinning—of wheels in the bureaucracy. It is not unusual for major regulatory proceedings to last five years or more.

President Reagan added another layer to this complex process. Through an executive order, issued in 1981, the president established the Office of Information and Regulatory Affairs within the Office of Management and Budget. Agencies are required to submit proposed regulations to the Office of Information and Regulatory Affairs, together with a justification explaining that the benefits of the contemplated regulation exceed their costs. No Advance Notice of Proposed Rulemaking may be published before the White House accepts the agency's justification for proceeding further. The Office of Information and Regulatory Affairs has thus obtained, in practice, a veto power over an agency's ability to proceed with rule making. In addition, before an agency issues its final ruling, the Office of

Information and Regulatory Affairs possesses a similar veto.[9] Economist George Eads has compared these changes with the establishment of the Bureau of the Budget, as an organization directly subordinate to the president, whose job it was to examine agency budgets before they go to Congress. The change marks, he argues, "the final emergence of regulation as a governmental function deserving the same level of attention as the raising and spending of money."[10] (In fact, that is not quite true. Unlike the situation with budgetary appropriations, formal authority to issue regulations remains with the agencies and not with Congress.)

Creation of the Office of Information and Regulatory Affairs represented the culmination of many years of efforts to change bureaucratic decision-making procedures to include the White House. The first major such change resulted from the National Environmental Policy Act of 1969. That law required agencies to develop environmental impact statements on their actions, to be submitted for comment to a newly established Council on Environmental Quality in the White House. During the 1970s, however, the focus of presidential concern turned more to the economic costs regulations imposed. In 1975 President Ford required, by executive order, that agencies issue an inflationary impact statement for major regulations. He authorized the Council on Wage and Price Stability in the White House to testify before regulatory hearings, just as other participants do. President Carter established, also by executive order, a Regulatory Analysis and Review Group in the White House to comment on proposed regulations. This body did not have the authority to veto agency actions, but it was able to flag issues and bring them to the president's attention for possible direct involvement. The Reagan changes, however, represent a qualitative increase in the level of White House involvement, both in terms of authority and in terms of size of its staff.

The courts have been significantly involved in the political process in the bureaucracy for significantly longer than the

White House. From its beginning, the political process in the bureaucracy was made to appear as similar as possible to procedures used in courts, so that bureaucratic decision making could be justified in terms of its resemblance to courts. Thus, the involvement of courts as a venue for appeal of agency decisions was a natural development. Over time, the scope of judicial review has been expanded so that an agency's choice is often reviewed in toto. In theory, courts review agency determinations on questions of law only, not on questions of fact. This makes little difference in practice, however, since "the adequacy of the evidence adduced to support a finding of fact is a question of law."[11]

All this may be so familiar to us as Americans that its uniqueness is not fully appreciated. In fact, no other country in the world prescribes such a detailed set of decision-making procedures for government agencies. Nor does any country provide for such extensive involvement and review by the courts. Many European countries do establish fairly detailed and courtlike procedures for situations in which an agency is making a determination in an individual case, such as whether to grant a license or to deny coverage for government-provided insurance. There are, however, generally few requirements governing procedures that agencies must follow before issuing general rules. No other country requires anything even resembling our panoply of public hearings, cross-examination of witnesses, posthearing comments, and statements of reasons. Many countries do not even require texts of proposed rules to be published in advance. Few countries require anything resembling the openness of the American process. Outside the United States, government agencies generally undertake a simple process of informal consultation with affected parties before promulgating regulations. These consultations often take the form of meetings with affected parties, assembled as a group, together with the appropriate agency officials, where the goal is informally to hammer out a decision as widely acceptable as possible. The agency selects who is to participate, meaning that representation is generally limited to well-established interest groups—both individuals and representatives of newly emerging groups are generally excluded—and meetings often take place behind closed doors.[12]

More so than with Congress, the procedures used for political choice in the bureaucracy are open to change. Advocates who do not like procedures that are used for decision making in the bureaucracy will probably therefore have an easier time getting them changed than is the case for procedures used in Congress. Americans remain uneasy about handing formal authority to the bureaucracy and are thus always seeking ways to rein bureaucrats in. The expansion of the role of government during the 1960s and 1970s dramatically expanded the importance of the bureaucracy. In the early 1970s the main thrust of changes in procedures was to make it easier for citizens to force a reluctant bureaucracy to act, by authorizing suits against nonaction in court and by widening in other ways the access of outsiders to the process. The biggest change in recent years has been the increased participation of the White House in the rule-making process.

The Bureaucracy and the Political Process: Informal Input Into Legislation

The role of the bureaucracy in the political process is not limited to situations where government agencies have been given formal authority to make rules in legislation that Congress has passed. Government agencies are involved in the early stages of the political process as well, providing inputs to the White House and Congress when legislation is being drafted. But procedures for such involvement are informal, because the bureaucracy has only informal influence, not formal authority. On legislation whose topic does not extend beyond the confines of one agency, informal cooperation between the agency and the relevant congressional committee (or committees) often occurs. In other situations, an agency may become involved in whatever policy development procedures have been established in the White House.[13]

The agency officials who provide legislative input are seldom the same people as those involved in rule making. Rather, input at this early stage comes mainly from offices of policy and evaluation, often staffed by academically oriented personnel, frequently with Ph.D.s, and from offices of legislative affairs, often staffed by people with staff-level legislative experience.

In systems outside the United States with traditionally strong bureaucracies, the role of the bureaucracy in developing legislation is often far greater than the informal advisory role the bureaucracy plays in the United States. In parliamentary systems, legislation is drafted within the executive and given what generally amounts to rubber-stamp approval by parliament. This means that agency officials often play a key role in preparing actual statutes. The process of preparing legislation takes place to a much greater extent behind closed doors than it does in the United States, where congressional involvement is so prevalent. Richard Rose describes legislative proposals developed in Britain as a "conjoint product of work by top bureaucrats and (politically responsible) ministers."[14] Such a statement could probably be made about the role of the bureaucracy in most countries outside the United States.

The degree of agency influence in parliamentary countries over legislation varies with how visible and politically important an issue is. How much the bureaucracy consults with interest groups and elected officials while drafting legislation, and the procedures for such consultation, vary by country. In Japan and France such consultation is often relatively perfunctory. In Sweden, by contrast, an elaborate system of "state commissions" brings politicians, interest group officials, and bureaucrats together to develop proposed legislation.[15]

Elected Officials and the Bureaucracy

One way we express our hesitation about granting unelected officials formal authority over political choice is to ring that authority with extensive procedural requirements, requirements that are more stringent than in other countries. A second way is to give elected officials more influence over the bureaucracy than is the case abroad. How Congress and the president can influence the bureaucracy were discussed in earlier chapters.[16]

It is a subject of some debate how much the various ways that elected officials can influence the bureaucracy in fact end up limiting the freedom of unelected agency officials to make the choices they wish to make. Probably the dominant view among political scientists studying government organizations has been to emphasize the limitations on the influence of elected officials.

What limits the ability of the White House to influence political choices made in the bureaucracy? The basic problem is the problem that produces delegation of formal authority to the bureaucracy in the first place—the number and technical complexity of so many of the decisions that are to be made, and the far greater organizational capacity in the agencies than in the White House. Beyond that are the difficulties the president has influencing his own agents within the executive branch, the assistant secretaries who actually run government programs.

One of the first problems presidents face is that they must appoint many assistant secretaries at the beginning of their administration, when there is so much else to do and the most poorly developed organizational machinery to get it done.[17] If a president does not decide that this is an extremely important priority, these appointments are not likely to be appropriate from the president's point of view. With President Carter, for example, an "early interest [in appointments] faded quickly as other substantive concerns captured his attention."[18] By contrast, President Reagan realized how important assistant secretaries were to the political tone of his administration. To do things right, he was willing to delay these appointments, often by several months, until an organizational capability had been established in the White House to make such appointments carefully.

A second thing that limits the ability of the president to exert influence through his assistant secretaries is that, even if the president takes the time to care about the appointments process, he does not really have a free hand in making his appointments. Dean Mann and Jameson Doig found, for example, that in half the cases they examined, the cabinet secretary and not the president or his staff was the dominant participant in the selection process.[19] Organized groups that supported the president in his election campaign often have favored candidates as well. Furthermore, the increasing policy expertise these positions require also hamstrings the president in many agencies. In agencies, the policy issues involved are too complicated to allow an assistant secretary appointed solely on the basis of loyalty to the president to have any chance at succeeding. As a result, the tendency has grown to appoint assistant secretaries from the ranks of the policy community in the substantive area with which the agency deals. Thus, less than half of recently appointed assistant secretaries had had any significant record of party political activity prior to their appointment. Only an eighth had been delegates to at least one of the two previous presidential nominating conventions.[20] In fact, between one-fifth and two-fifths were career civil servants before their appointments.[21] The danger for the president is that the loyalties of such assistant secretaries may be as much to the values of their agency or policy community as to the president.[22] And it is difficult to recruit and retain good top management if they are mere messenger boys for decisions reached above them.

Finally, use of the formal authority that the president possesses to fire appointed officials is politically costly and can be tapped only sparingly.[23] The public can easily perceive, and the media can easily portray, such dismissals as an embarrassing admission that the initial appointment was a mistake. The dismissed appointee may leave the job claiming to have been the victim of devotion to the public interest, unwilling to cave in to some nefarious special interest the president sought to heed. An extreme example of these difficulties was the reaction to the "Saturday Night Massacre" when President Nixon dismissed the attorney general for refusing to fire the Watergate special prosecutor. Generally, the threat of resignation by a high political appointee gives him leverage against the president, more than the other way around. John Quarles, deputy administrator of the Environmental Protection Agency during the Nixon-Ford years, reports in his book *Cleaning Up America* that William Ruckelshaus agreed to continue serving as administrator in 1973 only after President Nixon promised that the agency, not the White House, would make final rule-making decisions. Nixon presumably feared the consequences of a Ruckelshaus resignation enough to accede to the request.[24]

All this limits the ability of the president to influence agencies through informal means. The final success the Reagan administration enjoyed with the regulatory bureaucracy required changes in decision-making procedures themselves, so as to increase the formal authority and not just the indirect influence of the White House. Furthermore, for that formal authority to be meaningful, the White House must create the organizational capacity to examine key agency decisions. Otherwise, the advantages the bureaucracy gains from its expertise and continuous involvement remain overwhelming.

An analogous story of the difficulty that elected officials have influencing the bureaucracy can be told for Congress. The conventional view, that congressional oversight committees have trouble influencing the bureaucracy, has been challenged recently in an interesting and important article by economists Barry Weingast and Mark Moran on congressional control of the Federal Trade Commission.[25] Weingast and Moran point out that the relative infrequency of intervention from congressional committees should not be taken, as it often is in the literature, to prove the inability of elected officials to influence agencies. Rather, they note, infrequent intervention might also result from a system of control (based on control over budgets and statutory mandates) so effective that it deters the necessity actually to intervene; the effectiveness of ex ante sanctions could make frequent ex post interventions superfluous. (Although their argument involves the influence of congressional commitees, a variant of it could be made for other elected officials.) Weingast and Moran argue that the activist Federal Trade Commission of the mid-1970s had appeared in response to a Senate oversight committee that was extremely liberal. In 1977 the composition of this committee changed, and in response, the authors argue, the commission changed the mix of cases from industry-wide probes to less controversial investigations, such as actions against companies giving textiles improper country-of-origin labels.

There are serious problems with the specific argument about the Federal Trade Commission the authors have made.[26] The agency was indeed disciplined by Congress at the end of the 1970s, when the agency's appropriations were threatened and its jurisdiction limited. But the influence came in an open confrontation in 1979 and 1980, not through the quiet changes that Weingast and Moran incorrectly believe they have discovered. Moreover, it took a major shift in the popular mood regarding regulation, a mood to which the agency failed to respond, to accomplish that congressional influence. Such occasional successful interventions may then merely show that there are limits to how far an agency can ignore elected officials and popular moods. They would not argue against the structural limits on the ability of Congress to intervene. In this view occasional interventions would reflect the necessity to ration intervention to a few very big situations.

The ability of elected officials outside the bureaucracy to

influence the political process inside should be, I think, seen as a variable. The degree of influence depends on the policy area and on the institutional arrangements that have been established. First, the more technical an issue is, the more influence the bureaucracy will have. Examining a number of decisions about occupational safety and health in the United States and Sweden, I noted that the content of the decisions was similar, despite the extremely different political balance of forces in the two countries. The technical content of these decisions (who knows much about benzo(a)pyrene?) did not determine the choices, for they were political choices that involved values. It did, however, serve as a barrier to entry to keep elected officials out of the discussion.[27] By contrast, in policy areas where the expertise of government officials is more lightly regarded, such as education policy or consumer protection, elected officials have an easier time influencing the process.[28] Second, the more a government agency has a monopoly or quasi monopoly on information, the more influence the bureaucracy will have. This suggests greater bureaucratic influence over national security decisions.[29]

The way various political forces outside an agency interact with each other affects the degree of bureaucratic power. An agency operating in an environment with few organized groups, such as the State Department, may have greater independence because organized group pressures are less. At the same time, the presence of *competing* interest groups may cancel out any effect and also leave the agency with more independence than one would otherwise think, a conclusion suggested by my study of occupational safety and health rule making, where the agency was besieged by business and labor interest groups demanding the opposite decisions. The same may occur if an agency can play off the president and its congressional committees. Finally, if an agency interacts with only one interest group but that group has views similar to those within the agency itself (such as is the case for the Department of Agriculture and farm groups), the organized group may deflect the ability of elected officials to influence the agency.

Consequences of Granting Formal Authority to the Bureaucracy

By far the most important effect of granting the bureaucracy formal authority to make political choices is that this lodges authority in the hands of people who tend to support the program in question. That applies equally to programs generally regarded as "liberal" and "conservative," to environmental protection and to defense. Strong environmental policies—or a strong defense—may be highly controversial in the political system as a whole. They are far less controversial in the Environmental Protection Agency and the Department of Defense. As it has been evocatively phrased, where bureaucrats stand is often determined by where they sit. Speaking of situations where different agencies are involved in political contention within the executive branch, Graham Allison writes:

A proposal to withdraw American troops from Europe is to the Army a threat to its budget and size, to the Budget Bureau a way to save money, to the Treasury a balance-of-payments gain, to the State Department Office of European Affairs a threat to good relations with NATO, to the President's congressional advisors an opportunity to remove a major irritant in the President's relations with the Hill.[30]

The impact that giving the bureaucracy formal authority has on the content of political choices is an important example, then, of the impact that decision-making procedures have on results.

The reasons for agency support for programs under their jurisdiction may be found in agency missions and often their recruitment patterns. The mission of most government agencies, reflected in the statutes that create them, is to promote certain values. These values can range from defense to environmental protection to restoration of downtown business districts in urban centers. A mission is more than just a statement of tasks: to become an organization's mission, a statutory statement of tasks must be tied to the idea that these tasks are important to making the world a better place.

Furthermore, many agencies hire people with specific professional backgrounds to carry out the organization's work. Thus, inevitably, the Federal Trade Commission must have lawyers, since its statute directs it to bring cases against firms suspected of consumer fraud or of antitrust violations. The Occupational Safety and Health Administration must have safety engineers and industrial hygienists. The Army must have military officers, the Public Health Service doctors. These organizations could never get anything accomplished without such professionals.

Professionals, however, frequently come not only with a set of technical skills but also with a set of values and orientations, often received as part of their professional training. The agencies must hire these people for their expertise. But they often come only as part of a package deal. To hire the expertise, you must hire the values.[31] Frequently, such values and the mission of the agencies act in the same direction. Thus, for example, occupational safety and health professionals highly value protection of life and limb, a set of values consistent with the mission of the Occupational Safety and Health Administration.[32]

The effects of mission and recruitment can also be seen when the bureaucracy acts as a source of information for Congress and the White House in the early stages of the political process. The generation of alternatives is often far from serendipitous when undertaken by large organizations. If asked to come up with alternatives for how best to deal with unemployment, the Employment and Training Administration is likely to recommend something in the area of job creation or retraining rather than, say, abolishing the minimum wage or putting more money into preschool education. Which organizations become involved in generating alternatives therefore plays a role in determining which alternatives will be considered. Furthermore, agency officials often go beyond providing information. Although they are prohibited by statute from lobbying members of Congress—a reflection of our unease about bureaucratic participation in the political process—in fact agency officials do frequently campaign informally for specific political choices in Congress. As early as the turn of the century, for example, Harvey Wiley, head of the Bureau of Chemistry of the Department of Agriculture, campaigned for many years to get Congress to pass a pure food and drug law.

One result, then, of giving the bureaucracy formal authority is to increase the chances that decisions will promote the values embodied in an agency's mission. Second, agency officials are affected by outside advocates somewhat differently from elected officials. For starters, contacts outside of the formal procedures between agency officials and outsiders—whether they are representatives of interest groups, congressmen or staffs, or people from the White House—are now strictly limited. In a 1977 ruling, the Supreme Court struck down a decision by the Federal Communications Commission that had occurred after informal contacts between agency staff and parties to the proceedings that were not reflected on the official hearing record.[33] In the wake of that Court decision, agencies issued internal regulations often prohibiting any contacts outside of public hearings or written communication. In some cases, agencies allowed informal meetings, but only if a verbatim transcript was kept, to be entered into the formal rule-making record. Such prohibitions go far beyond anything that exists for Congress or the White House, where such informal contacts occur every day.

In addition, interests in the political process who can amass large sums of money cannot use it directly to influence the bureaucracy, because bureaucrats do not stand for election and thus do not need campaign contributions. To the extent that campaign contributions influence the behavior of elected officials, and their behavior in turn affects an agency, money can exert some indirect influence. And there have also been hints, under the suggestive rubric called "revolving door," that agency officials become biased in favor of wealthy interests by a hope of obtaining postgovernment employment with organizations able to pay handsome salaries.

Neither of these sources of indirect influence should be totally discounted. Nonetheless, the limits of the ability of money to influence the bureaucracy, compared with Congress, should be remembered. Since the process by which money can influence the behavior of agency officials is indirect, it can be expected to have less force than in a process where it is more direct. The opportunities for slippage are greater. And any effects of the influence of future nongovernment jobs on behavior of agency officials while they work in government are reduced by a possible countertendency for nongovernmental organizations to seek to hire people who are competent and aggressive, even if those traits had previously been displayed on behalf of government goals. Paul Quirk's interviews at a number of regulatory agencies showed that officials at the Civil Aeronautics Board and the National Highway Transportation Safety Administration did indeed believe that strong antiindustry stands might hurt their chances for subsequent private employment. But officials at the Food and Drug Administration believed this would be a problem only for individuals with "extreme" or "lunatic fringe" antiindustry opinions, while lawyers at the Federal Trade Commission, in fact, generally believed that aggressiveness helped their future prospects outside government.[34] One may ask, however, to what extent even the instances of perceived influence over a career outside government succeed in influencing agency policy. Of the two agencies where officials perceived such influences, one (the Civil Aeronautics Board) generally made "proindustry" decisions while the other (the National Highway Transportation Safety Administration) generally made "antiindustry" ones. And it is unlikely that a "lunatic fringe" at an agency will have much influence over decisions an agency makes.

All this makes it more difficult for advocates to attempt to wield influence, other than persuasiveness, in the bureaucracy than in Congress. In addition, the requirement that agency decisions be justified by evidence on the formal rule-making record does not apply to congressional decisions. It is probably also the case that the typical agency official is more at home in a world of facts and substantive arguments than are elected officials.

The role of persuasiveness in influencing agency officials tends to equalize power among interest groups whose financial resources or number of members differ, because inequality among organized groups' ability to muster argument and do research is almost certainly less than the inequality of financial resources or membership.

It is not only interest groups with a lot of money or members that are relatively disadvantaged in the bureaucracy compared with Congress. Also hurt are advocacy groups with a visible, popular issue about which they can make a case to the media or to elected officials, but a harder time summoning up detailed arguments. Agency officials meet "real people" less than politicians do. They become used to well-argued briefs and have a hard time with inchoate pleas. The political process in the bureaucracy is more sanitized than is politics in Congress, more removed from direct contact with reality outside Washington. Thus, for example, John Chubb found that consumer-oriented energy groups had an easier time with Congress, where many members were responsive to public outrage over high oil prices, than in the Department of Energy, where they could not present technical arguments.[35]

A final consequence of placing formal authority in the bureaucracy is that it reduces the likelihood of quick or dramatic policy departures. Elected officials are more likely to be willing to take risks, for they have entered a much riskier profession. Government officials, by contrast, have entered a system where job security is often one of the attractions of the work.[36] Furthermore, the procedures according to which the bureaucracy must operate virtually preclude rapid choice, because they frequently mandate certain time periods for interested parties to comment and require examination of often voluminous evidence prior to decision. Congressional procedures are cumbersome in number, but there are no time or evidence requirements. Thus, while Congress also typically acts slowly, it is more capable of acting with great speed in a crisis than are agencies.

Perhaps the best way to summarize the results of giving formal authority to the bureaucracy rather than Congress is to ask what kinds of outside advocates would rather deal with agencies and which with Congress. Advocates whose views are out of line with the mission or recruitment values of an agency would generally rather take their chances with the more unpredictable process in Congress than rely on an agency predisposed against them. An advocate representing a group with many members or a visible and popular issue or a lot of money generally prefers to deal with Congress. An advocate who wishes to take advantage of a crisis to seize the moment before the crisis has been forgotten almost certainly prefer to deal with Congress. So does, usually, an advocate who seeks radical change in current policy. The advocates who prefer to deal with the bureaucracy are generally those like government officials themselves—skilled in careful argument, relatively unemotional, and patient enough to stand fast over the long haul. In his book *The End of Liberalism,* Theodore Lowi argues that vague legislation placing lots of formal authority for political choice in the bureaucracy increases the influence of interest groups over the political process.[37] I do not think one can make such a generalization. Rather, some interest groups will prefer to deal with the bureaucracy, but others will prefer Congress.

Is the Bureaucracy Too Powerful?

As we have seen in this chapter, the bureaucracy is a political place. Those who wish to shield the bureaucracy from the influence of elected officials sometimes inveigh against the "politicization" of the bureaucracy. This is plain silly. If by "political" is meant involving controversial value choices, then the bureaucracy cannot *become* politicized, for it already *is* so. We should not deny that or even be ashamed about it. Both the substantive expertise and the political point of view that government officials have are important resources in the political process.

In a world where nonelected officials have significant independent influence over the results of the political process, it becomes important to think about how such a state of affairs could be justified. The justification is relatively straightforward as long as government officials merely make proposals to elected officials about what the problems might be and how they ought to be solved. Bureaucrats are then participants providing valuable input into a political debate in which their expertise and continuous involvement certainly legitimate their ability to participate. Even when government officials act as advocates for the programs their agency represents, I would argue that they are acting legitimately as ongoing institutional representatives for values that Congress has chosen to grant legitimacy by enshrining in statutes.

However, eyebrows may justly be raised when advocates are given the formal authority to make actual political choices, even when these choices are constrained by various procedural and other checks. The problem is what in the erstwhile language of the Communist Chinese would have been called the dilemma of being "red" as well as "expert"—of having the appropriate values, and not only appropriate knowledge.

Perhaps the best approach is to make positions where political choices must be made more subject to political control, but to appoint many of the people for these slots out of career civil servants with values appropriate to the administration in power. An excellent reform in this direction was the provision in the Civil Service Reform Act of 1978 to permit politically appointed executives to transfer career senior managers to other senior career jobs within an agency. This allows politically appointed managers greater freedom to select career people who share their values. It is good to have career people because they have the expertise. It is also good to have greater leeway for political criteria in the choice of *which* expert to use. Meanwhile, the expertise of the senior managers who are transferred to other senior management positions can be used in less politically sensitive areas. Opponents of such moves often evoke a fear of what they refer to as politicization, using the word in a different sense to mean the infusion of incompetent cronies into government agencies. In fact, though, selections for the positions in question are made only from among those who have already attained senior rank in the career service. So, that fear should not be allowed to stand in the way of greater political responsiveness.

The Bureaucracy and Public Spirit

In the research they did comparing attitudes of high-level civil servants in several countries, Joel Aberbach and his colleagues found that the American officials were considerably more "likely to see themselves as promoters of and advocates for policy ideas than were their counterparts in Europe."[38] There are several possible reasons for this difference.[39] One that strikes me is that, given the lower prestige of the bureaucracy in the United States than in Western Europe, a stronger motivation for people to go into the civil service in the United States is the desire to promote what they believe are the right policies,

policies often associated with the mission of the agency they join. In Europe, by contrast, the greater prestige of elite civil service jobs may attract more people who simply want prestigious jobs.[40]

When agency officials act as advocates for the values embodied in the missions of their agency, their ability to examine issues in light of a broad range of considerations is endangered. Where they stand depends on where they sit. The design of the political process in the bureaucracy, however, encourages agency officials to broaden their perspectives. Decisions must be supported by a statement of reasons based on arguments and evidence that have appeared on the record. Opposing arguments must be answered. Courts review them and elected officials examine them, all against a standard of adherence to a disinterested search for good public policy. Perhaps these checks against "where you stand depends on where you sit" thinking are insufficient to deal with that problem. Perhaps though, we should not want them to be complete. The presence of an institutionalized governmental voice for values that have been embodied in legislation provides an anchor against each shimmer of shifting opinion.

6

Institutional Settings for Politics: The Supreme Court

No court in any democratic country plays as important a role in the political process as does the United States Supreme Court. This is so because American courts have formal authority in four areas not typical in other countries.

First, there exists in the United States a significant body of judge-made "common law" rules that have grown up alongside laws legislatures pass. Common law rules, mostly of contract and tort law, regulate interactions among private citizens and are an important part of how government has an impact on people's lives. Generally, judges, not legislatures, have determined rules for what constitutes negligent behavior by an automobile driver involved in an accident or for when people may legally renege on contracts they signed. This role for judges exists not only in the United States but in other common-law countries (that is, Great Britain and her ex-colonies) as well.

Second, American courts have the authority to interpret the language of laws Congress has passed. Courts may lay down requirements they determine to be demanded by a law, even in cases where such requirements are not explicit in the statutes. Thus, on the basis of general language in the Clean Air Act of 1970 that the purpose of the law was to "protect *and enhance*"* air quality, it was ruled that the Environmental Protection Agency had to adopt policies, not specifically required in the legislation, to prevent air quality from deteriorating in areas (such as wildernesses) where it was already better than established quality standards.[1]

Third, the decisions of administrative agencies, whether adjudications involving individual cases or rule-making decisions of general applicability, may in the United States be appealed from the agency that made them to the courts. The Supreme Court reviews only a tiny proportion of agency decisions, and it upholds most such decisions it does review (although it is more common for lower federal courts to overturn administrative rulings).[2] Nonetheless, the formal authority remains, and overturning one decision can have significant impacts on future agency decisions.

Fourth, and most widely noted, the Supreme Court, virtually alone among courts in democratic countries, has the authority for judicial review. The most obvious use of this formal authority is in declaring laws that Congress has passed to be unconstitutional and hence void. (By contrast, as Walter Bagehot once wrote, "There is nothing the British Parliament cannot do except transform a man into a woman and a woman into a man."[3]) The Supreme Court can rule not only that the Constitution *bars* certain political choices, such as laws banning abortions. It also rules that the Constitution *requires* certain choices, such as establishment of protections for criminal suspects. The Supreme Court has (through 1985) ruled 114 provisions of federal laws and 1,088 provisions of state or local laws unconstitutional.[4]

*Emphasis added.

Decisions the Supreme Court makes are political decisions because they have the force of law and people disagree over them. In many instances the Supreme Court is the last waystation of the political process. Choices made in other forums are not final until the Supreme Court has ruled—or declined to rule —on them. In an account of the political process in most democratic countries, courts could be mentioned only in passing. In the United States, that would be impossible.

The considerable formal authority of the Supreme Court has arisen not at once but rather over time. Common-law authority was taken over from England and existed from the beginnings of American history. Judicial review is not specifically authorized by the Constitution, although Alexander Hamilton made a case for it in Federalist Number 78. The Court proclaimed such authority in its 1803 decision in *Marbury* v. *Madison.* Judicial review of administrative decisions was established in a 1902 Supreme Court decision declaring that administrative actions not in accordance with authorizing legislation could be struck down by the courts. Provisions for judicial review of agency decisions were then written into most federal regulatory statutes and incorporated as a general rule in the Administrative Procedures Act of 1946.[5]

We might think that the relative importance of the Supreme Court has increased during the twentieth century. If we look at the early years of the Republic, the Supreme Court indeed appears to have been less important than the other two branches. A number of prominent people refused offers of nomination to the Supreme Court or left the Court for other public offices.[6] Until the 1930s the Court met in the basement of the Capitol, and justices did most of their work at home.[7] Most of the instances where provisions of federal and state laws have been struck down have occurred during the twentieth century.[8]

The impression of the increased relative importance of the Supreme Court may be misleading, however. Take the increasing frequency with which provisions of laws have been declared unconstitutional. This is not necessarily a sign that the *relative* role of the Court is growing, because the number of laws has itself increased dramatically during this century.[9] Likewise, it has been noted, generally by critics of the courts, that courts have become increasingly involved in prescribing specific policies regarding prison conditions, public schools, or welfare assistance that earlier courts avoided—even, in some extreme cases, placing government agencies such as schools or prisons in "receivership" and appointing officials to run them. Courts have, to quote Donald Horowitz, been "very busy, laboring in unfamiliar territory."[10] Yet this need not constitute a *relative* increase in the influence of the courts. It is true that courts have been getting involved in public policy in ways they rarely did in the past. But government as a whole has become more involved in these areas, and other parts of government have been laboring in unfamiliar territory as well. It is also noteworthy that, although the number of cases appealed to the Supreme Court has expanded quite dramatically—increasing by 400 percent between 1943 and 1983—the number the Court actually agrees to hear has been quite stable.[11] In sum, we may state unequivocally that historically there has been a relative shift in influence from Congress to the presidency and the bureaucracy. It is harder to make a clear case for such a relative shift over time in the influence of the Supreme Court.

Indeed, the work-load pressures that have produced increased reliance on staff in Congress and the presidency have not been as severe in the Supreme Court. Most justices currently have four clerks each (generally recent law school graduates who serve for only one year, unlike congressional or presidential staff). There have been isolated allegations of excessive influence by the clerks, including at least one call that they be made subject to Senate confirmation. But the general view is that their substantive input is very small, certainly compared to that of congressional or presidential staff.[12] R. Shep Melnick has made the interesting point that efforts by judges to search in congressional committee reports for the "legislative intent" of vague statutory language increase the influence of *congressional* staff, because committee reports are generally staff-written.[13]

Decisions the courts themselves make about their procedures affect the scope of judicial formal authority. The political decisions courts make occur in the context of cases among litigants (the litigants may be private parties, or they may be private parties and the government). A court cannot make a decision on a policy question unless court procedures classify the policy question at issue as something appropriate for a court to hear in the first place. The Constitution limits the jurisdiction of the Supreme Court to situations involving a "case or controversy." The way that constitutional language was traditionally interpreted, only people with a direct—often direct economic—interest in an issue at hand were allowed to bring legal action. By contrast, the simple fact that a person regarded some existing policy to be wrong did not suffice to give that person standing to bring a case in court. Thus, for example, the traditional procedures for determining whether a case could be brought would allow somebody the paint on whose own house was corroded by acidic air emissions from a nearby plant to go to court, but not an environmentalist in the next town who suffered no personal damage. The traditional rules thus limited the ability of the courts to make political choices, because they limited the situations eligible for court review.

Rules about standing, however, were altered by a number of Supreme Court decisions during the 1960s. Thus, for example, in a 1968 ruling the Supreme Court held, overturning previous doctrine, that taxpayers alleging that money was being used for an unconstitutional project could use their status as taxpayers to give them standing to challenge the legislation in court. In another decision, the Supreme Court ruled that injury to "aesthetic and environmental well-being" gave standing to sue in environmental cases, not just economic injury.[14] The liberalization of rules about standing opened the doors for the direct involvement of organized groups in bringing suit, for the growth of public interest law firms of the left and right, and hence for an expansion of the scope of judicial formal authority.

Another example of changes in rules interpreting the "cases and controversies" requirement involves whether someone should be allowed to bring suit when the court would be unable to provide relief in the specific situation over which the suit has been brought. Under the traditional doctrine of mootness, courts would not accept cases where it would be too late to provide a remedy by the time a ruling could take place. Under traditional doctrines of mootness, for example, antiabortion laws could not be challenged in court because it would be too late for the court to allow a woman bringing suit to have an abortion even if the court ruled she was entitled to one. Similarly, election laws that excluded a certain candidate from appearing on the ballot could not be challenged in court, because they would have become moot by the time a decision could be handed down. In the 1960s the Supreme Court liberalized its rules about mootness to allow cases to be brought where there were recurring situations that might happen to the same litigant again. This change in procedures allowed the Supreme Court to hear cases it would otherwise not have even heard—such as the case that led to the legalization of abortion in 1973.[15]

Similarly, decisions about procedures for class action suits—that is, suits where a number of plaintiffs band together to demand damages that would be far greater than if the suit were brought by a few individuals—will also affect the scope of judicial authority. Since class action suits increase the potential damages a plaintiff can win, prosecuting such suits becomes more attractive for lawyers. Hence, the more willing the courts are to accept class action suits, the more political choices will come before them. In recent years, there has been some liberalization of procedures for determining who may legitimately participate in a class suit and how damages are awarded. The Supreme Court has, however, ruled that when federal statute requires a certain minimum monetary damage for bringing suit in federal court, that amount applies to each member of a potential class. It is not, therefore, possible to meet a $10,000 injury requirement by pooling a $10 per person injury of a thousand victims.[16] Were the procedures different, more cases would certainly come to the courts, and the substantive results of the political process might be different from what they are.

The liberalization of procedures that has allowed more kinds of cases to come before the courts has not necessarily increased the relative role of the Supreme Court in the political process, because other institutions have also gotten more work to do as the role of government has expanded. It has, however, allowed the courts to avoid being a laggard compared with other political institutions.

The Supreme Court and Democratic Control: Insulation and Influence

If the Supreme Court is to have formal authority separate from that of democratically elected officials, institutional arrangements should be established that encourage justices to behave at least somewhat differently from elected officials. Otherwise, there would hardly seem to be any reason to grant them separate authority. Thus, in a number of ways, the Supreme Court has been designed to insulate justices.

The Constitution establishes that justices have life terms and that their salaries may not be reduced while in office. Furthermore, a number of practices, of an informal and customary nature, have grown up over the years. Supreme Court deliberations are secret, and no written notes are kept.[17] The secrecy limits the ability of outsiders to put pressure on the Court before decisions are made. It also reduces any sense of pressure felt by justices to conform to the views of people to whom they feel close. Furthermore, secrecy is not the norm of American democratic practices, and one way of making something sacred is consciously to differentiate it from the every-day run of activities with which it otherwise might be confused. Hence, secrecy contributes to an aura of solemnity and even mystery surrounding the activities of the Court and hence to the justices' own conception of the special nature of their role.

Norms have also developed over time that inhibit attempts by elected officials or interest groups to influence court decisions. The Court itself has contributed to development of these norms by a number of acts of self-abnegation where it passed up opportunities to become more closely involved with the rest of the political system. For example, the Court turned down a request from President Washington to give advice on legal issues relating to the Neutrality Proclamation of 1793.[18] When Franklin D. Roosevelt entered office, he proposed that he get together with the chief justice on an ongoing informal basis to discuss his plans and "to get the Court's slant on them before acting." The chief justice icily rejected the offer, noting that "the strictest separation between the Court and the White House was not only advisable but necessary."[19] Some justices have given informal advice to presidents, but the practice has been very limited. Justice Abe Fortas got into trouble for continuing too close a relationship with President Lyndon Johnson after being named to the Court.[20]

Similar norms severely limit the interaction of justices with interest group representatives. To be sure, there are ways interest groups can influence the Supreme Court. Many suits are filed directly or supported financially (for individual litigants) by organized groups. Thus, for example, many important Supreme Court decisions involving the environment grew out of actions filed by the Natural Resources Defense Council or the Sierra Club. The litigants in *Brown* v. *Board of Education,* where the Court declared school segregation unconstitutional, were supported by the National Association for the Advancement of Colored People. Furthermore, organized groups can file amicus curiae briefs arguing for one of the parties even if they are not themselves litigants.[21] When the Supreme Court heard the case of *California* v. *Bakke,* involving racial preferences in university admissions, there were a total of *120* such briefs.[22]

But direct interest-group lobbying of the Court is considered highly improper. In *The Brethren,* Bob Woodward and Scott Armstrong recount an incident where Thomas Corcoran, a Washington lawyer and former New Deal associate of Justice Hugo Black, made an effort privately to discuss with Black an antitrust case in which Corcoran was representing one of the parties.

> Black was shocked. No one came to the Supreme Court to lobby, even to "put in a good word" for a petitioner. The mere mention of a pending case at a cocktail party was forbidden . . . Black cut his old friend off quickly. *No.* He shooed Corcoran out of his office.[23]

Justice William O. Douglas, a man hardly insensitive to improper influence by the powerful over the processes of government, wrote in his memoirs that, except for the Corcoran incident, he knew of no case where any "corporate interest even tried to tamper with the Court," adding that he could "say the same of any labor union, any senator, any congressman."[24]

All these efforts to insulate the Court, involving both institutional design and informal norms, have worked in the sense that the Supreme Court has been able to act in a way more insulated from democratic pressures than other political institutions. One justice, a former member of Congress, when asked the difference between Congress and the Supreme Court, replied, "Have you ever gone direct from a circus to a monastery?"[25] In his memoirs, William O. Douglas contrasts his life on the Court with his previous years as director of the Securities and Exchange Commission. At the agency, "the hours were busy, the appointments many, the days long." On the Supreme Court, "there was no need to see anyone; appointments dropped off; the routine of reading and research set in."[26]

At the same time, the institutional design of the Supreme

Court has allowed for some democratic influence. Most important are the constitutional provisions that justices be named by the president and confirmed by the Senate. Two out of three presidents have been able to appoint at least one Supreme Court justice within their first two years of office. A president who serves two terms is likely to be able to appoint a significant number of justices.[27] And presidents normally appoint people whose views they expect will be relatively similar to their own. Almost every Supreme Court justice ever appointed has been of the same political party as the president who appointed him. Presidents have personally known about three-fifths of the justices they appointed.[28] Furthermore, "most justices," according to Lawrence Baum, "have had significant involvements in partisan politics prior to their selection, as holders of partisan offices and participants in political campaigns."[29]

Congress has influence as well. Senate approval of Supreme Court nominees is by no means automatic. One-fifth of all such nominations have been rejected, a figure far higher than for any other type of presidential appointment, although rejections were considerably more common in the nineteenth century than they have been in the twentieth century.[30]

The Constitution establishes other forms of democratic control over the Supreme Court. Laws (or constitutional amendments) may be passed nullifying the effects of Supreme Court decisions or modifying the original legislation only marginally in order to meet constitutional objections. According to Henry Abraham, this has occurred in about one-third of the cases where the Court declared federal laws or provisions of federal laws unconstitutional.[31] Laws may also be passed to change the kinds of appellate cases the Supreme Court is authorized to hear or the number of justices sitting on the Court. Such efforts have rarely been successful, but they have frequently been threatened. In 1866 Congress actually forbade President Andrew Johnson to fill the next three Supreme Court vacancies, and in 1937 President Roosevelt made his famed, failed effort, in reaction to decisions striking down various pieces of New Deal legislation, to expand the size of the Court.[32] In its renowned "switch in time," the Court majority upheld a number of New Deal laws just following Roosevelt's court-packing attempt. Likewise, Walter Murphy's careful analysis of the disposition of Supreme Court cases before and after strong congressional attacks on decisions on national security/civil liberties cases shows an increased tendency by the Court to reject civil liberties claims after such criticism.[33]

Democratic control over the Supreme Court is also a matter of informal norms as well as institutional design. There is considerable evidence that justices do not adopt an attitude of Olympian indifference to popular reaction. Justices try especially hard to issue unanimous opinions when their decision is likely to be controversial. Chief Justice Warren, for example, exerted considerable efforts to achieve a unanimous decision in the 1954 school desegregation case. As William O. Douglas notes in his memoirs:

A five-to-four decision was the last thing any of us wanted. It would not be a decisive decision historically. It would make the issue a political football, and would make the filling of the next vacancy on the Court a Roman Holiday . . . [With a unanimous decision] we could present a solid front to the country.[34]

In the same vein Abraham noted, "the Chief Justice will normally make it a practice to assign so-called 'liberal' opinions of the Court to 'conservative' Justices and so-called 'conservative' opinions to 'liberal' Justices . . . in the hope of making them more palatable."[35]

Sometimes such concerns may lead the Court to duck an issue or to modify the content of a decision. The Supreme Court is not required to consider cases appealed to them. The Court refused, for example, to consider whether the war in Vietnam was unconstitutional (because undeclared by Congress). It added language about "all deliberate speed" to its 1954 school desegregation decision, perhaps to blunt the decisions's revolutionary impact.[36]

The degree of democratic control in the institutional design of the Supreme Court is greater than for the courts of most other countries (although, to be sure, these courts, in turn, have less influence over politics). In France and Germany, judges are chosen from a judicial career track. They are generally part of a civil service system independent of any political control.[37]

The Impact of Court Power on the Results of the Political Process

Since courts issue legal decisions, considerations that are especially convincing or relevant in a legal context will have more influence over political decisions made in the court than if courts were not involved. Furthermore, since so many decisions made by other political institutions, particularly the bureaucracy, can be appealed to the courts, considerations especially important in legal thinking tend to become more important in the political process as a whole, and not just in the courts themselves.

Respect for precedent is one such consideration, and this gives a continuity to Court decisions that is less present in congressional ones. Courts sometimes do overrule legal precedents, but respect for precedent forms an important part of legal reasoning. It is easy to remember the times when the Court has overturned established doctrine—such as in the *Brown* v. *Board of Education* ruling that overturned the earlier acceptance of separate but equal schools—and easy to forget how many times advocates do not even seek to change policies through the courts because legal precedents make their chances of success so small. Changing existing policies is difficult in other political institutions as well, but it is more difficult to revise established policy in the courts. This is less likely to be the case when the Supreme Court becomes involved in new areas where there exist few readily available precedents.

Perhaps the most crucial consideration that is disproportionately important in a legal context is the concern for rights and obligations. Legal rules are generally defined in terms of rights they recognize for one party and obligations they impose on others. The importance of courts in the political process thus means that rights are taken more seriously than they otherwise would be. This is the most obvious for "First Amendment" cases and other cases involving the Bill of Rights, but it plays a role in other kinds of decisions the Supreme Court makes as well. Consistent with this view of its role, the Court, as Lawrence Baum notes, is a major participant in only a few substantive policy areas, those where issues of rights are important. The Court plays a smaller role in the bulk of policy areas.[38]

Beyond the fact that rights and obligations are reciprocals and that concern over one perforce creates concern over the other, the importance of obligation in legal thought has an independent impact. For if public policies are seen as actions that lay down obligations for some citizens, then policies will tend to take the form of requirements or prohibitions rather than incentives. Economists, for example, believe (for various reasons not relevant to the discussion here) that it is generally a more sensible idea to tax undesirable behavior than to prohibit it, say, by placing a charge on pollution emissions rather than prohibiting emissions above a certain amount. Yet legal thought does not encourage people to think that way. The influence of courts encourages political choices that require or prohibit, rather than encourage or discourage.

Some commentators downplay the role that legal considerations play in Supreme Court decisions and argue that general ideological considerations are far more important than sometimes assumed. But even such commentators grant that, at a minimum, legal considerations act as a "constraint from which legislators are free" and that it is often difficult for judges to decide precisely whatever they want.[39]

The relative insulation of the Supreme Court from democratic opinion, compared with Congress and the presidency, makes it easier for the Court to give effect to the values embodied in legal arguments and approaches. As Martin Shapiro has noted,

Aside from school desegregation, which was spurred by long-term well-financed lobbying by the NAACP, the major policies and many of the minor ones were judicially initiated without the support of substantial organized constituencies, interest groups or identifiable blocks of voters . . . Indeed, the Court could readily anticipate more political opposition than support—and opposition from sources with a lot of political clout such as state political elites and the Catholic Church. Few American politicians even today would care to run on a platform of desegregation, pornography, abortion, and the "coddling" of criminals. If, as we are so often told, the Supreme Court follows the election returns, it nevertheless does not act in a directly election-oriented way.[40]

One effect, then, of lodging formal authority in the Supreme Court is to increase the ability of arguments and approaches that are unusual for legal reasoning to have an influence over the content of political decisions. A second effect of locating political choice in the courts comes from the fact that courts hear only specific cases. This may create a tendency for the courts, compared with other political institutions, to establish general rules based on the kind of egregious or extreme situations that often become the subject of legal action. Just as lawyers often say that "hard cases make bad law," so it is probably true as well that "horror story" cases make bad law. Requirements designed to deal with the worst of prison conditions, for instance, may be excessively burdensome for the average penal institution. To be sure, the tendency of the Supreme Court to make general determinations based on atypical cases is reduced by the use in litigation of social science data regarding general conditions. Furthermore, other political institutions are hardly immune from the tendency to make policy on the basis of dramatic stories; such horror stories can affect which face of an issue people see and hence influence the results of the political process in all the institutions of government. However, the problem may go deeper into the institutional design of courts, which decide specific cases, than it does with other institutions. Furthermore, because courts hear cases individually, they are in a poor position to make judgments of relative urgency—they do not have a budget, like Congress does, in the context of which they must make tradeoffs.

Is the Power of the Supreme Court Legitimate?

The same kinds of questions about legitimacy as are raised about the bureaucracy are raised about judicial review, and about the judicial activism of which judicial review constitutes a part. This is unusual for an institutional arrangement so well established and of such long duration. The idea of giving courts authority as impartial resolvers of private disputes among individuals has deep resonance in our traditions. American self-assertiveness creates a situation where people tend to get into many disputes with each other, compared to the situation in other countries where the lowly are more inclined to defer to the mighty or where people might try to work things out among themselves more often. Thus we have high litigation rates in the United States compared with other countries; this gives the courts a prominent role in our society. But our democratic traditions, which distrust any lodging of formal authority in non-elected institutions, make any greater role for the courts problematic. That role probably developed, historically, because the founders wanted to place a further check on the uninhibited sway of democracy. The courts benefited, in terms of formal authority granted by institutional design, in a way the bureaucracy, the other nonelected institution of the political process, never did, because the latter, initially small and part of the executive branch headed by the president, was not seen as an effective check against anything.

How can it be justified in a democratic society for the avowedly nondemocratic Supreme Court to make political choices?[41] The answer, if there is one, must in some sense be along the lines suggested by the constitutional scholar Edward S. Corwin, who once described the Supreme Court as "American democracy's way of hedging its bet."[42] The most common view is some form of the observation that not everything—and, in particular, not the rights of minorities—should be subject to democratic control. The role of the Supreme Court, then, is to secure such rights. As Justice Robert Jackson, reflecting this view, once wrote:

> The very purpose of a Bill of Rights was to withdraw certain subjects from the vicissitudes of political controversy, to place them beyond the reach of majorities . . . One's right to life, liberty and property, to free speech, a free press, freedom of worship and assembly, and other fundamental rights may not be submitted to vote; they depend on the outcome of no elections.[43]

Not only recent civil liberties decisions have been framed as protections of the rights of a minority. So were earlier ones striking down regulatory or social welfare laws that were viewed as attacks by democratic majorities on rights to keep or use property.[44]

The justification of the Supreme Court's authority because a non–democratic institution is needed to protect rights raises problems, however. It is true that no widely held philosophical theory of what constitutes good public policy holds that such determinations can be made simply by toting up whether a majority of those concerned would be made better off or not by a proposed policy. But the situations where simple majority rule will fail to produce good public policy are not limited to issues of rights. Simple majority rule may also be inappropriate if the majority holds its views weakly and the minority holds its views intensely, even where no issues of rights are at stake. At the same time, there are few who believe that considerations of rights are absolute, such that political choices involving rights should be fully outside the world of numbers and intensities.

Given this, it is hard to make a case for a fast distinction between issues involving rights, insulated from majorities by the courts, and all other issues, subject to untrammeled democratic choice. Arguments for removing questions of rights from democratic control could easily be extended to a far broader range of issues involving any minority with intense interests versus a majority with weak interests. Arguments for ways that democratic institutions can be shaped to mitigate the problem of intense minorities can be applied to issues of rights as well.

Perhaps a more cautious argument is in order. In situations where appeals to rights must be made to justify a policy, the policy will have a more difficult time in the democratic process than in situations where the justification involves a calculation involving intense minorities and indifferent majorities. This is true as a conceptual and not simply an empirical matter. If the minority interest were large or intense enough to outweigh the majority, considerations of intensity of interest would suffice to justify the policy. No argument based on rights would be needed. If it is necessary to appeal to considerations of rights to justify a policy, that means that the minority is not large enough or sufficiently intense in its interest to outweigh the interests of the majority. When appeals to minority rights are required, those holding the rights will therefore be less able to fend for themselves in the democratic process—at least one where public spirit plays no significant role—because they will be smaller in number or less intense in their preferences than are other minorities.

At the same time, this difference is one of degree only. One would not, I think, wish the general argument for democratic decision making to pass unnoticed in the constitutional design of the courts. And this, luckily, seems to be the basic form that the institutional design of the Supreme Court has taken. Justices are insulated from the democratic process, but not completely so. And the use of the courts does represent a hedging of bets (or a redundant protection, to anticipate language I will use later on), not a replacement for public spirit in the democratic institutions of government.

The justification of a role for the Supreme Court as a guarantor of rights that should not be subject to majority vote is a persuasive one. The only problem is that it is not the one the Court itself has given for its judicial review authority. Rather, that authority has been based, since *Marbury* v. *Madison,* on the idea that the Court is measuring political choices in the other branches against the standard of conformity to the Constitution. In constitutional litigation, Justice Owen Roberts stated, in striking down a piece of New Deal legislation in 1936, the Court "has only one duty—to lay the Article of the Constitution which is invoked beside the statute which is challenged and to decide whether the latter squares with the former.[45]

There are three problems with this alternative justification. Two are problems on the argument's own terms. First, as legal scholar Alexander Bickel has noted, the statement that laws contrary to the Constitution are void does not itself establish the authority of *courts* to proclaim such unconstitutionality. Jefferson's view, for example, was that each branch had the responsibility to see that it (and other branches) adhered to the Constitution. This is the arrangement used in countries that have written constitutions but no judicial review.[46] A second problem with this alternate justification is that, as noted by virtually every commentator on judicial review, many key provisions of the Constitution are vague and give anything but clear guidance. What is the "due process of law" that government must follow before depriving people of life, liberty, or property? What is a "cruel and unusual punishment"? And then there are joker provisions, such as the Ninth Amendment, which states that "the enumeration in the Constitution, of certain rights, shall not be construed to deny or disparage others retained by the people." The fact of constitutional vagueness often makes it inappropriate to speak, as some do, of "strict construction" of the Constitution, since there frequently is no construction available for strict obedience.[47]

The biggest problem with the "apply the Constitution" justification for judicial review is that it tracks the protection of rights so imperfectly. It is true that some provisions of the Constitution do involve recognition of rights, such as freedom of speech. Clearly, however, many constitutional provisions do not purport to involve rights. The Constitution, for example, reserves to the federal government the authority to regulate interstate commerce, and a state law that regulated interstate commerce would, by hypothesis, be clearly unconstitutional. Yet, certainly, the constitutional provision reserving this authority to the national government has nothing to do with rights. Furthermore, there are many rights people might plausibly be argued to have that are not protected in the Constitution. The Constitution recognizes, for example, no right to property or to liberty of action, although it does stipulate that people cannot be deprived of property or liberty of action without due process. Nor does the Constitution recognize welfare rights to a minimum standard of living.

The view that judicial review is justified as a mechanical interpretation of constitutional provisions is comforting because it suggests, in a burst of power denial, that the Court exerts no real power at all, acting instead, in Robert McCloskey's phrase, as a "passive mouthpiece" or "helpless instrument" of the Constitution, simply enforcing judgments made by the founders and not by the justices themselves.[48] Such review, Alexander Bickel notes, would be "a nearly automatic act . . . which in turn gives rise fatally, if unintentionally, to the inference that a nine-man court is an instance of featherbedding."[49] If such a modest view fails, however, the typical underpinning for judicial review disappears. There remains a case for the Court as securer of rights. But that justification has little basis in, and therefore little authority from, the Constitution itself, as appealing as it might be as a general intellectual proposition. One is left then with legal scholar Michael Perry's argument that "many of our contemporary political practices and institutions . . . go far beyond anything the framers likely contemplated," so why pick on the Supreme Court?[50]

The Supreme Court and Public Spirit

Courts are the political institution most explicitly designed to encourage those making decisions to examine policies in the light of what is right rather than what is in the personal interest of the decision maker. The norm of public spirit for courts goes back to the very foundations of why we have courts in the first place—to obtain the impartial arbitration of disputes. For such a system to be legitimate, those given formal authority must engage themselves in a disinterested search for the right decision. Such an attitude constitutes the essence of public spirit.

The norm of public spirit in the courts is promoted in many ways, even including the way judges dress. Neither members of Congress nor presidents wear any special clothing when performing their responsibilities. Judges wear robes. The sartorial transformation is designed to signal (and promote) an attitudinal transformation. "To the often-heard 'Does a person become any different when he puts on a gown?' " Henry Abrahams writes, "Mr. Justice Frankfurter's sharp retort was always, 'If he's any good, he does!' "[51]

The sense in which justices display public spirit is, however, controversial. The claim that courts merely interpret and examine cases against a standard of preexisting constitutional rules is highly questionable. A somewhat more defensible version of this claim is that judges examine cases in light of overall judgments about the meaning of various vague constitutional provisions or of general views about whether the Court should show restraint or activism in its review of decisions made by the more democratic branches.

Even the view that justices decide cases in terms of overall constitutional philosophies has come under attack from so-called judicial behavioralists. These scholars have specialized in performing quantitative analyses of the voting behavior of Supreme Court judges, and their results indicate that justices' votes tend to fall consistently into "liberal" and "conservative" patterns on a wide array of issues.[52] The point of such studies is generally to show that divisions on the Court are "political," involving general, not legal, ideologies.

Several points may be made about such studies. First, taken by themselves, they do not really demonstrate what they purport to show. Consistency can be the result of a consistent constitutional philosophy as well as of a consistent political philosophy. The question, presumably, is the extent to which justices simply find legal language, or develop legal philosophies, to support political views they hold on independent grounds. Data about judicial consistency across issues have nothing to say about that issue. Second, it would certainly not be surprising to discover, given the fact that most Supreme Court justices have had significant political careers, and a good many had no judicial career before being appointed to the Court, that the source of consistency did indeed turn out to be general political views and not general legal philosophies. One good test of this hypothesis is to see the extent to which Supreme Court justices have acted differently on the bench from the expectations of the presidents who appointed them. Robert Scigliano has calculated that the behavior of about one-third of all justices has been a disappointment to the president appointing them.[53] Whether that is many or few will be left to the reader's judgment.

It should be noted that, from the point of view of public spirit, the debate about constitutional philosophies versus political philosophies is somewhat irrelevant. This is so despite the debunking tone of much judicial behaviorism. In fact, decisions based on political ideologies can be just as public spirited as those based on constitutional philosophies. Like so much other academic writing of a debunking nature about the political process, the contentions of the judicial behavioralists fall flat.

7

Production: A Framework for Analysis

The dividing line between the political and production stages of the policy-making process may be drawn in different ways. The political process generally continues after a law is passed, in the bureaucracy and often in the courts. But eventually the shouting subsides. It never stops entirely, of course. Organizations, or even units within organizations, are not monoliths, and some disputes about what should be done continue until final government actions occur. Furthermore, power can be exercised within organizations just as in political processes, when, for example, managers use various inducements to try to improve the performance of subordinates. Finally, citizen dissatisfaction with what a government organization produces will frequently open up political battles again as efforts are made to get the organization to change what it is producing or to do a better job.

Production, according to my definition, is the stage of the policy-making process when political contention involving people outside an agency has died down and the organization is left with the job of creating the outputs it has been decided that the government should make. I recognize that any dividing line such as this is likely to be fuzzy around the edges. Conceptualizing the dividing line this way allows using research on organizations and on operations management to see what happens when production becomes the issue and to examine how the quality of the operating performance of governmental organizations can be improved.

Many features of what citizens observe when they see final government actions are the results of what occurs during the production process.

- How welfare recipients perceive welfare policy depends not only on political choices about eligibility requirements or payment levels, but also on how those requirements are interpreted on a daily basis, on how long the lines are at the welfare office, and on how caseworkers treat recipients.
- In the early 1970s the federal government established a Supplementary Security Income program to aid the blind, the handicapped, and other disadvantaged groups. But when the first checks went out, millions were for the wrong amount.
- How worthwhile a program is depends on its costs as well as on its benefits. "Waste in government" is a major concern of citizens, and waste is a problem of the efficiency of organizational performance.

This is why, as noted earlier, production is part of the policy-making process. If final government actions bear only indistinct resemblance to earlier political choices, this is because something has gone awry during the production stage of the policy-making process.

Sometimes government sets about to do something, and nothing happens. Indeed, lots of the interest in implementation began around the time of Lyndon Johnson's Great Society, when just such implementation busts were perceived.

The earliest classics of organization theory did not see the quality of performance of bureaucratic organizations as problematical. Max Weber never questioned the effectiveness of bureaucracy as a means to accomplish goals. "The decisive reason for the advance of bureaucratic organization," he wrote, "has always been its purely technical superiority over any other form of organization. The fully developed bureaucratic mechanism compares with other organizations exactly as does the machine with the non-mechanical modes of production."[1] Similarly, in traditional microeconomic theory it is simply assumed that firms will perform to the best of their potential, thus taking for granted much of what managers sweat long hours to achieve.[2]

More recently, theories about organizational performance (or at least the performance of government organizations) have taken the opposite tack. The publication, in 1973, of *Implementation* by Jeffrey Pressman and Aaron Wildavsky, which in short order succeeded in becoming a minor classic, launched the new tack.[3] Pressman and Wildavsky examined efforts to implement decisions to create jobs for the disadvantaged in Oakland, California, through two government-assisted construction projects. They note that "some programs are aborted because political agreement cannot be obtained. Others languish because funds cannot be secured." But in the case they examined, neither was the case. "Everyone agreed. . . . Essential funds were on hand at the right time."[4] Yet the marine terminal and the airport hangar that were planned were never built.

Many of the problems the authors described in *Implementation* were political, involving contention among different views at the local level. Nonetheless, Pressman and Wildavsky drew a generally pessimistic conclusion that went far beyond the limited scope of their case study. And (as often happens) the conclusion is better remembered than the details of the case. This somber view was reinforced by the spate of studies appearing around the same time suggesting that many social programs had not succeeded in solving the problems they were intended to solve. In fact, what the research results, if correct, demonstrated was that the original political choices had been ill conceived. (To use the language of this book, the final government actions envisioned would not achieve the real-world outcomes desired.) The problem may not have been at the production stage at all; ill-conceived policy choices may be produced flawlessly. Nonetheless, such subtle distinctions tended to get lost in the discussions. The impression grew that government could not accomplish anything.

I steer a middle course between views that take successful production for granted and those who regard the achievement of good performance as hopeless. Organizations can accomplish great feats. If it proves impossible to create the needed capacity, or if unintended consequences of establishing it distort performance, then an organization may founder: experience teaches that the production stage can be a land where dreams die. And the quality of performance may be poorer than it need be even when a program does not fail completely, if the organization's design does not encourage the best performance. The central focus of this chapter, then, is on how organizations develop the capacity to produce—including attention to why the development of such capacity may be problematic and to the unintended consequences of the establishment of organizational capacity for the results of the production process. The view I take comes closest to that in management literature, which sees success as a challenging task that can be met. Such a view has a double virtue: it realistically describes the production process in government and also fits nicely this book's orientation toward the participant, or potential participant, in the policy-making process.

Why Organizations?

Organizations are formed because people cannot accomplish certain tasks at all, or at least as well, by themselves. It is sometimes physically or otherwise impossible for an individual to accomplish a task alone. Even in a lifetime, an unaided individual could not build one of the Great Pyramids. No single individual could handle the millions of telephone inquiries that taxpayers make each year with questions about their taxes.

More often, however, having individuals undertake tasks by themselves is not so much unfeasible as inefficient. Assume I am good at wood carving. I might choose to locate wood, chop it down, take it home, carve it, and go out and sell my carvings —all by myself. But it does not make sense for me to spend time locating, chopping, and transporting wood, or selling what I have produced, if what I do best is *carving*. I should instead spend all my time carving so as to have more products to sell and then use some of the proceeds to hire people to do the other tasks. I should, in other words, form an organization.

Organizations are systems for accomplishing an activity by dividing it up among individuals. Sometimes, such division of labor consists simply of having large numbers of people perform a similar task, thus allowing activity to be undertaken on a scale otherwise impossible. Often, however, organization involves specialization. Whether it is the woodcarver in my example, the fabled pin factory of which Adam Smith wrote in *The Wealth of Nations,* or the division of responsibilities in the Occupational Safety and Health Administration between those who write the regulations and those who inspect factories to enforce them, the principle is the same. Specialization can improve quality and increase productivity.

It does so, basically, by making it easier for people to do a better job. Specialization can make it easier to perform better for several reasons. In some cases, dividing up a task allows it to be performed by people with relatively low skill levels. It would require great skill to assemble an entire automobile from scratch, but it is easy to attach a door. In other cases the advantages of specialization are of a very different sort. If the knowledge and skills required for a task are complex, it is all a person can do to become good at one job. Somebody who tried to become a good research chemist and a good lawyer would likely fail at both. In still other instances, specialization improves performance because people have greater talent or inclination for doing some kinds of jobs than others. It would be foolish for someone good at sports but weak in math to divide his time between jobs as a professional football player and an accountant. Finally, frequent repetition of a task, which specialization permits, improves performance. Heart surgery, for example, is better undertaken by specialists than by general surgeons.[5]

Division of labor allows an organization to accomplish great feats, but designing an organization to achieve that division of labor is a challenge. An organization's capacity for work consists of its ability to get good performance from its people and of the way it designs the jobs the organization does. Good performance is attained by recruiting the right people, training them, seeing that they are inclined to work hard, establishing performance measures for their work, and using inducements to reward or punish performance depending on how it compares to performance standards. All this is the domain of what used to be called personnel management and is now often called human resources management. Organizational job design establishes the degree of job specialization, decides the extent to which behavior should be regulated by rules and the extent to which people will be given discretion, and creates mechanisms for coordination among the various tasks into which the organization's work has been divided. This is the domain of the organization of production.[6]

Organizing Production: Job Design

Because an organization's work is done on a large scale, jobs must be designed to achieve reasonable performance quality on a routine basis and not simply as an occasional virtuoso result. And when specialized tasks within an organization must be meshed, jobs must also be designed so that performance of each individual task is predictable. If one cook is responsible for the steak and another for the potatoes, one item will get cold if the other is not ready on time.

One of the things that makes job design such a challenge—and, often, such a frustrating failure—is that frequently jobs must be designed not only to encourage uniformity and predictability in performance but also to encourage adaptability and flexibility in the face of unusual circumstances or environmental change. The sources of unusual demands are legion. Clients may ask for something they have never asked for before. Methods of dealing with situations that worked before may stop working. The problem for job design is that these two requirements often work against each other. Uniformity and predictability suggest detailed rules and procedures, whereas adaptability and flexibility suggest the opposite.

The most fundamental issue in job design is thus the extent to which behavior is regulated by standard operating procedures and the extent to which people are left to decide for themselves the most appropriate way to behave. Standard operating procedures are rules, developed in advance, that establish how people doing a job are to behave in specific situations they face. Examples of standard operating procedures in organizations are countless. Welfare offices require that applicants for welfare fill out a form listing information about income, assets, and family status. Occupational Safety and Health Administration inspectors, early during an inspection, must interview a random group of workers about possible hazards. Other standard operating procedures for these inspectors describe at great length how the size of monetary penalties for violations should be calculated.[7] Standard operating procedures for maintenance workers in office buildings prescribe how often preventive maintenance is to be performed on heating units or other equipment and what specific steps should be performed during maintenance on a given piece of equipment.

Standard operating procedures solve the challenge of predictable quality and of uniformity by reducing the skills required to do a job. Tasks are divided up so they become less difficult. Responses are preprogrammed so that tasks require less discretion. In terms of assuring reasonable performance on a large scale, standard operating procedures allow a wondrous achievement: they allow ordinary people routinely to perform extraordinary feats. Although standard operating procedures can help even highly skilled people, because they save time, it is where a job is to be performed by people of average skill and accomplishment that routine procedures can become crucial.

What would be the alternative to having standard operating procedures for preventive maintenance on a machine? Professional maintenance engineers, with advanced degrees, could be hired as maintenance workers. But that would be an expensive way to proceed, and it would still be time consuming, and hence even more costly, for such people to make ongoing individual determinations about procedures to follow for each machine. However, people with only modest skills can do the job if they "go by the book" (or, as is actually the case with the standard procedures developed for equipment maintenance, follow the instructions on a laminated card they take with them). The alternative to having prescribed routines to establish eligibility requirements for food stamps would be that skilled home economists or social workers would have to make time-consuming case-by-case determinations.

Standard operating procedures can also address the problem of assuring reasonably uniform behavior. Fast-food chains such as McDonald's attract customers, including out-of-towners who have never eaten at a local McDonald's, by using an elaborate variety of standards for food preparation to create a product of uniform quality.[8] In government, standard operating procedures can establish under what circumstances "rush" passports will be issued, what will count as proof of eligibility for registering to vote, or how high welfare payments should be for people with a certain income. This is important because equitable treatment of citizens provides a signal of equal recognition that has an effect on us as people.

Since they do not respond to preprogrammed solutions,

unusual situations are the enemy of the standard operating procedure. Organizations use several strategies to deal with this. One is to develop large numbers of procedures for different contingencies, including rare ones. The *Field Operations Manual* for Occupational Safety and Health Administration inspectors, for instance, tells them how to act if threatened by an employer with a deadly weapon. The Internal Revenue Service has a procedure for dealing with a spouse who filed a joint tax return, became estranged in the weeks between filing the return and the mailing of a tax refund, and now complains that the estranged partner cashed the entire tax refund check sent to them jointly rather than dividing it between the spouses.[9]

If change in the environment is predictable, it can be subject to standard operating procedures. Because banks and supermarkets know when they typically get the most and the fewest customers, they can regularly vary their staffing levels to deal with (predictable) environmental change.[10] Because the Internal Revenue Service knows that each year around tax time the number of telephone inquiries to its local offices will triple, it can establish procedures for hiring and training temporary personnel, and renting additional telephone circuits.[11]

An organization can also be designed so that standard procedures are in place to transfer responsibility from an employee who can only summon a limited repertoire of responses to one who is more skilled. When taxpayers call a local Internal Revenue Service office with questions, the person taking the calls has a relatively low level of training. Questions that this individual cannot answer are transferred to a back-up person. A health maintenance organization using nurse practitioners will design procedures for handing over the more difficult cases to a physician. One danger of excessive reliance on standardized procedures is that they overload higher levels of the organization with demands to make decisions that those below, if given more responsibility, might have been able to make themselves.

However, discretion is inevitable even in many jobs based on standard operating procedures. If an event is truly unexpected, rather than simply unusual but predictable, there can be no routine procedure for it. And decisions must often be made on the spot, without time to refer them to a higher authority.

Although standard procedures may solve one challenge of job design—the challenge of developing predictable quality and uniformity—they do so at the expense of adaptability and of potential excellence. The more rules are established, the more people are left at sea when faced with new situations, because they are incapable of thinking for themselves. A maintenance worker who always works by the book may be unable to perform emergency corrective maintenance. And while standard operating procedures may assure reasonable competence, they will not call forth outstanding performance. By establishing a model of acceptable conduct, standard operating procedures may discourage behavior that is better than acceptable. Instead of defining minimum performance they may come to define maximum performance.[12] As management consultant Tana Pesso reports in her account of the behavior of intake workers at a state welfare office:

> Intake workers rarely offered advice to applicants about how to improve their chances of being found eligible or how to accelerate the process. Nor did they often inform them of the range of services the Welfare Department provides. . . . Applicants often directly asked for or implied that they would like assistance in solving immediate problems, such as imminent telephone disconnection. Intake workers never responded to these requests by drawing on their personal experience or common sense.[13]

Having said that, I hasten to add that this description of standard operating procedures may miss the big picture. An organization's procedures constitute a core element of its capacity. If we see standardized procedures predominantly as an obstacle we miss the point that much of what we seek to accomplish through organizations would never be possible without them. If production is difficult, it is typically not because standard operating procedures are a *barrier,* but because it proves impossible to develop them in the first place. And, images of the assembly line to the contrary, employees frequently like standard operating procedures—although perhaps for the wrong reasons—because they relieve them of thinking for themselves and hence make their lives easier.

An alternative strategy for job design is to make tasks more skilled and give people substantial freedom to determine how to behave. Often, but not necessarily, this requires hiring more educated, and hence more expensive, employees. Designing jobs around highly trained people represents a different solution to the challenges of getting operating tasks performed. Reasonable quality comes from the high level of skill of those performing the job. And one of the things an organization buys when it hires professionals is an increased ability to get judgments in unusual situations. Uniformity, to the extent it is achieved, comes from the similar training people in the job have received: legal aid lawyers can generally be counted on to provide clients with a good defense because they were taught to do so in law school.

If work is both highly skilled and also idiosyncratic—for example, the work of spies in the CIA—the organization is likely to take intelligent people with a liberal arts education and train them on-the-job. On the other hand, if the work is common to many organizations, such as that of lawyers, doctors, or engineers, it is less expensive to hire people with prepackaged skills learned in professional education. In recent decades, as the tasks of government have become more complex, recruitment of professionals has increased. Some agencies have come to be dominated by certain professions: the Federal Trade Commission is dominated by lawyers and economists; the Occupational Safety and Health Administration by safety professionals; the National Bureau of Standards by engineers. Professionals constitute twice as large a percentage of the federal government work force as they do of the work force as a whole.[14]

The choice between high-skill and low-skill strategies is influenced by the nature of the task being performed. Some difficult tasks, such as building an automobile, can be subdivided into simpler tasks without difficulty. Others, such as playing a violin or performing surgery, cannot. Furthermore, in jobs where there are routinely many contingencies, a job can be designed around standard operating procedures only if it is possible to determine relatively easily which procedure should be summoned. This is the case for an employee at a social security local office who deals with complaints about social security checks, but it is not the case for the job of a police officer.

Is it better to use standard operating procedures or to give people more freedom? The answer is that it depends. Routine, unchanging tasks, or tasks where demands for tight coordination are important, are candidates for standardized procedures. The more complex and changeable the task, the more appropriate it is to give people freedom to decide what to do. Sometimes choices about job design depend on a decision about exactly what it is one is producing. For example, in the Soviet Union, surgical operations are sometimes conducted on an assembly line, with different doctors responsible for different parts of the operation. Presumably this is done because it is cheaper per operation. But if the goal is skilled doctors who can intervene in an emergency situation all by themselves—or a feeling of security and dignity on the part of the patients—this way of designing the job, although cheapest, may still be inappropriate. Job design decisions are thus strategic decisions that have implications for the nature of what one produces.

Organizing Production: Putting the Organization Back Together

Organizational specialization has costs. One cost is to make coordination of the various tasks that make up the organization's work more difficult. If the woodcarver does everything himself, he knows to chop down more wood when he needs more and not to offer his carvings for sale until he has enough ready. Once tasks are specialized, however, the carver can run into problems if his woodcutter is sick when he needs more wood or if the sales agent he has hired has his regular sales trip planned at a time when the carver has few pieces available. Having been rent asunder by specialization, the organization needs to be put back together again.

If delinquent loans from the Department of Housing and Urban Development are referred to the Department of Justice for prosecution but get delayed there because dealing with such cases has a low priority, it is unlikely that the government will ever get much of its money back, because experience shows that quick legal action against delinquent debtors is generally necessary to get results. If the central computers are down at the headquarters of the Social Security Administration, employees at local social security offices who handle complaints from the public will not be able to access the information they need to handle the complaint.

The coordination of work flow among units is often handled through standard operating procedures. These dictate the order in which various tasks are performed—the sequence in which parts of a car are mounted on an assembly line, the order in which cases proceed from the district attorney's office to trial, or the days when college classes start and end. The uniformity of the behavior emanating from one unit of the organization, which standardized procedures promote, also aids coordination. "Co-ordination is achieved on the drawing board, so to speak, before the work is undertaken."[15]

When operating tasks are performed by highly trained people with lots of discretion, work-flow coordination can potentially be a special problem, because there is less assurance of exactly how the people will behave or when they will complete their work. These problems can be dealt with by making the system a "loosely coupled" one not dependent on split-second interactions among its various parts.[16] Professors teach courses separately, so that if one professor does a bad job, a student's whole education need not be ruined. Lawyers at government agencies who review documents that agency scientists have prepared will generally be working on several matters at once so that, if one document is several weeks late, the lawyer still has other things to work on.

Specialization can also create problems when one unit in the organization has an idea for something it wants to do that has implications for the organization as a whole and not simply for the unit concerned. This occurs frequently in government. New organizational initiatives that affect more than one unit can be handled by letting the unit proposing the initiative also pursue it. They may be handled by formalized mutual adjustment mechanisms such as committees or task forces, or they may be handled by clearances through higher-level managers.

Lower units and higher management may have different views on whether a proposal, substantively, is a good idea. Given the fact of specialization of tasks, those originating the proposal generally will have the most knowledge about the particular situation to which the proposal represents a response and the greatest technical expertise about the subject of the proposal. This is the case for the procurement officer who wishes to approve a contract or the manager of a social security office who worries about the effects of tattered furniture on clients.

Specialization also creates problems, however. It creates a tendency on the part of each unit to look at an idea from the perspective of the unit's specialized activities rather than from that of the organization as a whole. Take the design of a new television set. If left to the engineering people, a fancy set with loads of spiffy technical features might be designed. However, such a set could be complicated to manufacture and might create quality problems that would bedevil the service people. The advanced technical features might not be those the public wanted, and the set might be too expensive and too unstylish to market easily. The same problem can arise in a government agency. Those who are to enforce an agency's regulations may want them to be easy to understand because this promotes voluntary compliance. Agency lawyers, on the other hand, may want the regulations to be able to stand up to court challenge, which prompts the lawyers to write them in complicated and stilted legalese. In situations such as these, different units of an organization are like different participants in a political process (albeit an intraorganizational one). Where each stands may be influenced by where he sits.[17]

This suggests a dilemma for the design of organizations. Centralizing decisions about proposals that come from one unit may ensure consideration from the perspective of the organization as a whole. But it has costs. If the assumption is always that proposals coming out of one unit will be bucked up to higher levels, this does nothing to encourage members of the individual units to see things from the perspective of the organization as a whole. It can simply entrench "where you stand depends on where you sit" reasoning. Like making an organization too dependent on standard operating procedures, referring upward too many decisions creates a cycle of dependence, whereby low-level employees never learn to be competent decision makers because they never get the opportunity to do so.

Human Resources Management

A crucial feature of individual behavior in organizations is that, to quote Chester Barnard, its "significant aspects are not personal." Instead, they are "determined by the system either as to manner, or degree, or time."[18] When people are doing things they want to do, it can generally be assumed that they will do their best. But since what an organization wants individuals to do with their time may not be what they would choose to do if left to their own devices, the quality of performance in organizations becomes problematic. The organization must create capabilities to help it obtain good performance from its members.

That good performance cannot be taken for granted is clear not only from the widespread perception that *government* organizations perform poorly. There are also a considerable number of empirical studies demonstrating wide variation in the output per worker in different *business* firms, producing the same articles, even after the amount and quality of machinery being used has been held constant.[19] To quote economist Harvey Leibenstein, "Effort in its broadest sense is a variable."[20]

The most rudimentary capability that all organizations create to obtain good performance from their members is the contract between employer and employee at the time a person begins work. Chester Barnard uses the phrase "zone of indifference" to refer to those actions that people will undertake simply because it corresponds to their understanding of what they agreed to do when they took the job.[21] Thus, workers who accept jobs on an automobile assembly line are presumably willing to appear at the position on the line to which they have been assigned and to more or less carry out the tasks they have been given.

Employment contracts, however, are far more incomplete than other typical contracts. When the post office arranges to buy sorting equipment, the agreement very carefully specifies its performance characteristics, price, and delivery date. The post office's contracts with its employees are much more vague. Salary may be specified (although it may not be completely so, given a possible performance component). But much remains unspecified—the exact amount that employees will produce, the employees' willingness to innovate under unexpected circumstances or to make suggestions for how to do things better, their effect on the production of their fellow-workers through their degree of helpfulness or general attitude, and a host of other things that would tell the post office exactly what it is getting for its money. An employer purchases labor time, not effort.[22]

To try to increase the chances of obtaining good performance, organizations establish capabilities to select appropriate employees in the first place, to train people, to cultivate an organizational culture that promotes good performance, and to provide inducements contingent on good performance.

Accounts of how organizations elicit good performance, certainly in the literature of organization theory and even to an extent in management literature, tend to emphasize inducements that can be used to change employee performance from what it otherwise would have been. This preoccupation is analogous to the psychological fascination of many observers of the political process with power. It also reflects the hope that incentives can be crafted so that self-interested behavior still produces outcomes that are acceptable to the organization.

Just as the fascination with power leads the observer of the political process astray, so too does a similar fascination with regard to organizational behavior.[23] Recent business management literature—and not all of it of a pop management nature—has emphasized the importance of selection, training, and culture—over carrots and sticks—in developing organizations that can meet the challenges of international competition. Good organizations, private or public, try in the first instance to attend to the ability and inclination of the people who work in them. They try to recruit people who have abilities and inclinations the organization needs, to train them, and to create an organizational culture that further leads them to act in certain ways.

Initial selection of people into an organization is crucial, writes personnel expert Jonathan Brock. "Trying to motivate a person who is basically mismatched to a task or work unit may be like pushing on a string."[24] Walter Wriston, the chairman of Citicorp, has stated:

The only game in town is the personnel game. My theory is that if you have the right person in the right place, you don't have to do anything else. If you have the wrong person in the job, there's not a management system known to man that can save you.[25]

Wriston's observation may be exaggerated, but it is excusable. Proper selection is not only a matter of getting people with the right skills, but also of looking for people with the appropriate inclinations. Government organizations, for example, that recruit public-spirited people get people who are disposed to do a good job for the organization even before they are on board. An organization's eyes shouldn't be bigger than its stomach. Tasks should not be designed for which the organization cannot recruit people.

Managers differ in the attention they pay to selection. An observer of Japanese and American electronics firms concluded that the Japanese firms paid closer attention to selection of their blue-collar employees than did the American ones.[26]

Training, formal and informal, occurs both when an employee starts a job and, often, at periodic intervals on the job. When employees first start, they are generally at their most receptive to signals the organization can give about what is expected of them, not only about the nuts and bolts of the job, but about attitudes and orientations as well—about what a "good" police officer or a "good" Federal Trade Commission lawyer is like. This is why early training is so important.

An organization's culture consists of the values that are common to most of the organization's members.[27] For example, James Q. Wilson detected different kinds of organizational cultures in police departments he studied. Some departments emphasized keeping order through informal dispute resolution and tended in general to underenforce the law. Others saw the maintenance of order as a law-enforcement problem and fought tendencies to underenforce the law.[28] If an organization can establish a culture that embodies values promoting good performance, the organization's members will more likely have the inclination to perform well. If a culture is organization-wide, it can also counteract tendencies toward parochialism of the "where you stand depends on where you sit" variety in units within the organization. As management scholars George Strauss and Leonard Sayles have pointed out, using a dramatic but arresting example, "The Catholic Church operated for centuries on a decentralized worldwide basis, long before the advent of modern communication, largely because the strength of the priest's faith made it unnecessary to receive constant instruction from Rome."[29] In a classic study, Herbert Kaufman concluded that the Forest Service succeeded in getting forest rangers, dispersed over the expanses of the country's national forests, to behave in the spirit top management sought in part by careful attention to the inculcation of an identification with the historic mission of the service as a steward for multiple uses of the nation's forests.[30]

How do the features of an organization's culture become established? Partly, they relate to the nature of the organization's work itself. In business firms, write management experts Terrence Deal and Allen Kennedy, "if hard selling is required for success, the culture will be one that encourages people to sell and sell hard; if thoughtful technical decision-making is required, the culture will make sure that happens too."[31] The culture of the FBI can be calm and deliberative because agents generally investigate crimes after they have been committed, interviewing people whose emotions have had time to cool. Police on the street, by contrast, frequently must intervene in the midst of crisis, where authority must be established and decisions made quickly. The culture of police officers therefore is more gunslinging.[32] In the CIA, the environment for spies— where exposure ends the agent's ability to accomplish his tasks and could lead to the agent's imprisonment and possibly execution—puts an enormous premium on the importance of secrecy. A CIA dominated by people whose background is spying is likely to resist undertaking covert operations to overthrow governments, which are harder to keep secret and may threaten the secrecy of information about intelligence agents, safe houses, or modes of communication.[33] If the work of government organizations involves production of good public policy, then a public-spirited culture will be promoted. When managers working on developing the Polaris missile-carrying submarine faced the challenge of getting submarine people committed to the new idea that the role of submarines might be to carry missiles rather than to sink ships (as had traditionally been the case), they were very methodical in trying to create an organizational culture conducive to the change by appealing to overall desires to enhance the nation's defense ability. Families of those working on the project were given periodic lectures on the importance of the new mission "so that they would appreciate the personal sacrifices required of them if the program were to succeed." At the conclusion of his standard speech to those working on the project, the admiral in charge would often ask his audience to grasp the back of their necks. "Those are the necks that will be saved when the Polaris is developed," he then declaimed.[34]

The backgrounds of people before they joined the organization, if they are similar enough, can also influence the nature of the organization's culture. If an organization recruits lawyers, the culture is likely to value litigation skills and the ability to win a case. If an organization recruits safety professionals, it is likely that the culture will value efforts at saving lives, consistent with the values of the safety profession.[35]

Very importantly for government organizations, an organization's culture is influenced by its mission.[36] An organization's mission, which is often embodied in its statute, is the purpose for which it is established. The mission of the Occupational Safety and Health Administration, as stated in the preamble to the act establishing the agency, is "to assure, so far as possible, every man and woman in the Nation safe and healthful working conditions."[37] The Age Discrimination in Employment Act gives the Equal Employment Opportunity Commission the mission to "promote employment of older persons based on their ability rather than on age."[38] The mission of the Department of State is to promote the interests of the United States in the world by diplomatic means, of the Department of Agriculture to help farmers.[39]

An organization's mission is generally rather vague. It may be difficult to translate a mission into specific standards for good performance. Nonetheless, the significance of the mission should not be underestimated. Frequently, the nature of the mission tends to preselect the kind of people who choose to work for the organization. Given the mission of the organization, strong civil rights advocates are likely to be attracted to the Equal Employment Opportunity Commission, because work at that agency represents a way to realize the ideals in which they believe. Strong advocates of farmers are likely to seek employment at the Department of Agriculture. Often, the mission of an agency and the values of professionals whom the agency must recruit to do its work reinforce each other, such as in the case of industrial hygienists working for the Occupational Safety and Health Administration or of military officers in the armed forces.

Culture is inculcated by symbol and by incantation as well. There is a reason why soldiers and police wear uniforms—indeed, the Forest Service uses uniforms as well to remind rangers of the traditions of the Service. To emphasize the importance of the Polaris project to the nation's security, military officers assigned to the project were urged to wear uniforms on the job rather than the civilian clothes normally worn by those with such desk assignments.[40] John Dilluo discovered that the best prison he examined—but not the others—proudly displayed "prison memorabilia" (such as handmade weapons guards had discovered).[41] Drivers at the United Parcel Service are required personally to wash their delivery trucks each morning when they start work, in an effort to inculcate a culture of personal responsibility for quality.

Controversies over goals that a government organization should pursue, left over as a residue from the political process, imperil the climate for the production process. Hard feelings over past fights may make cooperation more difficult among people within an organization who need to cooperate to assure successful implementation. This problem is exacerbated because political choices for a given program activity are ongoing.

Political fights, with the same participants, may proceed at the same time that production of earlier choices is to occur. Such controversies are not unknown in private business firms. Different parts of a business organization (such as marketing and manufacturing) have different perspectives, and this can lead to controversies. A manager whose pet project failed to gain approval may not be in a particularly friendly or cooperative mood the next time around. Yet these controversies are generally kept within bounds by a consensus within the firm about something like a profit maximization goal, a consensus that generally does not exist about the purpose of government organizations. A sense of mission in government organizations counteracts these divisive tendencies.

Finally, choices about job design have implications for the disposition of people to perform well. Generally, standard operating procedures motivate less than freedom and discretion. But if people are given discretion that exceeds their ability, the result can be frustrating and demotivating. Similarly, to require that new ideas always be bucked up to higher-level management for decision has implications for the inclination to perform well. When people want to do something, they don't like to be told by others that they can't—or even that they must go to others for permission. (Accounts of the formation of small, new, high-technology companies often recount that the firms' founders had been working for a corporate giant such as IBM and then left, frustrated with complicated review procedures for proposals they had made or upset that an idea of theirs had been turned down.) The more obstacles a proposal must run before it gets approved, the less likely it is that people will come up with new proposals.

We turn now to the role of inducements. They affect the results of the production process, just as they do of the political process. Some organization members are not disposed to perform at levels beyond the minimum, and inducements are needed to change their behavior. Even those who are so inclined frequently can use encouragement. And, of course, behavior initially elicited by inducements may eventually turn into behavior toward which one is inclined.

To use inducements to improve performance, the organization must first establish performance standards that employees can use to measure their own contribution. For people to *meet* goals, they must *have* goals. A diplomat needs to know if he or she should seek agreement even at the expense of making concessions or should try to avoid making concessions even at the expense of failing to reach agreement. An office worker whose job is to respond to letters from the public needs to know if answering twenty letters a day is a lot or a little.

Second, an organization must be able to determine what the quality of a person's performance has been. Hospitals need to know how individual doctors perform in the privacy of a hospital room, and police sergeants how officers act on the beat, before it can be ascertained whether performance merits reward or requires punishment.

Performance measures, which establish what constitutes good performance, may be of various sorts.[42] The standard operating procedures of an organization constitute one set of performance standards, for they are statements about how organization members are expected to behave in different circumstances. Performance standards may also be expressed as quantitative measures—what was the cost of collecting the garbage per household served; how many inspections did the restaurant inspector make last month; what proportion of the determinations of a social security administrative law judge were overturned by a higher court; what proportion of a teacher's students passed a standardized test? But quantitative information accumulates too slowly and is too disembodied to serve as the exclusive source of performance information for managers. Thus, despite formal information systems, most managers rely heavily on snippets of information gathered informally in conversations and through observations of how people handle themselves in specific situations.

Organizations possess material and normative inducements

for trying to improve performance. (Few organizations have coercive inducements available.) The most ubiquitous material inducement available is, of course, money. Yet, starting with the writings of the "human relations" school of industrial psychology of the 1930s, going through the "hierarchy of needs" writings of psychologists such as Abraham Maslow and Frederick Herzberg in the 1940s and 1950s, and up to the "participative management" writings of Rensis Likert and his colleagues at the University of Michigan in the 1960s and since, there has been a gigantic academic assault on the view that money is an effective inducement to better performance.[43] According to these writers, attention from supervisors, fulfilling work, or ability to participate in decisions are more important than money. This is not a book on how to motivate employees, so this debate will not be discussed here, except to note that these findings run so counter to common sense that it appears more justified to jettison the research than to jettison common sense. Indeed, Edward Lawler's more comprehensive (although for some reason less noticed) analysis of studies of pay as a motivator concludes that pay ranks higher as an important job factor than Herzberg believed.[44] Even if it were true that money is not an important motivator once someone is on the job, that would say nothing about its ability to induce able people to take one job rather than a different one in the first place, as well as to encourage people to remain within the organization rather than to leave.

Money (or other benefits) is not the only material inducement organizations have available. Organizations may offer the prospect of more interesting work assignments or promotions to more interesting jobs. In every police precinct there are beats that most officers would rather have or avoid. A staff attorney at a given grade level in the Department of Justice can be assigned to a glamorous "sting" case against a famous politician or to recovering defaults on government loans.

The normative inducements organizations have available to influence performance include recognition for good work and criticism for bad work. In government service, one such inducement is recognition for promoting the public-spirited goals of the organization. Many material inducements are also seen by those receiving them as a normative recognition of status in the organization. Sometimes, a reward that is purportedly material serves mainly to signal recognition. Offices near the boss may be no nicer than other offices (indeed, in the case of the offices in the West Wing of the White House compared with those in the Old Executive Office Building next door, the opposite is the case). But certain office space signals recognition.

Normative inducements are extended more in the context of daily organizational life than during formal performance reviews. A manager who ignores this "extended personnel system" (to use the expression of Jonathan Brock) simply lets it operate by default, giving employees unintended signals either that the quality of their work has not been recognized (because nobody has bothered to praise it) or that there are no problems when in fact there are (because nobody has bothered to point them out).[45]

The establishment of performance standards and the offering of inducements related to performance of those standards are often seen as inseparable. This is not the case. There can be evaluations without specific performance standards, and performance standards can be established without rewarding people who do well or punishing those who do badly. Interestingly, the simple establishment of performance measures, independent of any reward following positive evaluation, appears to improve performance. Performance measures help subordinates figure out where they should be concentrating their efforts and improve morale by giving people something concrete to point to having accomplished as a result of their work. Management expert Paul Mott's study of effective organizations showed that the perceived clarity of organizational objectives related to good organizational performance.[46] An assistant secretary in a government bureau, with private-sector experience, in an interview with Dorothy Robyn noted that "in an auto plant, there's satisfaction in seeing the product at the end of the day," but govern-

ment often failed to provide such satisfactions.[47] An empirical
study of differences in job commitment among public and private-sector managers by management expert Bruce Buchanan
showed higher average levels of commitment among private
than among public managers. Buchanan found that the best
explanation of this was the difference in the perceived ability
of the individual to make a contribution to the organization's
success, because of the greater ability to measure results of
one's activity in the private rather than the public sector.[48]

Implementation

Sometimes implementation failures occur. Let us take an extreme example—the kind of experience that gives the sixties a
bad name. A local school district, described by Neal Gross and
his colleagues in their book *Implementing Organizational Innovations,*
introduced in one of its elementary schools a new program in
which teachers were to move from a traditional teaching style
to a so-called catalytic role.[49] Rather than directing the whole
class, teachers would allow students to move around the classroom and work in small groups; the students would choose
from among an array of educational material made available to
them. In the program Gross and his colleagues described, teachers in the school were sympathetic to educational innovation
and to restructuring the classroom situation. But no organizational capacity was created to make this change possible. The
meager written material on the innovation discussed mostly
how *students* were to behave under the new arrangements. There
were no new procedures or other kinds of guidance for *teachers*
about how they were supposed to behave. Furthermore, little
textbook material was available of the self-instructional type
the new approach required. On top of all that, teachers were
given a *one-month* lead time to prepare for the transition. Abject
failure was a certainty. Indeed, from the jaded perspective of

the eighties, it is hard to imagine how anyone imagined such a program had the slightest chance of being successfully implemented. Yet some people did so imagine.

Implementation busts generally occur for quite straightforward reasons. It may prove impossible to develop ways of accomplishing the specific tasks the organization has been assigned. If nobody knows reliably how to rehabilitate criminals while they are in jail, it is quite certain that an organization charged with this task will fail. Somewhat more subtly, if a tiny number of very talented individuals is able to judge the situations of individual criminals so they can adapt interventions accordingly, that does not imply that the job can be done routinely, unless the extraordinary performers can teach their skills to the ordinary run of those who can be expected to work at the job. If tasks can be performed only by people whom it costs $50,000 a year to hire, and the organization only has sufficient money to hire people at $20,000, the tasks cannot be accomplished as they have been designed within the organization's budget. Organizations also run into problems if jobs are designed so they require skills available individually, but rarely found together. If the job of a police officer requires psychological finesse as well as ability to use physical force, there are likely to be problems.

Two special types of situations where the most extreme kinds of problems can arise merit more detailed examination. They are (1) the production of new programs and (2) situations where the creation of organizational capacity brings with it unintended consequences for the organization's behavior.

IMPLEMENTING NEW PROGRAMS

Some of the impression that government is unable to make anything happen comes from the focus in many studies on new programs. An emphasis on examining new compensatory education programs for disadvantaged children or new ways to fight crime is likely to produce a different perspective from an examination of the ability of the Department of Defense to field a several-million person army, of a community library to provide books to the public, or of the post office to deliver the mail. With respect to the latter activities there may well be complaints about the quality of performance, but there is no room for saying that government decided to do something and nothing happened.

New programs require establishment of new organizational capacity. Doing so generally requires dealing with many problems that are distinct enough so that solving one provides no assurance that a solution will be found for another, although it can provide psychological momentum and inspiration. Furthermore, failure to solve any one problem can cause the entire enterprise to fail. If thirteen things need to happen, it isn't good enough to say that one has failed at "only" one of the thirteen. To apply in a somewhat different context an exercise in the simple mathematics of probability undertaken by Pressman and Wildavsky in their book *Implementation*: even in a situation where the chances of success at any one of the steps required successfully to implement a new venture are 90 percent, it takes a total of only seven steps to bring the probability of final success below one-half.[50] To establish mechanisms for doctors in hospitals to review the performance of other doctors, it is not enough to get doctors to be willing to serve on the committees and to develop a system for getting patient care data, if it turns out that data on the original patient medical records are so hard to locate that medical records personnel miss a great deal of it.[51] Each step here is distinct; solving one does little to help solve another. Yet all tasks must be completed if final success is to occur. This is what produces the sense of dread that often occurs with the production of new government programs.

To have a fighting chance of success, planners must think carefully about implementation early. They must be ready to run into dead ends—conceivable ways of accomplishing a task that turn out not to be feasible—and then good-naturedly to go back and start down another road. They must be ready to encounter unforeseen problems—contingencies that need to be dealt with, work that is more difficult than it initially appeared —and to address them.

Implementation planning is best done in group brainstorming, or at least by consulting with several individuals. What is needed early on is essentially an enormous list of questions and concerns. Groups are best for coming up with lists; rare is the individual who can think of as many things alone as can several colleagues.

When the government made the decision, in 1976, to attempt to vaccinate the entire population against a possible outbreak of deadly swine flu, those responsible for the program did not think carefully enough in advance about what needed to happen for a swine flu program to be successful (and what could go wrong). Predictable problems resulted. It was known that single doses of any vaccine can produce excessive reactions in children and that children might therefore require two smaller doses. No provision was made, however, for organizing the program to take account of this eventuality. When the eventuality occurred, children ended up being excluded from "universal" vaccination. It was known that what doctors refer to as "coincident deaths" would likely occur in connection with vaccination (that is, cases of people who just happen to die shortly after they are vaccinated). But no plans were made for briefing the press or in any other way preparing for this, despite the effects publicity about such deaths would have on the willingness of the public to be vaccinated.[52]

Implementation planning will teach that "God is in the details." I had occasion during the mid-1980s to work on an implementation plan for an idea to deal with possible future energy emergencies by rebating increased revenues from the windfall profits tax on oil back to the public in the form of a check to every adult American.[53] The production challenge was how to get a check out to everyone quickly, during a national emergency, when there existed no central list with the names and addresses of all adult Americans. Developing the plan required investigations of the most diverse sort into scores of small details, each of which affected the viability of the plan as a whole. For example, I wanted to propose that computer files from different agencies be matched to purge them of duplication; that meant I needed to figure out how one would deal with the situation of somebody listed as Mary Smith on one computer file and M. Smith on another. I needed to find out how many complaints about nonreceipt of checks could be expected; that meant I needed to figure out what percentage of letters sent to mailing lists that are six months out of date get returned as undeliverable by the post office (a search that led to discussions with the people who run the *Reader's Digest* annual sweepstakes, among others).

Since development of the needed organizational capacity can by no means be taken for granted, it makes sense to try to keep the design of a new program simple. Procedures for each task should be straightforward, with as few different units involved as possible. As little coordination as possible should be needed. Rube Goldberg plans must be avoided.

The successful production of a new program may not call for creation of new organizational capacity from scratch but rather for changes in the behavior of an existing organization. Changing the behavior of existing organizations is notoriously difficult. This is so especially when the change is initiated by top management or by a legislative body outside the organization rather than by the organizational units being asked to change. Such change is difficult not only in government, but in business firms as well, as the large body of business-oriented literature on the subject attests.[54]

The most difficult part of change is generally the human change it requires. This is not simply because people are stubborn and hidebound, although they can certainly be both. A proposal to introduce a $1,000 bonus every Christmas is unlikely to be resisted, although it constitutes a change. People are likely to resist change if it creates problems for them, and, as in the political process, pain brings out self-interest. And change can create problems because previous ways of doing things frequently constitute more than simply the technical capabilities of the organization. They also constitute important aspects of the lives of the organization's members, a fact that hardly should be surprising, since people spend such a large part of their waking hours on the job.

Producing a new program frequently requires changes in an existing organization's standard operating procedures. This is often very hard, because standard operating procedures can become deeply embedded in people's lives. Partly, they become embedded psychologically. When a child cuddles in bed with the same teddy bear every night, eventually the child develops an attachment to it and would be upset if it were suddenly replaced by a stuffed giraffe, even though the teddy bear has no more intrinsic significance than the giraffe. The force of simple habit is illustrated by a time-and-motion investigation in the army around World War I showing that artillerymen stood at attention and paused before firing their artillery, thus slowing down the speed of fire. It turned out that this represented a simple continuation of behavior that had originated when cannons were horse-drawn and soldiers had to pause before firing to "hold the horses." The behavior persisted even after artillery became motorized.

The attachment to standardized procedures may go deeper. If one procedure was originally selected as the best way to accomplish a goal, organization members attached to the goal may worry that changing the procedure signals a change in priorities. When a proposal was made to change the academic calendar at Harvard University in the early 1970s, so as to start the academic year earlier, have exams before Christmas, and end the school year earlier, many professors resisted. Elimination of a "reading period" before exams in mid-January, they protested, would remove an opportunity for students to integrate the semester's material before taking exams and for professors to assign a term paper over reading period. The worry was that this might signal a downgrading of the university's commitment to academic excellence.[55] Similarly, army sergeants may resist efforts to change rules regarding hair length for recruits on the grounds that they signal a loosening of the commitment to discipline.

Standard operating procedures frequently become embedded in the lives of members of an organization not only psychologically but concretely. An important reservoir of skills may be tied up with existing procedures. Medical records technicians in hospitals who have devoted a lifetime to mastering a highly complex system for classifying diseases may well resist when efforts are made to introduce a simplified system designed to make it easier to assess the quality of patient care.[56] Changes in routines for coordination may change patterns of interaction among organization members, interrupting arrangements that allowed each to accomplish his or her work better. If, for instance, changes in standard operating procedures for scheduling police deployment require reassigning police on the beat, police may lose the ability to work together with buddies whom they have come to trust, making good police work harder.

People in organizations may also arrange other parts of their lives around the patterns procedures establish. If the mail is picked up from an office at noon each day, secretaries get in the habit of leaving it off before lunch. This is disrupted if the mail starts getting picked up at eleven. The annual meetings of many scholarly organizations had come to be scheduled around Labor Day, adapted to the mid-September beginning of term rather than to the first week in September opening as was proposed for the changed calendar of Harvard.

Finally, standard operating procedures may become embedded in an organization in the sense that one procedure becomes tied together with others, so that if one is altered without altering related ones, the goals of the change may not be accomplished. In order to speed up the leasing process, the General Services Administration has streamlined procedures for examining compliance with the Historic Preservation Act when the government rents office space. That change, however, would not have accomplished its purpose unless procedures for examining compliance with rules regarding access for the handicapped, a process undertaken simultaneously, were also streamlined.

Like its procedures, an organization's culture is an important element of its capacity. But once an organization has gotten inside its members' heads, it is not easy to turn around and request that people take it out. So if producing a new program requires an organization to change its culture, that feat will also be difficult. Politically appointed agency leaders who are unsympathetic to an agency's traditional mission run into this problem when they try to change the agency's orientation toward its work. Morale in domestic-policy agencies plummeted when President Reagan took office. Occupational Safety and Health Administration inspectors who had been inculcated with the belief that tough enforcement was the only way to achieve compliance, for example, did not want to start being nice to employers.

The resistance to something that goes counter to an organization's culture need not be ideologically tinged. The Internal Revenue Service has opposed proposals to get the agency involved in activities outside of tax collecting. Many such proposals would involve making use of the information on tax forms for nontax purposes, such as to establish eligibility for government health insurance. The Internal Revenue Service has been afraid that this would interfere with the agency's mission by reducing voluntary compliance with the tax laws.[57] Drug Enforcement Administration agents resisted efforts to change the agency's emphasis from pursuing many small-time drug dealers to going after a few big-time ones. The agents lived in an organizational culture that emphasized action and visible accomplishment. Small-time cases permitted both in abundance. By contrast, writes James Q. Wilson, the large-scale cases

involve fewer chances to kick in doors. Months of patient tedious work are required—checking motel registrations, long-distance telephone toll slips, and airplane reservations, or sitting for many dull hours eavesdropping on telephone conversations in order to establish that the alleged members of a conspiracy are in fact acting in concert.[58]

Something similar occurred when the Antitrust Division of the Department of Justice first brought large-scale monopoly cases against industry giants such as IBM and Exxon. The problem was that these large "industry structure" cases took forever to prepare, and this ran counter to an organizational culture emphasizing litigation and hanging coonskins on the wall. Morale was thus low and turnover high among attorneys assigned to the big cases; the quality of organizational performance on such cases was poor, and (doubtless for a host of other reasons as well) the government failed to win any of them.[59]

A conscious effort to change an organization's behavior thus involves difficult, often intractable, problems when doing so requires changing standard operating procedures or the organization's culture. (Indeed, the difficulty of changing procedures is one reason to be cautious about their excessive use in the first place.) The assumption that efforts at change will fail is probably the most appropriate one; at least it induces an appreciation for the difficulty of the undertaking.

Success requires, first of all, a proper diagnosis of the situation. If management seeks to change standardized procedures it must determine how deeply embedded they are within the organization. How closely are they tied to organizational goals in which employees believe? Do they embody important skills that employees either are proud of or will not want to relearn? How will training of new employees need to be changed in light of the new procedures? The more embedded they are, the more difficult procedures will be to change.

A similar diagnosis is necessary prior to any effort to change an organization's culture. Are the attitudes simply inculcated on the job or do they also reflect preexisting values among the type of people the organization recruits? Are there elements of the culture that could support the new behavior as well as the old?

Are there ways the new behavior can be made to fit better with the existing culture? Are there outside threats to the organization that require some adaptations if the broad contours of the organization's culture are to survive? In the final analysis, managers must decide whether the game is worth the candle. Standard operating procedures and an organization's culture are not just obstacles to change. They are also crucial elements of an organization's capacity. To try to change them and fail risks destroying capacity and producing nothing in its stead.

Two attempts to change standardized procedures in New York City during the administration of Mayor John Lindsay in the 1960s, one involving the police and the other the sanitation department, illustrate the difference that attention to diagnosing a situation can make. Each involved a new program to improve the delivery of a service. Each involved a change in the way the existing organization operated. One effort, to change police deployment so that more police would be on the streets during high-crime hours, failed. The other, to change garbage pick-up schedules so that more pick-ups occurred on Mondays after the weekend garbage accumulation, succeeded.[60]

Getting more police on the streets during high-crime hours required a change in the standard operating procedures for deploying police. Existing procedures divided police into three equal-sized platoons rotating through three shifts. The proposal was to add a new fourth platoon. This sounded like a narrow technical change, and management treated it as such. It turned out, however, that the existing three-platoon system was deeply embedded in the organization; it had originally grown out of a 1910 law limiting the number of hours police had to work and hence had become a symbol of worker rights vis-à-vis management. Beyond that, people had adapted other parts of their lives to the existing system, arranging for moonlighting jobs or bowling league games so as not to conflict with the established work schedules. New standardized procedures for deployment would have taken police away from their old beats and partners. This had negative implications for the existing organizational capacity built up in the form of an officer's knowledge of his beat and his buddy.

Even after a diminished fourth platoon, consisting only of volunteers, was fielded, failure to learn what additional procedures had to be changed once the deployment plan was altered led to further problems that reduced the effectiveness of the fourth platoon in fighting crime. First, the new platoon would be working at a different time from any of the existing platoons (overlapping two other shifts). Yet it was assigned no special supervisors, so that the fourth platoon lacked supervision. Second, existing standardized procedures for deployment called for officers to be assigned to the highest-crime beats first, with lower-crime beats covered only to the extent that manpower was available. No effort was made to change this procedure when the fourth platoon was introduced. The result was that the extra officers made available by the fourth platoon were assigned to the lowest crime beats.

The change in garbage collection schedules, by contrast, was successful. Getting more garbage picked up on Mondays required shifting work schedules so that garbage collectors had fewer Mondays off. The Department of Sanitation was far more sensitive to what was required to change standard operating procedures successfully. They spent time before the new procedures were made final talking with workers at the operating levels about how to fashion the system so that the new procedures minimized disruption of old patterns. They discovered that many garbage workers had developed carpooling systems around the existing schedule; this enabled them to program the new system so that a sufficient number of workers stayed with their previous teams to carpool together even if the teams worked on different days. They discovered that garbage collection was easier if at least somebody on the truck knew the route being serviced; this enabled them to modify the new system so that enough workers having experience with the old routes would still work each day of the new schedule. They also learned that although the workers did not relish the idea of losing a few three-day weekends, they appreciated the possibility of getting more Saturdays off, which the new system would provide. And when the new system began, each garbage collector was given a wallet-sized calendar with his new days off circled in red.

Finally, those involved in implementation realized that the new schedule was far more complicated than the existing one and that the scheduling clerks at each station would need to be trained in how the new system worked. Training was carefully planned, including seeing to it

> that the clerks from any one district attended different training sessions, each session several days after the preceding one. [The hope was] that the men who did not understand the material could go back to their districts and either find the answer from another clerk or send the next representative to bring up the question the next time around.[61]

Furthermore, at least one clerk in each borough was selected to be responsible to answer questions within his own borough, creating a cadre of clerks who were knowledgeable and active supporters. This also gave the other clerks a chance to bring up questions with "one of their own" about how to fold into the new system practices they all used that went against official rules.

Failed efforts to change an organization's culture are so common that Washingtonese has an expression to describe the fate of political appointees who have stopped trying. They "go native"—adopting the culture of their organization rather than adapting it to their own purposes. The most sustained attempts to change an organization's culture are generally undertaken by political appointees so hostile to what the organization had previously been doing that they are indifferent about the effect of their efforts on the organization's capacity to perform. Often, at a minimum, a new culture requires wholesale changes in the existing staff. Caspar Weinberger succeeded as Chairman of the

Federal Trade Commission in 1970 in changing the organization from one that recruited Southerners into a "good ol' boy" culture into an organization made up of aggressive consumer advocates. But he had to get rid of many of the agency's existing lawyers to do so—and was willing to try because he was convinced that nothing else would work.[62]

A fascinating example of a successful change in an organization's culture that occurred without destroying the organization's capacity or replacing its staff was the effort in the early 1970s to reduce police corruption in New York City. These changes occurred in the aftermath of the Serpico revelations of widespread corruption in the department and the widely publicized hearings of an investigative commission appointed in the wake of those revelations.[63] Patrick Murphy, the newly named commissioner, took advantage of outside pressure to change the organization. The investigative commission had chosen a high-visibility strategy with televised public hearings featuring dramatic accounts of corruption. Murphy was able to tell his organization that outsiders—who were far more extreme and did not have the interests of the force in mind—would come in and institute more draconian changes if the department did not reform itself.

THE UNINTENDED CONSEQUENCES OF
ORGANIZATIONAL CAPABILITIES

Sometimes what goes awry during the production stage is not that a program simply fails to happen or even that the quality of performance is poor. It is rather that the behavior coming out of the government is inappropriate or anomalous. For example, between the 1930s and 1960s the government ran a program to distribute surplus food to the needy. Under this program food was indeed distributed. The problem was that the kinds of food distributed often turned out not to be very nutritious. And the warehouses from which the food was distributed were often located far from where the poor lived.

There is a tendency in instances such as these to assume that the paradoxical final government action is intentional. In reality the anomalies often arise from unintended consequences of the capacity the organization has created. Organizations create standard operating procedures, they recruit professionals, they nurture an organizational culture, all to help them do their jobs. In certain situations, however, any of these capabilities can render the organization incapable of dealing appropriately with a certain type of situation. If creating certain organizational capacity produces a situation where the organization's performance will be poor in some types of circumstances, the organization may simply need to learn to live with this problem, unless it can find a way to deal with the side effects without risking the capabilities themselves. It is difficult not to keep the bathwater along with the baby.

Standard operating procedures create organizational capacity by telling organization members how to react in a given situation. Having created those standard responses, it should not be surprising that organization members "go by the book." That is what they have been told to do. Yet that will inevitably create inappropriate or anomalous behavior in some situations. As the sociologist Robert Merton pointed out in a classic argument, rote application of the rules to every situation will often produce behavior perceived as "rigid" or "bureaucratic." If a standardized procedure was established that all applications must be typed, so as to get rid of problems with illegible handwriting, a handprinted application may be rejected though it is completely legible. The rigid behavior is not an intended policy of the organization; it is an unintended consequence. In a somewhat similar vein, the repeated rote application of standard operating procedures can produce a mechanical behavioral style. Employees who have dealt with a situation innumerable times may fail to realize that it is new and threatening for the people with whom they are dealing; welfare intake workers may simply rattle off a question to applicants about whether they own a car, not realizing that applicants are afraid that if they answer yes they will be declared ineligible.[64] Standardized procedures can produce inappropriate or anomalous behavior in situations where the world has changed, making a previously sensible routine inapposite. The example of police from the fourth platoon being assigned the lowest-crime beats in their precincts, discussed earlier, is a good example of this problem.[65] To assign police first to high-crime beats and only later to low-crime ones normally makes perfect sense. It was perfect nonsense, however, as a way to deploy the fourth platoon. The small number and inconvenient location of the warehouses from where surplus food was to be picked up by the poor under the commodity distribution program resulted from procedures that the Department of Agriculture had developed for storage of government surplus. These procedures, perfectly reasonably, included requirements for warehouse construction quality sufficient to prevent spoilage, and it made sense to build a few large warehouses to meet these requirements because of economies of scale. Such arrangements were fine as long as food was simply being stored for pick-up by large food processing purchasers. They became inappropriate when surplus food was to be distributed to individuals. And if the food distributed was not of high nutritional quality, this resulted from operating procedures determining distribution of food based on what food the government had in excess supply. In all these cases, unfortunate final government actions resulted not from bad intentions but from the application of standard operating procedures to inappropriate situations.

Professional values can also produce inappropriate or anomalous behavior. Doctors in VA hospitals order excessive tests and practice high-tech medicine just like their colleagues in private practice, even though they are salaried and thus have no economic incentive to do so. Doing so, however, reflects the values of the medical profession.[66] The police department recruits "tough guys," and the organizational culture encourages toughness, because frequently police need to be tough. But this can produce inappropriate behavior in situations where more subtle behavior is called for. The Federal Trade Commission hires attorneys because the agency's statute calls for it to bring legal action against perpetrators of consumer fraud. But attorneys generally want to bring legal actions against bad guys even in situations where there would be better ways, such as encouraging provision of more consumer information. Those in the CIA whose mission it is to undertake covert actions must have a "can-do" attitude if the difficult and risky jobs they undertake are to have any chance of success. These attitudes, however, lead covert operatives to overestimate the chances of an operation's success even when they are asked for a dispassionate judgment, and to develop wild schemes even when more conventional ones would do.[67]

Anomalous results of the predispositions growing out of an organization's culture can easily be misinterpreted by outsiders. In 1961 President Kennedy asked the CIA people who were planning the Bay of Pigs invasion in Cuba for an estimate of the plan's success. He thought he would be getting a sober judgment based on intelligence information. Instead, he was getting the judgment of covert operations people, who did not have the intelligence information the agency's own analysts had and who were inveterate optimists. He thus failed to discount the estimates he got.[68]

The Results of the Production Process

Much of what occurs in organizations is routine. People often plod on, doing more or less the same thing day in and day out. This encourages the view that production is dull compared with politics, and that there is less room for strategy or for creativity. The media generally are a good guide to what kinds of things we want to learn about (because if they don't get that right, people will not buy their product), and they pay enormously more attention to activities in the White House or Capitol Hill than they do to the production process.

There is, nonetheless, ample room for creativity, and for developing strategies to make things turn out better, during the production stage of the policy-making process. The kinds of challenges, and the kinds of room for creativity, are different from the challenges that face people in trying to be good individual performers. The challenge of management is not simply to do a good job yourself, but to get a group of people to do a good job of producing something together. In organizing for getting the work done, members of organizations participate in a lower-visibility aspect of the policy-making process, but still in an engaging one—and indeed the decisive one. For policy ideas and political choices, even when accompanied by all the fanfare of congressional enactment or presidential announcement, cannot affect society, cannot produce results, save if they are translated into final government actions at the street level, at the level of citizens whose lives the policy-making process is to improve.

8

The Civil Service as an Institutional Setting for Production

Government organizations face the same basic challenge as other organizations—to create organizational capacity to accomplish their tasks. They must manage human resources and organize production. Government organizations seek to meet these challenges in an environment of institutional choices that have been made about the design of the civil service. These choices are sometimes reflected in statutes, sometimes in executive orders by the president, sometimes in regulations, sometimes through informal practice.

Many of the choices about the institutional design of large government organizations are unusual. They are so in the literal sense of the word: they are different from choices typically made in the design of large private sector organizations and, sometimes, even of government agencies in other countries. Furthermore, many of these institutional features make it more difficult to create organizational capacity in government compared with more usual practices. Therefore, one purpose of this chapter is to explore how it happens that government ties one hand behind its back when it designs institutions for production.

Managing Human Resources

Government organizations are public organizations. This fact creates both opportunities and problems for the development of organizational capacity in government.

Publicness creates opportunities, because people wishing to display public spirit come to work for government organizations with an inclination to perform well independent of any contingent rewards or punishments the organization has available. Public spirit is a source of an organizational culture promoting good performance.

At the same time, the fact that government organizations are part of the public political process creates a dilemma for their management. Because commitment to the values of the organization helps employees perform well, managers tend to want to have on board as many subordinates as possible who share the political values of the organization's top management. This motivates managers toward bringing in new people from the outside whenever there is a new administration. On the other hand, technical skills and knowledge are also crucial in the production process, and politically driven staffing upheavals would thus be devastating, because such upheavals can put people in important positions who are unfamiliar with the work of the organization. This dilemma resembles the "red" and "expert" problem in Communist China that was discussed in the context of the participation of the bureaucracy in the political process.[1] Private firms do not face this dilemma to the same degree because there is greater agreement on goals.

Similarly, the fact that government organizations are participants in the political process has, in the American context of fear of unelected bureaucrats, resulted in decisions to bring top management into agencies from the outside. (As noted in chapter 5, that decision is a matter of institutional choice; top managers are civil servants in most countries, although the bureaucracy is also a part of the political process there.) The resulting inexperience of agency top management creates problems for the creation of organizational capacity in government. In private business an individual who totally lacked management experience would not be appointed as chief executive officer. Yet their counterparts in the public sector, cabinet secretaries and assistant secretaries, frequently do not have any such experience. Corporate chief executive officers typically have always worked for the companies they head, and they often serve in their positions for many years. In large firms, about 90 percent of new chief executive officers are appointed from within, and these new chief executive officers have had, on average, nineteen years of prior experience in the company. The average chief executive officer has served in his current position for almost eleven years.[2] This means they generally have intimate knowledge of the company's business and a wide range of informal contacts available for gathering information and for working out problems among different parts of the organization. One empirical study shows a significant relationship between both the extent of prior experience within the company and number of years a chief executive officer has been at the helm of a business firm on the one hand, and the firm's relative success on the other.[3] By contrast, assistant secretaries often have had no prior experience in the government agencies they are appointed to head.[4] And their average tenure, because they are appointed politically, is only two years. All this produces public-sector chief executives who have less prior experience being given less time to do the job.

Another feature of the environment for government organizations should be mentioned. The bureaucracy in the United States has lower prestige than in Europe and Japan. Presumably this lowers the tendency of talented people to seek employment in government agencies, but it may increase the relative proportion of public-spirited individuals among those seeking government jobs.

Let us now turn to the institutional design of human resources systems in the civil service. There are three areas in particular where these design choices have been not only unusual but also counterproductive to the goal of creating organizational capacity: (1) hiring and firing, (2) use of performance standards for evaluating people, and (3) pay structure and the use of pay as a reward for performance.

The civil service system puts extreme limits on the discretion of managers to hire and fire employees. The corpus of rules regulating such decisions is embodied in statutes and in *6,000 pages* of personnel regulations. And it is not just the rules that managers must cope with. Perhaps just as important, the civil service has been designed so that many personnel decisions are not made within the organization at all but rather by (or with the participation of) the Office of Personnel Management and Merit Systems Protection Board, government personnel offices that are outside of the individual agency altogether.

The most dramatic example is the "rule of three" for government hiring decisions. Applicants for government jobs must take civil service examinations and fill out an employment application listing education, past experience, and other information. Test scores and information from the application then form the basis for placement on a centralized list of candidates compiled for the entire federal government by the Office of Personnel Management. When agency managers have to fill a job, they may not simply go out and fill it. They may not even simply go out and fill it from among those who have passed the civil service exam. Instead, they must send the Office of Personnel Management a job description. The Office of Personnel Management then compares the description with its master list of candidates and returns to the manager a list of the three individuals on the entire central list that the Office of Personnel Management has determined to be best qualified for the vacancy. Managers must then hire one of these three.

There are ways managers attempt to circumvent this system so as to have a chance to do something outrageous—namely to hire someone they have turned up through their own recruitment efforts. Managers may counsel the individuals they want to hire to put certain skills and achievements into their job applications so that they have a better chance of appearing when the central file is searched for the three best candidates. Alternatively, managers may tailor the job description sent to the Office of Personnel Management to the qualifications of the person they want to hire. Finally, managers may reject all three names provided (as long as they supply an explanation and request three more).[5] The fact remains that an organization external to the manager—and even external to the manager's own agency—is intimately involved in hiring decisions that are key to the ability to create organizational capacity. Nothing even resembling this exists in the private sector. It is as if a manager in General Motors had to make hiring decisions based on a short list developed by a personnel unit of the Motor Vehicle Manufacturer's Association.

The grade level (and hence salary) for a civil service position, as well as the description of the duties of the job, are also only under a manager's limited control. The agency's personnel office makes initial decisions about position classification, with the manager's own views being merely one input. These agency-level decisions are in turn subject to audit by the Office of Personnel Management, which frequently sweeps into agencies and departs, having downgraded a significant number of positions. Because the worst thing that can happen to an agency-level classification official is to be overturned by an audit, these officials tend to adopt a cautious attitude in their negotiations with line managers, generally urging them to lower the grade levels assigned to a given job.

The Office of Personnel Management or the Merit Systems Protection Board must grant approval to many other personnel decisions as well. For example, managers must get approval to pay moving expenses for a new employee, to extend temporary hiring arrangements, or to send employees on training assignments.[6]

To be sure, rules governing promotions from entry-level positions are not nearly as restrictive as those governing initial hires. Managers have a decent amount of discretion here. Contrary to an impression many have of the civil service system, promotions are *not* based simply on seniority. But higher-level jobs in government organizations, as in private ones, tend to be filled from the ranks of those who initially came into the organization at the entry level. Thus, any system that impairs the ability to recruit good people initially will have an impact on the quality of people in the organization as a whole.

A manager's decision to fire an employee may be appealed through a several-layered process culminating in review by the Merit Systems Protection Board. A manager must prove, if challenged, that the decision to fire is backed by substantial evidence. The extended appeals process, and the many procedural grounds on which such decisions may be overturned, make it in practice very difficult to dismiss a federal employee. Managers fear that an appealed dismissal will eat up enormous amounts of time for as long as several years.

To be sure, this situation should not be painted in colors more dramatic than they really are. New employees are dismissed relatively frequently during the one-year probationary period when the appeals provisions do not apply. And managers can frequently get employees to quit voluntarily. There is evidence that since passage of the Civil Service Reform Act of 1978 (one of whose purposes was to make it somewhat easier to dismiss people), the perception that unsatisfactory performance will produce some action by supervisors has increased. In a 1979 survey, conducted at the very beginning of implementation of the 1978 law, only one-third of respondents believed that poor performance would lead to demotion or dismissal. In a 1983 survey the percentage had increased to 46 percent.[7] Finally, in the spirit of recent arguments extolling lifetime employment in Japan, it could be argued that job security produces more productive workers and hence helps rather than hinders creation of organizational capacity.

Nonetheless, government managers do perceive significant problems with unsatisfactory employees. In the same 1983 survey just cited, over 40 percent of managers stated that during the previous two years they had personally supervised employees who performed unsatisfactorily.[8] I know of no comparable surveys among private sector managers, but this figure seems high. And while the difficulties managers have dismissing poor performers certainly aren't solely responsible for these numbers, it is hard to argue they do not contribute to them. And the private firms that guarantee job security seek to shield employees as a group against layoffs when business turns bad, not to protect individual employees whose performance is persistently poor.

What are the effects of these various institutional arrangements? Narrowly and immediately, they inhibit the ability of managers to hire people who they believe will do the best job and to eliminate those who are doing a poor one. The "rule of three" is a bizarre guardianship imposed on public managers. It cannot be expected that officials from the Office of Personnel Management, distant from an agency's style and culture, or a given manager's work habits and needs, can select the three most qualified candidates from hundreds of applicants on the basis of a test score and a form (with no interviews and no reference checks). Furthermore, the centralized process, involving information going back and forth between the agency and the Office of Personnel Management, delays hiring so much that the best applicants frequently are snapped up by other employers before the agency is able to make an offer.[9]

More indirectly, these arrangements for hiring and firing people send exactly the wrong signals both to managers and employees. Managers who want to slouch and avoid taking the responsibility for selecting good people have an easy time of it. They need do little work on their own, limiting their exertions to sending a job description to the Office of Personnel Management and hiring one of the three names provided. Conscientious managers, on the other hand, must undertake extra work to try to circumvent the established system. They may also be made to feel vaguely sleazy for their endeavors. Likewise, a manager who puts up with poor performance will run into little problem with the system. But one who attempts to deal seriously with an irremediable problem may be rewarded with exhausting efforts to shepherd a dismissal through a lengthy appeals process, during which time the work of the unit may get short shrift. Similarly, employees who want to cheat the public of the effort and competence expected of them can try to rely on the hope that their supervisors will not take action because the rules make action so difficult. Meanwhile, the initial experience of dedicated and enthusiastic individuals seeking their first government job is likely to be collaboration with their future employers in an effort to circumvent civil service hiring rules. Such episodes hardly reinforce the public spirit that may be an important part of what impels them to government service and a crucial resource motivating their future performance. In addition, the enforced toleration of poor performance that the system often produces is a constant insult and source of demoralization to the public-spirited employee.

One unusual feature of the institutional design of the American civil service for managing human resources, then, is the rules for hiring and firing. A second unusual feature has been the relative lack of attention, at least until rather recently, to development of objective performance measures for people working in government. The Performance Evaluation Act of 1950 required that employees be given overall performance ratings such as "outstanding" and "satisfactory." It did not, however, mandate development of criteria according to which such evaluations might be made. The problem is to find simple measures that relate closely to accomplishment of a government organization's goals. It is often argued that development of appropriate performance measures is more difficult in government than in the private sector. In government, the argument goes, goals are vague, there is more conflict over them, and it is difficult to use measures of what has been produced to establish the final outcome of an employee's activities.

Sociologists and political scientists who write about organizations are remarkably sensitive to the difficulty of crafting performance measures in government and to the limits of any such measures that a naive or inexperienced person might attempt to develop. The literature is filled with observations of the sort that judging the performance of a government inspector by the number of inspections encourages cursory inspections of small establishments.

Some of these worries are justified, but sometimes they are excessive. Those who practice private-sector management do not seem to be quite as somber as sociologists and political scientists on the subject of performance measures. Andrew Grove, president of the highly successful Silicon Valley firm Intel, for example, notes that unintended consequences from performance indicators can create problems, but suggests that frequently this can be handled by pairing measures. For example, companies keep inventories to avoid shortages. However, carrying inventory costs money. If only shortages are measured, this encourages overaccumulation of inventory. Therefore, he suggests, pair a measure of shortages with one of inventory carrying costs. Companies developing software packages, he continues, want to get new ones out with dispatch. Speed, however, can be an enemy of quality. Therefore, he suggests, pair a measure of speed with ones of performance and reliability.[10] As Professors Robert Anthony and David Young, writing from a business school perspective about the management of nonprofit organizations, argue:

Some measures of output is usually better than none. Valid criticism can be made about almost every output measure . . . There is a tendency on the part of some managers to magnify the imperfections and thus downgrade the attempt to collect and use output information. In most situations a sounder approach is to take account of the imperfections and to qualify the results accordingly, but nevertheless to recognize that some output data, however crude, is of more use to management than no data at all.[11]

What is referred to as the ability of the marketplace environment to spur good performance may in fact in considerable measure be a surrogate for two institutional differences between business and government. One is the ability of business firms to reward good performance handsomely with money and other perquisites. The other is the ability to establish output-oriented measures of performance. Both differences are spurred by the fact that businesses need to make a profit to continue to exist. But profit-seeking organizations are not the only enterprises able to design their organizations so they produce excellence.

Business firms do use output-oriented measures—of quantity, quality, and cost—to evaluate performance. But profits are only one such measure businesses use. A production manager's performance objectives for a given year might include producing 500,000 units of a new product at a certain cost per unit or reducing inventory costs by 5 percent without an increase in downtime attributable to stockouts. A salesman may be measured by sales volume. It is interesting to note that dissatisfaction frequently exists inside business firms with the performance of units for which it is difficult to develop good measures of performance, such as research and development departments or legal staffs, even though such units exist within a profit-oriented and competitive environment. Output measures in government might include how many complainants an employee of a social security local office sees each hour, how many complainants must return with the same problem, or how many complainants are satisfied with their treatment.

The ability of appropriate performance measures to spur performance applies to government organizations as well as private ones. James Q. Wilson noted in his classic study *Varieties of Police Behavior* that differences in the number of traffic tickets in different cities closely tracked differences in ticket quotas management had established: when performance could easily be measured, officers asked to produce more did indeed produce more.[12]

A second unusual institutional feature of the civil service, then, is relative lack of attention to developing performance measures. A third is the pay structure. It is not so much that federal pay scales are lower (or higher, to take the common misperception) than those in the private sector. It is rather that they are out of synch with private pay scales. Entry-level salaries for most federal jobs are competitive with the private sector. And pay for lower-echelon workers of all kinds is often higher in the federal government. However, salaries at the middle and upper levels are far lower in the federal government than in business.[13] One study showed that federal middle managers "earn at least 30 percent less than they would earn in comparable jobs in the private sector."[14] And while the chief executive officer of a large private firm earns hundreds of thousands of dollars a year (plus stock options), those managing multi-billion dollar government programs, often with tens of thousands of employees, in 1986 were permitted to earn no more than $75,000.

The pay structure produces a situation where government organizations frequently have a relatively easy time recruiting people for entry-level positions, but have difficulty keeping them as they advance in their careers. The best often leave after a few years for better-paying private-sector positions, having gotten on-the-job training in government for their private-sector jobs. (This training occurs at public expense, and government in this way subsidizes training for the private sector.) Based on the incentives the pay structure creates, we would expect the most talented people the government hires to leave after a few years, leaving the less talented ones behind. Furthermore, until recently civil service pay was tied in only a shadowy way to performance. The Performance Evaluation Act of 1950 did require performance evaluations for employees. Results of the evaluations, however, were not linked to pay determinations. Instead, all employees doing a certain job were given automatic pay increases. Employees could receive bonuses on special application by their supervisor, but this was not tied to the regular performance evaluation system. The system in government, then, not only deprived managers of the stick of dismissal but also of the carrot of money.

One should not imagine a black-and-white contrast between traditional civil service rules and private-sector practices. In business, performance appraisal systems are often unpopular and not used to advantage either. One book on the subject describes them as being "a lot like seat belts. Most people believe they are necessary, but they don't like to use them."[15] And studies of the correlation between performance ratings and salary rewards in the private sector have shown only weak links, leading one scholar investigating the topic to conclude that "many business organizations do not do a very good job of tying pay to performance."[16]

The American civil service system is unusual not only compared with the private sector but also, in some ways, compared with other governments. Differences are most apparent in the degree of centralization of hiring systems. Few countries give a central organization the kind of influence over hiring decisions that exists in the United States.[17] In Germany there are centrally conducted competitive examinations for entrance into the civil service. But the central authority simply certifies candidates as having passed. Agencies are then free to choose on their own from among the pool of successful candidates. In Sweden, there are not even competitive examinations. Agencies are required to advertise available positions, and it is up to them then to choose applicants they wish, subject only to a general requirement that selection be made on the grounds of merit.

The British and French systems are more centralized. In both countries, the civil service is divided at the entry level into elite and nonelite streams. It is difficult to pass between the streams; an individual entering the elite stream is relatively certain of a career path that will take him or her to (or near) the top. The elite character of recruitment into entry-level jobs for the higher civil service means, however, that agencies hardly need worry that they will not be getting good people. In France, entry into the elite service is based strictly on grades at schools that train civil servants. These schools are in turn the most difficult ones in France to enter. Initial job assignments are determined by a rank ordering whereby the very top students enter the most prestigious organ of the bureaucracy (the *Inspection des Finances*), those with the next highest grades enter the next most prestigious organ, and so on down the list. In Britain the system is somewhat less structured. Examinations are held centrally. The central authority then interviews successful candidates and subjects them to extensive role-playing exercises (what would you do if you were assistant to the Minister and . . .). On the basis of this evidence the central authority rates the candidates. Exact decisions about placement in a ministry are then determined by some mixture of the preferences of the candidate, of the ministries, and of the central placement agency. Although formally these British and French systems limit the hiring discretion of agency managers in ways similar to the American system, in fact these managers have little grounds for complaint, because they are assured of some of the top young people in their countries.

There are other features of civil service systems in Europe that resemble those in the United States, but grew up, historically, for different reasons. As in the United States, it is quite difficult to fire a civil servant. And promotions up to a fairly high level are, in some of these countries, much more automatic (seniority-based), and thus even less subject to managerial discretion, than in the United States. For example, according to Ezra Suleiman, it would not be unusual in France for a senior civil servant to be able to reel off "a list of posts and the names of those who would be filling them in the next decade and a half."[18] Performance evaluation is probably in general even less developed than in the United States. These institutional features should be seen mainly as reflections of the privileged status of the civil service as an elite group in European society.

Organizing Production

Institutional choices must also be made about how an organization's jobs are designed. The pattern of institutional choices in government is also unusual as compared to business firms. Job design in government organizations emphasizes, to an unusual degree, the use of rules and standard operating procedures to prescribe behavior. When employees face an unusual situation, or wish to behave differently from the rules, they are required to refer the situation to their superiors for review, rather than being allowed to make their own decisions. This applies up and down the line: to line employees vis-à-vis supervisors, to supervisors vis-à-vis top management, and to top management vis-à-vis elected officials and other overseers.

The civil service personnel rules discussed earlier in this chapter are a good example of the phenomenon of organizing a job—in this case the job of hiring and firing people—using excessive rules and clearances. Another is the system the government uses for procurement. The government procurement system for civilian products and services is significantly more formalized around open competitive bidding than procurement practices in the private sector. When buying something for the first time, private sector organizations frequently limit bids to a few invitees, leaving it to the discretion of managers which potential suppliers are good enough to be allowed to bid and which are not. Frequently private firms do not use formal bidding but rather informal negotiations between a firm and suppliers. Firms do not bind themselves to accept the lowest bid, but let managers judge reputation and past experience. And when they procure replenishment stocks, undertake new projects, or upgrade equipment, private business typically stays with the same supplier, relying on the supplier's interest in keeping the business to assure good performance, rather than undertaking the significant costs of new procurement (and reaping in turn the savings that suppliers gain from assurance of continued sales).

The government system allows neither procurement managers nor product users to exercise as much discretion. Certain rules must be followed: everyone must be allowed to bid; specifications must be written to insure that they do not favor certain suppliers; the low bid must be accepted. Requests to deviate from the rules must be justified through several layers of review. The system makes excessive use of standard operating procedures and insufficient use of the abilities and resourcefulness of its members.

It might appear that the purpose of the government's version of competitive bidding is to save money. However, were this the cheapest way to procure, this system would be used in the private sector as well, which is not the case. Furthermore, the system hurts general performance when it slows procurement of products or services the government needs to function properly. Government computers are thus significantly more outdated than those in the private sector, depriving the government of productivity gains and sometimes threatening delivery of government services. In the Social Security Administration, battles went on for years about whether the agency would be allowed to use IBM equipment for upgrades or would be required to open bidding to everyone; meanwhile, the computer system lurched toward near collapse.

Of course large corporations also have extensive rules, and frequently private managers need to get clearances for their decisions. Furthermore, the last chapter made it clear that standard operating procedures are in many circumstances an important way to create organizational capacity. The fact remains that, as a general matter, businesses show more concern in the organization of production for how to encourage achievement and accomplishment, and government shows more concern for going by the book.

Why Do We Make the Institutional Choices We Have?

The design of civil service institutions in the United States is peculiar because it does not seem to be prompted by the same factors that motivate the design of other organizations. Putting it perhaps too dramatically, we might say that our government organizations create the capacity to get things done in spite of the way we have designed them.

How has this happened? By looking at the historical context of these institutional choices we can see how they appeared and what concerns motivated them. I shall take the development of the civil service personnel system as illustrative of the institutional choices we have made—choices that emphasize rules and clearances rather than discretion and initiative.

In broad terms, that story is well known: starting during the administration of Andrew Jackson, government organizations became politicized with a "spoils system" that gave jobs to supporters of victorious politicians. After a long political battle in post–Civil War America, and precipitated by the assassination of President Garfield in 1881 by an unsuccessful seeker of patronage, the Pendleton Act was passed in 1883 to reform the civil service system. The new law established a "merit system" for appointing government officials.

Until the Age of Jackson there occurred relatively little turn-over in the civil service when administrations changed, except at the very top levels.[19] The Jacksonian change was a part of the democratic impulse deeply rooted in the United States and in the spirit of that age. Basically, the argument was that civil servants should no more hold office for life than should members of Congress or presidents. "Rotation in office," was thus seen as a phenomenon corresponding to the rotation of elected officials in a democracy.[20] The alternative, in this view, was oligarchy. "Those who prefer the calm of perpetuity in office," stated Jackson's postmaster general, "would certainly be better pleased that the Executive head be made permanent. This will not suit a Republic."[21]

In the post–Civil War decades, agitation to change the spoils system grew. The fundamental argument of the civil service reformers was that discretion to make civil service appointments was being abused to appoint people whose only qualification was partisan political activity on behalf of winning politicians. The expressed worry was over "politicization," used in this sense of bringing in incompetents solely on the basis of loyalty to a victorious elected official. Civil service reformers generally were quite explicit that the corruption of the appointments process represented a broader corruption in American society. Changing the procedures for appointing civil servants would set an example for the cleansing of society, not just its civil service.[22]

In important ways, the movement for civil service reform was antidemocratic. Opponents of civil service reform argued that reform would close office to all but an elite of the university trained. Given this, reformers tried to tie their argument to American democratic traditions by pointing out that the spoils system prevented Americans from competing equally for the civil service, since partisan loyalty tests served as a bar.

The goal of the Pendleton Act was to reduce the possibility of abuses by reducing the ability of those running government agencies to exercise discretion. One could certainly imagine other approaches to increasing the competence of government employees than establishing a system of centralized, competitive examinations to determine entry into the civil service. Most of these other means, however, would have required placing greater weight on the judgment of those doing the hiring. It was exactly such judgment that had produced the abuses the system was designed to eradicate.

During the next thirty years or so, the system established by the Pendleton Act was both expanded in scope and refined in method. The initial law included under its regime only about 10 percent of all federal employees. Between 1883 and the turn of the century, successive presidents expanded the number of positions covered by the act.[23] In addition, in the decades after passage of the Pendleton Act, rules were developed about decisions other than initial hiring determinations. The Pendleton Act was silent on questions of job classification, promotions, and dismissal. Reform advocates initially believed that control over hiring sufficed, because "if politicians could not name their henchmen to vacancies caused by removals, the incentive to remove would be destroyed."[24] The Civil Service Commission, however, quickly began urging additional rules to prevent possible abuses involving people already working for the government, on the grounds that harassment of merit employees would be a way to discourage other than patronage seekers from applying for office in the first place. "The Commission reported in 1894," writes the administrative historian Leonard White, "that the most common form of discrimination was to dismiss employees of one political faith for offenses which were allowed to pass unnoticed or with a slight reprimand when committed by employees of the opposite party."[25] In 1897 President McKinley issued an order that no employee hired under the competitive examinations system could be removed except for "just cause" and after the filing of written charges, to which the employee would have the opportunity to reply. In 1912 the Lloyd-LaFollette Act tightened the provisions both regarding grounds for dismissal and procedures to effect a dismissal.[26] The Civil Service Commission also took the initiative for the regulation of position classification and attempted, unsuccessfully, to require use of written examinations for promotion decisions.[27] Protections against the removal of civil servants came about, then, not from the initial reform legislation in 1883. They arose instead from demands by the Civil Service Commission itself that such rules were needed to make the merit system really work.

What generalizations can be drawn from this history? The major lesson is that the civil service has throughout our history been buffeted by the winds of the two jostling views Americans have of government: pride and cynicism. The prideful view holds government to a specially high standard. As early as 1792 Congress passed various laws prohibiting government officials from gaining personal profit from office and enjoining conflicts of interest. This legislation was far more advanced than British legislation at the time. Employees of the U.S. Mint, for example, were subject to the death penalty for counterfeiting.[28]

In the prideful view as well, people should have equal rights in their dealings with government organizations, whether as job applicants or as suppliers who would like the government to buy from them. Government officials should treat similar cases similarly—two people each wanting passports on a "rush" basis should not be treated differently because of bureaucratic whim or political favoritism. A lack of evenhandedness would mean that government organizations were failing to provide each citizen with a social recognition of respect and dignity they are due simply as citizens.

The problem for the bureaucracy, as with its participation in the political process, is that it does not have the democratic character that is so much a source of pride for the elected institutions of government. Hence the efforts to democratize the bureaucracy that are reflected in the original Jacksonian doctrine of rotation in office and the debate during the controversy over civil service reform after the Civil War about whether the spoils or merit system was "more democratic."

In our cynical view, by contrast, we suspect that left to their own devices government officials will behave terribly. We worry that in the political process that bureaucrats, left to their own devices, will make the wrong political choices. And we worry that in the production process that managers will name incompetent cronies to fill jobs and that procurement officers will accept bribes from contractors. We do this particularly because the bureaucracy is not under democratic control. We chafe at bureaucratic discretion in making political choices, and we chafe at it in the production process.

In the cynical view, the enemy is discretion. Note how this bias is seen in American political science literature on government organizations. Often in this literature, the surprising—and vaguely shocking—research finding is that bureaucrats, particularly lower or "street-level" bureaucrats, do, indeed, have some discretion. Such "irreducible discretion" is frequently regarded as if it were the name of some sort of disease. Even James Q. Wilson, at one point in his *Varieties of Police Behavior,* refers to "controlling discretion" as "*the* problem of administration."[29]* Writers about business organizations, by contrast, stress the need for promoting an environment where initiative and achievement are encouraged.

So, holding government to an especially high standard as we do, but worried that left to their own devices they will not meet the standard, we prescribe in detail rules that government officials must follow, lest a grant of discretion produce bad behavior. The problem in government is not lack of accountability as is sometimes incorrectly suggested. Government people do not lead sheltered lives. The problem is the nature of the accountability. Government organizations get a good deal of attention when they do something scandalous rather than when their operational performance is good. "Scandal" may be bribes, kickbacks, or other malfeasance. It may be a horror story of a bureaucrat somewhere who has harassed a small businessman to bankruptcy or of a patient at a VA hospital who died after being administered a recalled drug. The concentration on scandal reflects both our high expectations and our great worries about government.

*Emphasis added.

To design an organization to minimize scandal, jobs are encumbered with many formal rules and clearances that tell people exactly what they are supposed to do (and not do). The hope is that this will stop malfeasance. And, confronted by external attacks, officials are more secure if they are able to say that they at least adhered to the rules. There are other features of a job that motivate decisions about its design to emphasize rules rather than discretion, and most of these conditions apply equally to government and private organizations. Furthermore, the tendency to buck decisions up to the top of the organization gets rooted in government organizations because of their involvement in the political process, where decisions often have the force of law and it hence is natural to have them made at or near the top of the organization. But the views we have of government—both prideful and cynical—are an additional factor, present in government but not private organizations, that drives government toward rules and clearances.

What we do when we design organizations based on rules and clearances is to minimize the downside. But the cost is to stifle the upside. When government officials are deprived of the discretion that could produce misbehavior, they are, at the same time, deprived of the discretion that could produce outstanding achievement.

Reforming the Personnel System in Civil Service

As early as the 1940s, criticism of the consequences of the existing civil service system for the quality of the operational performance of government began. In a prescient 1948 article in the *Public Administration Review,* Professor Wallace Sayre complained of the "triumph of techniques over purpose" in the system. The complex rules regulating the behavior of government managers provided, Sayre argued, "merely the appearance, not the substance, of the measurement of ability and merit."[30] Over the years, criticism grew to include the way the system shackled a manager's ability to influence the behavior of his employees by removing many of the tools of such influence commonly available. By the mid-1970s, this line of criticism had become the accepted wisdom among professional students of public management, both academics and practitioners.

Such a consensus among public personnel experts hardly sufficed to change the system; it should not come as a surprise that organizations such as the National Academy of Public Administration are hardly the most powerful organized groups in Washington. Furthermore, once the system had developed, it was easy to see why nonmanagement civil servants—who were by the 1970s generally organized into unions—would be skeptical of change. Outstanding civil servants might be expected to prefer a situation where their performance could have been better recognized, but average performers are, by definition, more numerous. As a symbol of advances won by labor against management, the existing rules took on a legitimacy that to some extent was independent of their content.

Changes in the system became politically possible during the 1970s because the face of the issue changed. The fear of "politicization" had encouraged continuation of the existing system, but worries about how well government worked prompted demands for change. So increased disenchantment with the performance of government predisposed people to see the issue the way advocates of change, such as President Jimmy Carter, wanted them to see it.

Carter made "civil service reform" one of his early political priorities. (It is interesting that he used the same phrase, "civil service reform," as had been used one hundred years earlier to denote the movement to create the system that Carter was now criticizing.) The task force that President Carter appointed to come up with specific proposals was heavily dominated by public personnel management practitioners and academic public management experts (including Alan K. Campbell, former dean of the Maxwell School of Public Administration at Syracuse University, whom Carter chose as head of the Civil Service Commission). The task force came up with a laundry list of proposals about which public personnel professionals had agreed for a decade or more. Long-standing and widely accepted proposals from the "policy stream" thus got attached as solutions to problems identified in the political system.

The final task force report recommended reform along two basic lines. First, managers should be given more discretion to make personnel decisions, which meant reducing the role of civil service regulations and of the Civil Service Commission. Second, the newly freed managers should then be evaluated and held accountable for how well they had done in getting their jobs done.

Specifically, the proposals of the task force included

1. Delegation of examination to the agencies, so they could develop their own examinations if they wished
2. Abolition of the "rule of three" and its replacement by a system where the Civil Service Commission gave the agency a list of all those regarded as qualified for the job in question
3. Granting agencies the authority to make 5 percent of their new hires a year totally at their own discretion, outside of all civil service rules
4. Granting authority for managers to dismiss employees, subject to reversal only if the dismissal were determined to have been "arbitrary and capricious" (a considerably more lenient standard of review than the existing "preponderance of the evidence" test)
5. Elimination of some of the layers of review for appeals by dismissed employees, to reduce the time that such appeals could drag out
6. Establishment of an annual performance evaluation system, based on specific performance criteria agreed on between employee and supervisor, for all middle and upper level government managers (at grade level GS-13 and above)
7. Creation of a new Senior Executive Service to replace the existing "supergrades" (the highest-ranked civil servants). Managers in the Senior Executive Service could be demoted (although not

fired) without the possibility of appeal if their performance was
rated less than satisfactory

8. Abolition of automatic pay increases, simply on the basis of
   longevity, for middle managers (grade levels GS-13 to 15) and
   their replacement by pay increases based only on the results of
   performance evaluation

9. Establishment of the authority to grant Senior Executive Service
   managers bonuses of up to 20 percent of their base salary. No
   more than half of Senior Executive Service managers in an
   agency could be granted bonuses.

Not all the proposals of the task force survived in the bill the
Carter administration presented Congress. Of the proposals
mentioned above, the administration was not willing to go as
far as its task force recommended on elimination of the rule of
three (it proposed replacing it with a rule of seven). Also, the
administration bill replaced the proposal that all agencies be
allowed to hire 5 percent of their employees outside of civil
service rules with a less far-reaching proposal to allow selected
demonstration projects in a limited number of agencies.

And not all the proposals in the administration bill survived
legislative consideration. At congressional hearings, some witnesses and members complained that the bill was "unduly
management oriented." Others sought to change the face of the
issue back to the danger of politicization, by citing abuses during the Nixon administration.[31] The final law retained the rule
of three unchanged and established a compromise on the standard of proof required to uphold the dismissal of an employee.
The Civil Service Reform Act of 1978, however, gave reformers
a significant part of what they wanted.[32]

What has happened since passage of the 1978 law? Any
effects of the act on improving the performance of government organizations were confounded, unfortunately, by the
succession of insults to which the civil service fell victim virtually as soon as the act took effect. The tight budgets of the
last year of the Carter administration and of the Reagan years
made the salaries and benefits of government employees a

tempting target. Depending on the year, salaries for civilian government employees have been increased less than inflation, or frozen entirely, during every year since the Civil Service Reform Law was passed. In 1985, citing the example of workers in basic industry who had accepted salary cuts to make their firms more competitive, President Reagan suggested a 5 percent pay cut for federal civilian workers, although Congress endorsed "only" a pay freeze. The small or nonexistent pot of money available for pay increases eliminated most of the promise of bonuses for good performance for the middle-level managers in the merit pay system. (This was not the case, however, for the top managers in the Senior Executive Service program.) Simultaneously, serious consideration began to be given to cutting back retirement and health benefits enjoyed by federal workers. Finally, bureaucrat-bashing increased both in frequency and intensity during the Reagan years.

It would appear that, on balance, introduction of the Senior Executive Service has had a positive effect on the performance of government managers. Introduction of the system has brought about major changes in the nature of performance evaluation for these managers. In a 1983 survey, 97 percent of Senior Executive Service managers reported that they had received a performance appraisal during the previous year. Almost all these evaluations were based on written standards. By contrast, only half these managers reported having had received such appraisals prior to introduction of the Senior Executive Service.[33] Furthermore, 49 percent of respondents stated that "all or almost all" or "most" of the elements in their performance criteria used objective rather than subjective indicators. Another 20 percent said about half of their criteria were of that sort.[34] The new performance evaluations focused the attention of senior managers on performance as an important issue: one study of the effects of the Civil Service Reform Act on senior managers reported that "wherever we went we heard people discussing performance, what it meant, how it should be measured, who should get rewarded, and how poor performance should be handled."[35]

Surveys also show (what I would interpret as) positive results regarding managers' views of the effect of the new performance appraisal system on actual performance. (See Table 8-1.) Far more managers believed that the new system has helped rather than hurt performance. Though the largest group, and generally a small majority, do state that the new system had little or no effect, we should keep in mind that many people were probably already performing well, and that incentive systems of this sort generally function to influence the behavior of a minority. Furthermore, these results are biased on the negative side by the dissatisfaction that always exists during transition to a system where the individual is more closely watched.

The Reagan administration has put a high priority on increasing Senior Executive Service salaries. Several years of congres-

TABLE 8-1.

Self-Reports of Senior Executive Service Managers on Effect of Performance Evaluation on Performance

Effect on:	"Substantial" or "Some" Positive Effect (%)	Little or No Effect (%)	"Substantial" or "Some" Negative Effect (%)
My job performance	31	52	17
The job performance of my Senior Executive Service subordinates	43	43	14
The job performance of my non–Senior Executive Service subordinates	35	52	12
The overall performance of my unit or program	36	52	11

Source: General Accounting Office "An Assessment of SES Performance Appraisal Systems," GGD-84-16 (Washington: General Accounting Office, 1984), p. 34.

sionally mandated pay caps in the late 1970s had kept top career salaries at $50,000, even while salaries of the grade levels below them were rising. This created a situation where significant numbers of top career managers were being paid no more than some of their subordinates. Between 1981 and 1984, however, top Senior Executive Service base salaries (excluding bonuses) increased by 40 percent. By receiving the maximum bonus, it is now possible for Senior Executive Service managers to earn slightly more than members of Congress—an important breach of the pernicious principle of tying top managerial pay to the salary of members of Congress.

This picture should not be painted too rosily, however. Only two years after the Senior Executive Service Act was passed, Congress amended it to reduce the maximum proportion of Senior Executive Service managers who could receive bonuses from 50 percent to 20 percent. This made the bonus system a source of discontent. (The Reagan administration did succeed in 1984 in getting the proportion restored to its original size.)[36] Another problem with the operation of the bonus system has been that when political appointees seek to recruit people from the private sector for political Senior Executive Service positions, they often have promised them bonuses in advance as a way of getting around pay limitations. Such commitments created an impression of unfairness.[37] Also, Senior Executive Service pay is still low by comparison with that of private-sector managers with similar responsibilities. Senior Executive Service members still regard the salary levels more as a reason to leave government than to stay. Nor is the Senior Executive Service exempt from the general climate of attitudes about the bureaucracy: very few respondents in one examination of the Civil Service Reform Act felt that they were "part of an elite cadre of managers in the department by virtue of (their) membership" in the Senior Executive Service.[38]

Nor have the sticks created with the Senior Executive Service received much use. Very few Senior Executive Service members have received performance rating of "less than satisfactory" since the new performance evaluation system was initiated. And while large numbers of Senior Executive Service managers have been transferred within the service, few have been demoted.[39]

In 1983 the Office of Personnel Management moved, without specific statutory authorization, to extend a merit pay system down through the entire civil service.[40] These regulations have, as of the end of 1986, still not been put into effect, owing to congressional opposition and court challenges from unions of federal employees. The Office of Personnel Management has also established a clearinghouse for systems, permitted by existing statute, to allow clerical or production workers to share a portion of productivity increases in increased salary.[41]

The Civil Service Reform Act authorized establishment of up to ten demonstration projects to test experimental systems for personnel management. The first such project was an experiment at two naval research laboratories in California. In the experiment, civil service grade levels were conflated so that there would be a larger salary range within each level. Managers were given discretion to set pay within each level based on each employee's performance evaluation. They were also given greater freedom to establish position classifications. A control group of similar research laboratories where normal rules applied was also monitored. An evaluation showed both employees and managers to be generally more satisfied with the new personnel system than were their counterparts in the control laboratories. Both employees and supervisors saw a closer connection between pay and performance at the experimental laboratories. However, the evaluations did not specifically measure productivity differences, if any, between the laboratories.[42]

The attempts at civil service reform, at best only partly successful, at least in the short run, nonetheless convey a powerful message that not just politics but also production is essential to successful policy making, that the quality of the performance of government organizations will determine exactly how government policy ends up being experienced by citizens. Sending that message is enough to justify the entire exercise.

PART II

HOW *WELL*

DOES THE

POLICY-MAKING

PROCESS WORK?

9

How Should We Evaluate the Policy-Making Process?

How should we evaluate the policy-making process? I have proposed two standards, separate, yet—as will become apparent—related. One is whether the process tends to produce good public policy. The other is whether the process of government positively affects how we see ourselves, and how we act, as human beings.

Standard 1: Does the Policy-Making Process Tend to Produce Good Public Policy?

Certainly the most important standard for evaluating the policy-making process must be the extent to which it tends to produce good public policy. The word "tends" must be kept carefully in mind, since no institutions are perfect. Because it permits a good deal of imperfection, I use the word "tends" intentionally.

As obvious as this standard is, it is excruciatingly difficult to determine how well the policy-making process meets it. People disagree about what constitutes good public policy. And even if agreement were obtained, an evaluation of the entire range of actual government policies against substantive criteria for good public policy would be a stupendous undertaking, requiring massive attention to the details of large numbers of policies.

I therefore choose a more modest approach. I proceed from the view that if the policy-making process has certain features, then it will tend to produce good public policy. The first feature is a significant level of public spirit in the system. The second feature is a reasonable ability to create the organizational capacity necessary to produce final government actions that resemble earlier political choices. This latter feature is relatively straightforward. But the first criterion—the presence of public spirit—needs further discussion.

As noted in the Introduction, "public spirit" refers to an attitude on the part of individual participants in the policy-making process. The behavior of public-spirited individuals is motivated by an honest effort to achieve good public policy. This contrasts with the behavior of the self-interested, who do not ask what policy would be right overall but rather simply what policy would be best for themselves. The standard of public spirit assumes, at least as an ideal, honest efforts to seek and work for the right policies. It demands, again as an ideal, disinterestedness: whether as a participant in the political process or someone working for a government organization charged with responsibilities for production, one should act to achieve policies that take everyone into account, not just oneself. When public spirit is important in the political process, general ideas about what constitutes good policy are important in determining the results of the process.

My contention is simple: when people try to achieve good

public policy, the result tends to *be* good public policy. Public-spirited individuals can, of course, disagree about what indeed constitutes good public policy. The discussion and deliberation that constitutes the political process presuppose that people have different views. Public-spiritedness certainly does not preclude vigorous advocacy. But participants should be open to persuasion and learning. What occurs is a marketplace of ideas. Ideas jostle, and out of the jostling truth has a better chance of emerging.

Some may find this more modest approach of judging if the policy-making process tends to produce good policy by examining features of the process rather than specific policies to be somewhat unsatisfying. It is, however, very much in the tradition of previous efforts to evaluate how well the policy-making process works. When, for example, political scientists of the pluralist tradition, or commentators on American constitutionalism, have evaluated how well the policy-making process works, they have not looked at large numbers of specific policies. Rather, they have examined the process at a fairly high level of abstraction, just as I am proposing to do. Thus, for example, pluralists looked at whether all important social interests were able to exercise political influence. Deciding that they were, the pluralists then concluded that therefore the system worked well. Opponents of the pluralists, by contrast, believed that the interests of the wealthy were overrepresented and that therefore the process worked poorly.

Standard 2: Does the Process Itself Build our Dignity and our Character?

Government is more than simply an instrumental vehicle for accomplishing certain worthy substantive purposes. Although we should continue to judge it on how well it fulfills that role, at the same time, the policy-making process is not just about producing visible, material outcomes. Through government people seek recognition of their dignity and worth. In addition, the process of government should serve to function as a school for teaching ethical behavior toward others, for molding our character. The effects of the process of government on our feelings of dignity and on our character are important enough so that they should constitute a second standard against which to evaluate the policy-making process—with the emphasis here on "process" rather than "policy-making."

Other people are important for us. Their opinions of us have an important effect on our self-esteem and feelings of dignity. These opinions are communicated in our interactions with others. Governmental processes are one sort of interaction. One of the roles of government—one of the things people seek from the process of government—is recognition of dignity and worth. The fact that people seek recognition and not just material benefits from government is illustrated in an interesting way by the debates over budget cuts during the 1980s. A notable feature of these debates has been willingness of many groups to accept budget cuts *provided that others are cut equally.* This view is so common in political debate that it is easy to forget just how extraordinary it is. A retired person or a veteran whose social security check or medical benefits will decrease by $100 a month is out the same $100 whether or not others have also lost *their* $100 in benefits. The willingness to sacrifice provided others do the same suggests that the view that people seek only material benefits from government is too simple.

It strongly suggests that one of the things government does when it provides benefits to veterans, for example, is to make a statement that we as a society honor them for the sacrifices they have made in the service of our country. When government provides benefits to the elderly it makes a statement that we respect the contributions they made to building our land. Of course, government cannot create such recognition out of whole cloth. But government actions contribute to it. And since one feature of the desire for social recognition is that the very definition of what it is that people value includes its not being for sale, there is no way for the market to produce it. Recognition that has been purchased (or praise or friendship or love purchased) is different from recognition, praise, or friendship that is not for sale. Recognition that has not been purchased cannot be obtained through the market mechanism, which calls forth production only in response to a willingness to pay. The presence of such wants places an inevitable limit on the ability of the market to produce valued things and suggests a role for nonmarket institutions such as government to produce a separate category of valued things. It also suggests why we should evaluate the policy-making process against this standard: providing social recognition of the sort that cannot be purchased cannot possibly be left to the market.

Another way for our worth to be recognized is for others to pay us the compliment of sharing our values or way of life. We care about how others choose to live their lives. Their choices, if they are the same as ours, validate our own values, if different, assail them.

In such situations one role of government is to serve as a forum for public discussion of the value of different ways of life. Many people would like government to recognize and enshrine certain choices about how to live our lives. Public policy debates about environmentalism, gun control, and civil rights involve situations where the behavior of one person tangibly affects the situation of another. We would, however, miss something of the content—and, often, the fervor—of these debates if we failed to realize that part of what advocates are debating is what values people should pursue in their personal lives. Environmentalists care about how clean the environment is, but many of them also care about whether people stand in awe of nature, beyond any effect such values have on the tangible purity of air and water. Debates over gun control are as much about tough and tender-minded values in personal life as about guns as a societal phenomenon. In some public policy debates—such as those over pornography, homosexuality, or school prayer—the dominant issue is how we choose to live our own lives, more than the effects of such decisions on others. In these instances we can see how people try to obtain social statements of recognition of the worthiness of their own values, and hence of those who profess them.

Just as the presence of public spirit is important if the policy-making process is to function well in producing good public policy, so too is public spirit important if government is to function well as a source of the recognition of worth and dignity. For government recognition to be important, government must itself be considered to be an institution exalted enough to make its honor worth bestowing. It becomes so if it is seen as an embodiment of the public as a whole, less so if it is seen simply as a playground for private interests.

In addition to being evaluated against a standard of whether it helps provide recognition of dignity and worth, the policy-making process should also, finally, be evaluated against the standard of whether it successfully acts, to use the evocative metaphor of William Muir, as a "school" for teaching the inclination to behave ethically, for molding character in our everyday lives.[1] Note that here, as well, for the policy-making process to function successfully as a school for molding character, high levels of public spirit are important. For otherwise government teaches the wrong lessons.

I am arguing, then, that we should judge the policy-making process against the standards of whether it tends to produce good policy, using as an indicator whether the level of public spirit in the system is reasonably high, and whether it builds our dignity and character. Objections may be raised against both these standards. It may be argued that the system can be designed so as to produce good policy even without high levels of public spirit, or even that self-interest in the policy-making process is actually desirable. It may also be argued that it is not a legitimate function of government either to provide people with recognition of their dignity or to build character. I shall consider each of these objections in turn.

Objection 1: Public Spirit Not Necessary: Madisonianism and Pluralism

My view that high levels of public spirit are necessary for the policy-making process to tend to produce good public policy is a minority one. The most common defenses of the way the policy-making process works in the United States argue that our institutions have been designed so that the system can work well even in a world where people seek primarily power, domination, and selfish economic advantage through government. These views, related but somewhat different, may be called the Madisonian and the pluralist accounts of the functioning of the policy-making process.

By Madisonianism I mean the doctrine of American constitutionalism as presented in *The Federalist Papers*. The basic idea of *The Federalist Papers* is that political institutions should be designed to fragment and divide up power. With power divided, ambition can be made to counteract ambition. Selfish political actors will check each other, preventing any one from dominating the system. Policies can then be adopted only when there is wide agreement among these actors—and hence when the interests of the community as a whole are being served.

What is fascinating about the Madisonian argument is that it represents a political counterpart to the argument Adam Smith was making at around the same time for the free market. Smith argued that with market institutions that allow free establishment of business firms, competition for consumer favor would lead self-interested producers to serve the interests of the public. Altruism was not needed, because market institutions created an invisible hand that promoted such a result.

Similarly, Madison argued that our constitutional institutions would create a similar invisible hand, "supplying, by opposite and rival interest, the defect of better motives."[2] It would, then, be wonderful if we could expect public spirit, but if we cannot, we should design our institutions so we do not need it.

The doctrine of pluralism, a product in its full-blown form of American political science in the 1950s, was in some sense a development of Madisonian themes, although in other senses an amendment. Pluralists argued for the importance not only of spreading power among the various institutions of government itself but also for spreading power among interest groups that pressure government.

What was new about pluralism was the view that interest groups helped assure that interests held with greater intensity received greater representation in political decisions. In this sense, pluralists saw interest groups as something that complemented majority rule. In this view, the democratic principle of one person, one vote provides a voice for consideration of the interests of the greatest number. Interest groups provide an extra voice, beyond the vote, for people unusually concerned about an issue.[3] Thus, for example, if a city plans to build a superhighway and residents of the area through which the highway will pass organize an interest group to protest construction, then not only will the relatively minor interests of the majority in having somewhat more convenient transportation be represented, but also the interests of the minority who intensely oppose destruction of their neighborhood.

With pluralist institutions as well, public spirit is not required to achieve good public policy. If each individual votes his self-interest and groups are organized around intensely important self-interests, then the sum of the pressures on the political system will be a weighted sum of extent and intensity of interest that will automatically register, like an accurate scale, what constitutes the greatest good for the greatest number. (Note that this is different from "what is good for the greatest number," which would be a simple doctrine of majority rule that took no account of intensity of interest.)

I have a number of problems with these arguments, as common as they are. The connection I presented earlier between public spirit and good public policy was a straightforward one: if political discourse is conducted in terms of asking what public policy would be good in a given situation, then the competition of ideas can lead to good policy decisions. The argument that a certain institutional design, whether Madisonian or pluralist, will achieve good public policy is much more circuitous. It does not require—indeed, its very point is not to require—that any participant in the system actually intend to achieve good policy. The argument proceeds indirectly by establishing institutional mechanisms that tend to produce, not policies that are chosen because they are good, but rather *policies with certain kinds of features*. But policies with *either* of these sets of features are frequently likely, I believe, to be bad public policies. The pluralist utilitarian results of policies embodying the greatest good for the greatest number give insufficient concern to those rights to which people are entitled independent of utilitarian considerations. Madisonian institutions that make all government action difficult, by contrast, do a good job of protecting rights against government interference, but give insufficient weight to utilitarian considerations or to instances where people may enjoy rights not simply to government forbearance but to positive government action.

In the case of Madisonian institutions, government generally acts only where there is wide consensus—consensus sufficient to overcome the fragmentation of power in the system. Otherwise, government tends not to act. In the case of pluralist institutions, the policies tend to be those that weight number and intensity in such a way as to produce the greatest good for the greatest number. Before we can claim that these institutions tend to produce good public policy, we need to adopt some view of whether policies with the features so described do indeed turn out to tend to *be* good policies.

The Madisonian model protects certain kinds of rights against interference by an overbearing majority. These rights are those that might otherwise be repressed by government—

rights to freedom of speech, of religion, of assembly, and of liberty of action. But if one believes that individuals may enjoy not only certain rights against social *interference* but also certain rights to social *action*—such as a right to life that encompasses positive social actions to save lives that otherwise would be lost, or a right to a minimum standard of living—then the protection of rights encouraged by the Madisonian model is incomplete. The Madisonian model makes government action difficult. Although this benefits the minority that wants to stop government from bashing them, it is the bane of a minority that wants government to succor them. Similarly, the Madisonian model is good at protecting a minority with intense interests against government *interference* from a majority with minor ones. But it is poor at helping an intense minority against an indifferent majority when satisfaction of that minority's interests requires government *action*. Thus, for example, Madisonian institutions would help protect a community against building a superhighway without adapting the path of the highway to minimize disruption. But they would not help a group of community residents who would require government action to prevent airline flight patterns over their houses because of the noise. And it makes it more difficult for a majority to have its interests satisfied when the doctrine of the greatest good for the greatest number requires satisfaction of majority interests over minority ones. In short, Madisonian institutions cast far too wide a net. In order to protect either the rights or the intense interests of minorities against government interference, they make it more difficult to produce government action of *any* sort. Therefore, Madisonian institutions, absent public spirit, fail the test of tending to produce good public policy.[4]

Pluralist institutions, I believe, also fail the test, though for different reasons. A pure pluralist system, without Madisonian features, does not have the bias against government action that our constitutional institutions have. But they create two problems. One is the failure to protect rights in situations where those demanding recognitions of some right lack sufficient number or intensity to overcome a majority unwilling to grant it. Thus, for example, pluralism gives little protection to a small group of unpopular people whom the majority would enjoy persecuting. The second problem is that there are likely to be significant imperfections in the extent to which interest-group formation will be a proxy simply for intensity of interest, as it is supposed to be according to the system. In particular, as critics of the pluralists of the 1950s noted, differences in wealth can confound differences in intensity of view. A poor person whose very life is at stake might well not be in a position to influence the system as much as a wealthy one with only moderate interest in the results.

It is, of course, possible to dispute any of these philosophical contentions. But to establish institutional arrangements that tend to encourage either of these (different) types of policies would be to make a once-and-for-all edict, at a constitutional level, about a philosophical debate regarding what the features of good public policy are. Such a move seems extreme and undemocratic. And even if it is undertaken it would appear to require a public-spirited debate about the philosophical foundations of good public policy at the constitutional stage, if not in ongoing political life. So even this approach does not avoid the necessity of a public-spirited discussion about good public policy, a discussion whose possibility is denied by the suggestion that political behavior is legitimately self-interested.

So the basic problem with using either Madisonian or pluralist institutional design to assure by themselves a tendency to produce good policy is that policies with the features that these institutions encourage are not necessarily good policies at all. There are other problems as well with this approach. Even if these institutional choices could be counted on to produce good public policy, we would still need to ask how likely it would be that decisions to adopt the required Madisonian or pluralist institutions would get made in the first place, or be sustained, in a world where public behavior was simply motivated by self-interest.

If the goal is to establish procedures that have the largest chance of producing good public policy, then proposed procedures need to be evaluated not in terms of self-interest but in terms of which ones encourage good choices. We might imagine a division of labor between self-interested participants articulating their interests and others disinterestedly establishing procedures for mutual adjustment among the partisans. But it is hard to see how such a division of labor could be sustained in practice. If people think of politics as an arena for articulation of their own interests alone, from where are the public-spirited participants to be recruited? And if some emerge, how are they ever going to be selected to establish procedures for the process? The suggestion that self-interested parties all share an interest in choosing disinterested procedures seems inexcusably Pollyannish, to put it mildly. We know that different procedures bestow different advantages, so that advocates disagree about what procedures they want. Absent public spirit, arguments about procedures tend to be resolved by the law of the jungle.

Furthermore, the constitutional design of institutions for policy making leaves many details of how the system works undetermined. Choices must continually be made, on a level of detail far less cosmic than the Constitution of the United States, about what kinds of procedures should be used for making political choices. Should a certain bill be sent to the Finance Committee or the Commerce Committee of the Senate? Should the White House be able to stop regulatory agencies from initiating the process of establishing a certain government regulation? The impact of such "little" procedural choices on whether good policies tend to get chosen ends up being quite large. Yet such procedural choices must be made all the time, and there is absolutely no assurance that in a world without public spirit such choices will not badly distort a grand constitutional design.

The final problem with assuming self-interest and then relying on a certain institutional design to inhibit the problems self-interest creates is that it can generate a self-fulfilling prophecy. The controls inherent to the design signal that we expect people to behave badly. At a minimum, this removes inhibitions, suggesting people can leave it to "the system" to correct their depradations. People thus lose any sense of personal responsibility for their own behavior. At worst, a "Pygmalion effect" may operate, whereby people behave the way we expect them to behave, even if they might not have done so otherwise. When we assume self-interest in the design of our institutions, then we may get more self-interest. The more self-interest we get, the more draconian the institutions must become to prevent them from producing the wrong policies; the institutions do this by inhibiting any government action, lest the action be wrong.

None of this means that designing institutions to restrain the self-interested is useless. I would interpret such institutions as efforts to create room for public spirit by holding in check the ability of the rapacious to exploit those who are not out simply for themselves. James Buchanan and Gordon Tullock argue in *The Calculus of Consent* that even if many participants in the political process try initially to do the right thing, such a situation is unstable in a world where others behave selfishly. When selfish people refuse to look out for the interests or rights of others, and public-spirited people are led to regard their own interests or rights as only one consideration among many, then it is likely that the legitimate demands of the public spirited will get excessively short shrift. In such a situation, the public spirited will eventually conclude they are simply being chumps, and ethical behavior will fall victim to defections.[5] Institutions that place roadblocks against the ability of the selfish to get their way may thus be seen as bulwarks against the collapse of public spirit. By decreasing the rewards for greed, they create a space where concern for others may flourish. They act as a sort of fallback or redundant protection for the system.

It may, finally in this regard, be noted that a similar view, that we should try to design institutions so that we get good behavior despite self-interest, exists for the production process. Thus, we design checks into government organizations to prevent corruption and other malfeasance by government officials even if these officials should seek to act in a self-interested way. More broadly, relying on contingent rewards and punishments rather than a person's inclination to do a good job reflects a similar philosophy.

Here, too, I believe that while such efforts are not worthless, their limitations as a substitute for the inclination to perform well must be kept in mind. It would be difficult and costly to establish a system where inducements were always required to get people in organizations to perform well in situations where self-interest alone would lead them to do otherwise. At least a Smithian or Madisonian system arranges institutions such that bad behavior *naturally* brings forth a counterreaction. Shoddy products do not sell, and the ambitious behavior of one political actor is checked by that of others. Such a natural counter-reaction does not occur in situations in organizations where inducements are to be used, because there rewards and punishments do not occur automatically but must be meted out by conscious decision. Such an arrangement is not only very resource-intensive. Organizations relying solely on rewards and punishments would become incredibly intrusive in the lives of their members; at their worst they might come to resemble police states. Furthermore, there is now extensive experimental evidence that relying on rewards and punishments to induce behavior reduces the individual's intrinsic motivation to perform when not being observed. For example, subjects paid for undertaking a task such as playing cards stop doing it sooner after observation of them ceases than do those who were not paid.[6] The problem here is similar to one of the problems of relying on a Madisonian or pluralist system in politics: rewards and punishments can become like a drug that requires higher and higher doses to produce the same effects. My conclusion, then, is that in the production process as well as in the political process, public spirit is important—in politics to bring about the inclination to seek good political choices, in production, to bring about the inclination to do a good job. This, incidentally, is starting to be more and more the view of management scholars and practitioners, with whom an emphasis on the centrality of an appropriate "corporate culture" in producing good performance has replaced a single-minded focus on rewards and punishments.

We frequently hear from economists that concern for others is a rare commodity that must be husbanded carefully lest it turn out to be depleted when it is really needed. Political institutions, it is concluded from this reasoning, should not be designed to rely on altruism but rather to channel self-interest, a motivation that is abundant.[7]

It is, of course, true that the supply of altruism cannot be expanded infinitely. But the economists' view—an application of the general dictum from economics that people's preferences be taken as fixed—is an oversimplified account of much human behavior, whether it is playing the piano or showing concern for others. Observing public-spirited behavior—and practicing it—is likely to increase the extent of public spirit and get us better at being public spirited. There is good evidence as well that the actions we undertake frequently generate the attitudes we have, contrary to the view that the direction of the causal arrow always goes in the other direction. The drive toward reduction of cognitive dissonance suggests that if we start behaving in a certain way, our orientations will tend to move in the same direction. Selfish behavior thus generates selfish attitudes, and vice versa. Experimental studies confirm what Aristotle and the authors of the Talmud admonished long ago. "We become just by the practice of just actions", stated Aristotle. "Accustom yourself to do good, before long it will become your chief delight," is written in the Talmud. This applies both to development of public spirit in the policy-making process and to the spread of a similar orientation to behavior in our everyday lives. Should we foreswear public spirit in the design of our political institutions for fear that it will run out? Even if we were concerned about a limited supply of altruism, what better place to promote its use than government, where joint decisions affecting others are being made. If not altruism there, then where? Better, if need be, to rely on self-interest in the marketplace.

My own conclusion is that institutions that try to assure good public policy even in a policy dominated by self-interested behavior do help, but that they are not enough. Interestingly, this was even the view of Madison, when he asked:

> Is there no virtue among us? If there be not, no form of government can render us secure. To suppose that any form of government will secure liberty or happiness without any virtue in the people is a chimerical idea.[8]

It was also the view of de Tocqueville when he wrote in *Democracy in America* that "the best possible laws cannot maintain a constitution in spite of the customs of a country."[9] We cannot just leave things to the system and expect everything to be all right. Rather, we must realize that, in the words of John F. Kennedy, "Here on earth, God's work must truly be our own."

Objection 2: Public Spirit Not Desirable: The Argument from Unintended Consequences

Highlighting what Robert Merton dubbed "the unintended consequences of purposive social action" must certainly rank among the all-time favorite pastimes of social scientists.[10] By pointing to the pervasiveness of unintended consequences, the argument may be made that public spirit will actually produce bad public policy. Well-intentioned individuals advocate certain policies on the basis of good intentions, but it turns out, the argument goes, that such policies end up hurting rather than helping. We intend to aid the poor by passing minimum wage legislation, but instead we end up hurting the poorest of the poor, whom nobody wants to hire at the minimum wage and who thus are left unemployed. Or we may intend to help Jews in the Soviet Union by cutting off trade until more Jews are allowed to emigrate, but instead we end up stiffening the resistance of the Soviet leadership and decreasing the number of Jews let out. It is probably no exaggeration to state that by now the conventional wisdom has progressed beyond the injunction that good intentions are not enough to the more extreme view that good intentions count for nothing. And if they count for nothing, then public spirit counts for nothing.

How could it be possible that there is no relationship (or even a negative relationship) between trying to do the right thing and actually succeeding at doing right? The answer is that good intentions can fail to produce a proposal for good policy if a mistake is made about the best means to achieve the ends that are sought. The value statement, "It is right to help the poor," does not suffice to justify a conclusion about adopting a minimum wage. The contention of fact, "Adopting a minimum wage helps the poor," is required as well. If the contention of fact is mistaken, then the conclusion about the minimum wage would be wrong, despite good intentions. So good intentions are indeed not enough.

But do we really have reason to adopt such pessimism about the ability of people to understand empirical relationships in the world around us to draw the conclusion, often with a smirk, that there is *no connection at all* between trying to do the right thing and succeeding at doing so? Certainly it is possible to adduce examples of situations where bad policies were chosen despite good intentions. It is equally possible to cite examples where results have followed intentions. Government policies to support medical research have produced medical advances that have saved many lives, more or less as intended. Introduction of public schooling has produced a more educated population than would have otherwise existed. There are even instances where unintended consequences have been predominantly positive rather than negative. Defense research, for example, has produced many technological spin-offs with civilian applications.

Beyond the anecdotes, though, the point is that it would be perverse, and implausible in terms of the evolutionary fitness of the human species, to suppose that our understanding of the world around us is such that we fail more often than we succeed in choosing the correct means to achieve our ends.

Furthermore, the problems of unintended consequences are mitigated the more experience government gets at policy making. It would certainly appear unreasonably fatalistic to believe that unintended consequences are a constant, unresponsive to lessons from past experience or to efforts to think carefully in advance about the probable effects of various policies. As we gain experience in policy making in an area, our ability to learn by error grows. Furthermore, because taxes become higher and more visible as the role of government grows, there is less willingness to sign off on new policy initiatives simply on the basis of some vague good intentions. Demands for good information about the probable consequences of policy proposals are thus likely to grow as the cumulative monetary burden of government programs increases. Indeed, observations about the unintended consequences of public policies were most prevalent during the beginnings of the expansion of government's role in society. By now the lesson has been learned quite well that good intentions are not enough. In fact, one of the (probably) unintended positive consequences of the concern about unintended consequences has been to decrease the probability that policies with disastrous unintended consequences get adopted in the first place.

Objection 3: Public Spirit Not Desirable: The Argument from Information-Generation

A second argument for the view that participants in policy making should only express their self-interest is that if participants fail to advocate their own interests, information about citizen preferences that is important for making political choices will not be provided as completely.[11]

This argument begins with the observation that the information requirements for the determination of good public policy are extremely rigorous. They require an assessment of what values are at stake for those affected by a decision and of the consequences of various policy alternatives for those values. The best source of information about what is at stake, the argument continues, comes from the interested parties. They are most likely to be in a position to know where the shoe pinches. They also have the strongest incentives to make their concerns known. By contrast, detached, public-spirited participants, trying to determine on their own what policy would be right in a given situation, would be unable to conceive of all relevant considerations. For each participant to try to determine what political choice is right overall would, therefore, be a mistake, concludes Aaron Wildavsky.

It is much simpler for each participant to calculate his own preferences than for each to try to calculate the preferences of all. It is difficult enough for a participant to calculate how the interests he is protecting might best be served without requiring that he perform the same calculation for many others who might also be affected. . . . The danger of omitting important values is much greater when participants neglect the values in their immediate care in favor of what seems to them a broader view.[12]

Better to announce "We're thinking of banning pesticide X" and wait for reactions from self-interested participants. Those reactions will best reveal the interests at stake.

These critics, I suspect, frequently exaggerate the difficulties for someone well informed in a policy area to gain a relatively good idea of the major considerations at stake. Perfect information is, doubtless, extremely costly, but acceptably good information is often not.

Beyond that, the big problem with this argument is that information-generation constitutes only the first step toward making good political choices. Choosing good public policies requires not only good information about what is at stake but also conclusions about how to weight these considerations when they come into conflict. The objections raised earlier against the ability of institutional arrangements such as Madisonian constitutionalism or pluralism to assure the proper weighting of self-interested demands become relevant here. Self-interest may be good at generating information, but it remains insufficient for reaching good decisions. Just as good *intentions* do not suffice for making good policy choices, neither does good *information.*

Given the role of self-interested advocacy in generating information, it probably would be unfortunate if self-interest were to disappear entirely from the policy-making process. But, the world being the way it is, it seems curiously inappropriate, to the point of surrealism, to sound alarums about how much policy making would suffer if we were deprived of the input of the self-interested. The real causes for worry appear to lie in the other direction.

Objection 4: Public Spirit Not Desirable: The Argument from Fanaticism

A final argument in favor of self-interest in the policy-making process might be labeled the argument from fanaticism. One may point to the most terrible phenomena of contemporary history, such as Stalinism and Nazism, and note that they emerged from passionate ideologies, even passionate idealism. Concede, the argument might go, that we cannot expect great things from the politics of self-interest, but at least we can avoid great horrors.[13]

The world of the Final Solution and of the gulags seems far removed from a discussion of contemporary American society. The worry about idealism run wild also sounds peculiar to those immersed in the world view of economists and of many contemporary political scientists, in which people are seen as largely unable to summon up anything but self-interested behavior. Nonetheless, the point of the argument from fanaticism is that even if the risk is small, the potential evil is so great that steps should be taken to avoid it, even if it means sacrificing probable gains.

I am, however, not convinced. First, it is not at all obvious that when evil triumphs, those triumphs can be attributed to fanatic idealism. When large numbers of poor people are willing to see the rich murdered so that the poor can become better off, or large numbers of Germans are willing to see Jews killed because they believe this will solve their problems, this would appear to involve cases not of idealism, but of self-interest, run wild. People behaving that way would appear to be closer in motivation to mobsters than to idealists. I agree with the sociologist Nathan Glazer that "one can be quite passionate and unreasoning in the defense of interests, one can be quite calculating and rational in the pursuit of passions."[14] The defender of public spirit need certainly not defend every policy advocated in its name, any more than the defender of self-interest must do the same with every expression of self-interest. The issue is not self-interest versus idealism but reasonableness versus fanaticism. If one wishes to encourage public spirit, what is encouraged should include showing respect for others.

Objection 5: Is There a Legitimate Role for Government in Promoting Dignity or Molding Character?

I argued earlier that one of the standards against which the policy-making process should be judged is the extent to which the processes of government, over and above the tangible policies that result from those processes, make social statements of recognition of people's worth and dignity and serve as a school for teaching ethical behavior. I argued further that the extent to which the policy-making process is successful along these dimensions also relates to the pervasiveness of public spirit in the system. It is, however, one thing to state that many people see these roles for government. It is another to argue that such views of the role of government are justified.

Let me first examine the suggestion that there is no legitimate role for government in making social statements of recognition of dignity and worth. Some critics might concede that people may want opportunities to enhance their self-esteem through public statements of recognition but deny that *government* need become involved to satisfy the wants. There are, to be sure, many alternative institutions besides government, ranging from families to honorary societies, that provide recognition. However, only government represents the community as a whole. To the extent people wish to feel proud of being members of the community as a whole or to receive recognition from the entire community, there can be no substitute for government in providing at least some of these feelings.

Critics might similarly concede that many people might wish to gain the self-esteem that comes from social validation of values that they hold for how to live their own life, but still deny that government has a legitimate role to play providing such validation. Government should be neutral like an attitude toward personal ways of life, the argument goes, that tolerates diversity rather than enforcing one personal code over another.

Surely, however, the fact that discussion of the value of different ways of leading one's life occurs in the context of government does not mean that the outcome of such discussion lead to jail sentences for those with divergent life-styles. Indeed, in such debates, advocates of tolerance represent one important view about how we should lead our own life—a view that says we should not try to interfere with the decisions of others about how to lead their lives. Not to permit such discussion would appear to me, however, to send the wrong signal, namely that such discussions are not important and that decisions about what values should guide our personal lives are not crucial ones.

Similarly, it is hard to see a valid objection to the contention that government has a legitimate role to play in serving as a school for teaching the inclination to behave ethically. Citizens differ, of course, about whether particular substantive government policies are right or wrong. Those who believe in a minimalist government will generally conclude that the best government action is no action. But even those with minimalist views on the proper *substantive* role of government can agree to cherish a role for government in molding individual character. The views of both those who favor a minimal government and those favoring an active one are derived from arguments with ethical premises. Whatever our views on the substantive role of government, we can wish to see people in their everyday lives realize that the interests and rights of others set limits for how we may legitimately pursue our own self-interest. And since people must be taught ethical principles, and must get practice displaying ethical behavior, it would seem gratuitous to pass up the opportunity to use the process of government, with all its visibility, as one place to give the lessons.

Indeed, the role of government in recognizing people's worth and dignity can be justified not only by the fact that many people may want government to provide such recognition but by the contribution such a role makes to promoting ethical behavior. The more our individual satisfactions depend on recognition that others bestow, the more we are led to realize the importance of others and our own connection with them. The sense of the importance of other people lies at the root of the motivation to behave ethically. It is not the case (to paraphrase Jeremy Bentham) that, the amount of pleasure being equal, pushpin is equal to public spirit. It is legitimate for government to promote ethical behavior, not simply because people may happen to *want* it, but because it is *right* to be concerned about others.

Finally, the role of government in providing social recognition of people's dignity and in molding character suggests additional reasons for being worried about the Madisonian or pluralist solutions to the design of institutions. The democratic rule of one person, one vote makes a social statement about a basic human worth that all people share equally. But the Madisonian and pluralist solutions require that procedures be designed so that special weight is given to intense minorities. Such an institutional design contradicts the message about basic human worth. Furthermore, institutions that assume self-interest fail to provide the opportunity for government to help mold character. When self-interested advocates participate in the political process, at least they provide only input; they do not make final decisions by themselves. Yet in personal life, individuals are indeed called on to make by themselves decisions with impacts on others. If we abandon the effort to encourage individuals to think beyond personal considerations in political life, we miss the opportunity to have the political process function as a school for teaching ethical behavior in private contexts.

To sum up, I use two grounds for evaluating how well the policy-making process works. The first is whether it tends to produce good public policy. The second is whether the process itself helps provide recognition of our dignity and molds our character. I have argued that the presence of public spirit plays an important role in determining whether the policy-making process works well along both these dimensions.

It is also my view that most citizens evaluate government roughly according to the standards I have laid out. They ask whether government has produced good policies, whether public spirit is commonly displayed in the process, and whether the process does anything to make us better people. Prideful and cynical evaluations of government relate in good part, I think, to answers citizens give to these questions.

10

The Wellsprings of Public Behavior: Alternate Views

An important way I evaluate the policy-making process, I have stated, is by examining the extent to which public spirit prevails in the system. The common answer to this question is clear. Anybody who reads the newspapers or watches television—as well as most students who have studied the policy-making process in political science or economics courses in recent years—will surely have assimilated the impression that there is little in Washington besides self-interested battles for economic advancement or personal power. And those purveying such a view do not share the optimism of those who claim that the policy-making process can work well even if self-interest dominates it. Rather, the brunt of the argument is that self-interest dominates the process and that *therefore* the process works badly.

Self-Interest

The journalist's approach to the policy-making process is doubtless familiar to most of us. Why are federal regulations rolled back? Because business groups increased their lobbying efforts against them. Why do protectionist measures get passed? Because firms and workers that suffer from foreign competition pushed them through. Why did a certain member of Congress support the president on a particular piece of legislation? Because the president said he would see to it that the member's district got a new federal building located there if he did. Why does the Social Security Administration run into problems with its computers or the Defense Department with weapons that are overpriced? Because of the laziness, or corruption—or both—of bureaucrats who exploit their positions to live easy, or live high, at the taxpayer's expense.

Stories such as these are familiar ones, the stuff of which the evening news is made. Interestingly, though, similar arguments have been made with increasing frequency by academic economists and political scientists. And although the stereotype would have it that journalists are a bit wild, whereas academics are sober or even dull, in fact the zaniest of the theories about the domination of self-interest over the policy-making process have been concocted not in the newsroom but in the classroom.

For a long time, the view that the policy-making process works badly because of the dominance of self-interest was the special province of those on the Left, and particularly of Marxists. Marx wrote in *The German Ideology* that "the ruling ideas are nothing more than the ideal expression of the dominant material relationships," and Marxists have generally seen politics as a battle of interests where, in capitalist societies, those with economic power generally win out.[1] In this vein, the historian Gabriel Kolko argued that the food safety legislation of turn-of-the-century America was not passed because of popular revulsion against consumer fraud or against the unsanitary practices revealed in Upton Sinclair's *The Jungle,* but rather because big food-processing companies wanted regulation's help to drive smaller competitors out of business.[2] Others influenced by Marxism have seen government aid to the poor not as a way to help the disadvantaged but simply as a selfish effort to stave off revolution.[3]

More recently, though, the view that the policy-making process is dominated by self-interest and that this domination produces bad public policy has been taken up by people on the Right who argue that self-interest produces big government. Economist Gordon Tullock has argued that the fact that government officials are allowed to vote means that a government will inevitably be elected that is larger than the average non-bureaucrat would want, because bureaucrats themselves will always vote for bigger government so as to protect their jobs.[4] In economist William Niskanen's view, the budget will always be too large because bureaucrats have much more information than their legislative overseers about how much it really costs to supply public services and can thus claim they need a budget larger than they in fact do.[5] Morris Fiorina, letting his imagination run riot in *Congress: Keystone of the Washington Establishment,* has suggested that Congress establishes regulatory agencies so that they can gain support from constituents by handling complaints that the rogue behavior of these agencies creates. In his book *Congress: The Electoral Connection,* David Mayhew presents a picture of members of Congress motivated solely by the desire to achieve reelection, who have an interest only in posturing and claiming credit because that is what helps with constituents, rather than in actually accomplishing anything.[6] The economist E. S. Savas has argued that monopoly production of government services produces a situation where citizens are "subject to endless exploitation and victimization" by bureaucrats, where "so-called public servants have a captive market and little incentive to heed their putative customers."[7]

Twenty years ago the loudest voices criticizing the policy-making process for its domination by self-interest would have been those of the Marxists. Today, however, Marxism is largely discredited both in the world of ideas and in the world of public policy practice. Instead, the intellectual thunder comes from the efforts by economists to apply the perspective of their discipline to the analysis of the political process. This effort has produced what has come to be known in economics as "public choice" theory, pioneered by James Buchanan, the 1986 Nobel laureate in economics. Advocates of these ideas are now assaulting academic political science with the fury and the enthusiasm of Islamic moujahadin swooping down on the infidels. David Mayhew's *Congress: The Electoral Connection* and Morris Fiorina's *Congress: Keystone of the Washington Establishment* are two of the most widely praised and influential political science books of the last decade. As Marxism needed to be taken seriously in the 1960s, so does the "public choice" approach need to be taken seriously in the 1980s.

It is interesting to note the progression of brazenness that occurs from Buchanan and Tullock's *The Calculus of Consent* in 1962 to *Congress: Keystone of the Washington Establishment* in 1977. Early in the history of public choice, Buchanan and Tullock adopted a tone that was almost apologetic about their use of the self-interest assumption for the political process. Certainly, they regarded themselves as idiosyncratic in their views; earlier theorists, they note, had generally assumed that the average political participant "seeks not to maximize his own utility, but to find the 'public interest' or 'common good.' "[8] This tone of humbleness, however, disappears in later works. In an article published in 1979, Tullock noted that "the traditional view of government has always been that it sought something called 'the public interest' " but that, "with public choice, all of this has changed," adding, with a bit of contempt, that "the public interest point of view still informs many statements by public figures and the more old-fashioned students of politics."[9] By the time Fiorina writes, what might have once been seen as conspiratorial speculation has become scholarship that is not only respectable but highly acclaimed. Times, and academic fashions, have changed.

The behavioral supposition of the "public choice" approach is that behavior of participants in the policy-making process is motivated by self-interested efforts to get as much as they can of the things they personally want. (That these theories of rampant egoism are sometimes dubbed models of "rational choice" by proponents appears designed either to confuse or to give the word "rational" a bad name.) Self-interested motivation is seen to apply to participants in the political process, whether citizens or elected and appointed officials. It is seen to apply to the members of large organizations involved in the production process as well.

As noted, the "public choice" approach originated among economists. Economics has, since Adam Smith, developed a remarkable body of theoretical propositions about the production and exchange of goods in the marketplace based on the assumption of self-interest. These propositions have been powerful enough and (not unimportantly for scholars) often counterintuitive enough to earn economics the title of "queen of the social sciences"—and to generate among economists a powerful urge to apply their approach to institutions outside the marketplace, ranging from the family to the policy-making process.

These efforts emerged with publication of Anthony Downs's *An Economic Theory of Democracy,* in 1957, and of James Buchanan and Gordon Tullock's *The Calculus of Consent* in 1962.[10] Downs began his account with what he called "the self-interest axiom," that is, the view that political behavior is "directed primarily toward selfish ends." Following this general axiom, politicians, Downs assumed,

act solely in order to attain the income, prestige, and power which come from being in office . . . [They] never seek office as a means of carrying out particular policies; their only goal is to reap the rewards of holding office *per se.* They treat policies purely as a means to the attainment of their private ends.[11]

Buchanan and Tullock began with the same behavioral assumptions as Downs. "The average individual," they wrote, "acts on the basis of the same overall value scale when he participates in market activity and in political activity."[12] Or, as Tullock put it in a later book, "Voters and customers are essentially the same people. Mr. Smith buys and votes; he is the same man in the supermarket and in the voting booth."[13]

The prime claim to fame of economics as a discipline lies in its ability to demonstrate how self-interested actors, in a market setting, end up promoting the public interest. Indeed, many of the defenses of the role of self-interest in the policy-making process discussed in the last chapter partake of the same generous attitude toward the role of self-interest for which economists are renowned—and, as noted, the Madisonian system can be seen as envisioning creation in the sphere of political institutions of the invisible hand that market institutions create in the economy. It is therefore interesting to see how the public choice economists reach the conclusion that the operation of self-interest in the policy-making process produces bad results rather than the good ones economists see when self-interest holds sway in the marketplace.

Although the answers to that question among different public choice economists are as varied as they are inventive, two major strands dominate. One sees problems arising simply from the institution of majority rule voting for collective decisions. The other emphasizes the baleful effects of interest groups.

In a world where a majority may make decisions that have coercive force behind them and can bind a minority, the way is left open for interested individuals to use government to get something for nothing, something that can occur only because government may confiscate one individual's resources without his consent to benefit another individual in a way that cannot occur in the marketplace. "To the individual member of the effective majority," Buchanan writes, "the political process provides a means through which he may secure private gain at the expense of other citizens."[14] Buchanan and Tullock illustrate this problem with a simple case where a group of five farmers decides how much government money to appropriate for repairs to the roads leading to their farms. Under majority-rule institutions, three farmers may make a binding decision regarding the *total* level of such repairs. What will self-interested farmers do? Three of them will band together and vote repairs *for their farms only.* Each farmer in the majority will receive one-third of the benefits of the repairs. Since, however, the other two are also being taxed even though they receive no benefits, each of the three farmers in the majority will pay only one-fifth of the cost. Since the majority pays only one-fifth of the costs while receiving one-third of the benefits, the level of repair they vote will be greater than had they borne their full proportional costs. The majority thus exploits the minority. In addition, government ends up too big from *everyone's* point of view. This is because of the possibility of shifting majorities. Alternative coalitions of three farmers can arise and each vote themselves repairs at the expense of alternative minorities. By the time all the voting is over, everyone will have gotten himself into both a majority and a minority. The result will be a greater level of repair (and of taxes) than *any* farmer wanted.[15]

Another strand within public choice theory has emphasized interest groups. Many of these arguments are outgrowths of economist Mancur Olson's *The Logic of Collective Action.*[16] Political scientist critics of the pluralists had generally argued that the wealthy were indeed well organized but that the poor were not. Olson, by contrast, argued that *any* sort of organization into interest groups, whether by the wealthy or the poor, was problematic. The reason is that, in the technical language of economics, the benefits to be gained from group action are a "public good." That is to say, if they come about, they are shared by all, whether or not any given individual contributed toward their realization. A welfare mother, for instance, need not have organized to fight for a law providing higher welfare benefits in order to gain those benefits if such a law is passed. Given that, Olson argued, it is irrational for any given potential beneficiary of a government program to organize on its behalf. He should instead let the other guy do it and act as a free rider. However, of course, if everyone takes that attitude, nobody (rich or poor) will organize.

Economist George Stigler developed Olson's argument in his essay "The Theory of Economic Regulation."[17] Stigler argued that the propensity to organize increases the greater the stake a person has and the smaller the size of the group. Producer interests are in a position to capture enormous benefits from government and are often rather small in size. By contrast, the loss per consumer of government policies aiding producers is generally tiny, and the number of consumers is huge. (A benefit of $100,000 a year to a producer, if divided among 100,000 consumers, will cost each consumer only a dollar.) Stigler argues that producer interest will therefore generally be better organized than consumer interests. The well organized will then win out in the political process over the poorly organized, even though the well organized are a minority.

This tendency is compounded, the argument goes, by the development of "iron triangles" supporting established government policies—triangles consisting of a supportive interest group, an agency whose mission is in line with the program, and members of a congressional committee overseeing the program who have chosen to serve on the committee because they agree with the program.

For political science critics of the pluralists, "special interests" generally means the wealthy. The public choice analysis, emphasizing the benefits and costs of organization rather than the sociological status of the rich or poor, sees the danger of special interests in many contexts, not only when the special interests are wealthy. Special interests may include auto workers winning restrictions on foreign cars or even rifle enthusiasts winning limitations on gun control. In all these cases, the political process will tend to produce inefficient subsidies for the organized at the expense of individually small (but cumulatively large) costs to the unorganized.

Many of these arguments about institutional biases in a world of self-interests can be criticized more or less on their own terms. Indeed, this is the form that a good deal of the criticism has taken.[18] One can assume self-interest in the process and still be skeptical of the public choice (or Marxist) view that this will tend to produce bad public policy. Indeed, the whole point of the Madisonian and pluralist arguments is that institutions can be arranged so that good public policy can be produced in a self-interested policy-making world. It is also curious, for example, that conservatives tend to point to biases in the process that tend to produce government that is too large or too liberal (the influence of proprogram bureaucrats, the power of the media, even the fact of majority rule), while liberals point to features that tend to produce government that is too conservative (the bias in interest group organization in favor of the wealthy, the role of campaign contributions, the fact that the poor vote less than the rich). This is not just an amusing fact, but a piece of evidence about the institutional design of the process. Liberals focus on assets that conservatively oriented forces possess in the process, conservatives on those that liberally oriented forces have. Neither sees that the various alleged biases cancel each other out, or at least counteract each other. Furthermore, those presenting these theories frequently appear to be fighting the last war; as soon as the idea of "iron triangles" became the conventional wisdom of the political science literature, the influence of iron triangles in the political process began to dissipate under the assaults of media spotlights and the explosion of interest groups on many sides of previously single-interest group policy areas.

Public Spirit

An alternate view of the wellsprings of public behavior is also possible that does not so much challenge the arguments of the public choice approach on their own terms as it does criticize the terms in the first place. The alternate view is that public spirit is important in public behavior and that therefore the dolorous results for the policy-making process that result when one assumes self-interest do not occur simply because self-interest fails to dominate the way advocates of the public choice approach believe it does. In this chapter, I explore the basis for such an alternate perception at the theoretical level. In the next chapters, where I evaluate the political and production processes, I examine the evidence supporting the alternate views.

My argument for an alternate view begins not with the policy-making process directly, but with an alternate view of human nature—that not just personal self-interest but also concern for others can motivate behavior.

Only a foolish observer of the human condition would belittle the enormous role that self-interest plays in motivating people. I am neither a biologist nor a sociobiologist. From an outsider's perch, I will, however, confess to being convinced by the argument from the theory of evolution that self-interest has been selected over the long run because creatures who did not take a healthy interest in their own situation simply failed to survive and reproduce as well as those who did.

At the same time, according to the alternate view, concern for others can also motivate behavior. Why? The short answer goes back to Aristotle, namely, that man is a social animal who lives in a community. People depend on others for the satisfaction of both material and psychological needs. Materially, there is a division of labor in production even in the most primitive societies; psychologically, people gain approval, respect, and love from others. The alternate view is that the close webs that tie people to each other produce empathy with the situation of others as well.

And, indeed, there is ample evidence from experiments that confirms what anybody in Hollywood could have told us without such experiments: people experience empathy, and feel distress, when faced with the suffering of others. Laboratory experiments involving people witnessing scenes that appear to show an experimenter falling off a ladder, or having chairs crash down on him, confirm such reactions, based not only on self-reports but on measurable physiological changes. In one dramatic experiment, soldiers were exposed to highly realistic combat simulations and their responses measured. In one such simulation, soldiers were led to believe that they were in some way responsible for the injury of a fellow soldier in an explosion. Reactions to this simulation were compared with reactions to simulations of personal threats. "In comparison to the personal threat conditions, the simulation of personal responsibility for the injury to a fellow soldier produced the highest level of stress, as indexed by self-report, and a level of deterioration in complex motor performance that was second only to being under artillery fire."[19]

Research suggests that such empathy is largely involuntary. "It is hard for people to avoid emphathizing with someone in pain or distress unless they engage in certain perceptual or cognitive strategies such as looking away from the victim or trying hard to think about other things."[20] And there is good evidence that if distress is extreme and the time to react is short, many people will engage in what Piliavin and her colleagues refer to as "impulsive helping," helping behavior that occurs so quickly that it could hardly have been preceded by any extensive decision process. Thus, for example, in a staged experiment where a person with a cane collapsed in a subway car, 90 percent of the bystanders went to the victim's assistance in less than ten seconds.[21] Furthermore, these reactions appear early in infancy: there is research showing that infants two or three days old cry in reaction to hearing others cry.[22]

The seemingly involuntary nature and early appearance of empathy in humans suggests, although this is a somewhat controversial view, that like self-interest, altruism has a genetic, evolutionary base.[23]

How should we characterize behavior that displays concern for others? In a bizarre effort to define altruism out of existence, it is sometimes suggested that if an individual chooses to behave in a certain way, it "must" be because that behavior provided more rewards than costs, with the satisfaction at having helped someone counted as one of its rewards. Given that the behavior provided more rewards than costs, continues the argument, it was thus selfish and not altruistic.

What can we make of this argument, beyond any wonderment over the apparent eagerness to read altruistic motivation out of the human personality? The view that concern for others is part of our humanity does indeed enrich our view of the self and, indeed, of what is meant by "self-interest." We can also note how much of our views of what constitutes our own interest is defined socially and not by some isolated, asocial self.[24] If an individual feels bad when others suffer, this establishes a link between concern for oneself and concern for others.[25] In the typical situation where people display concern for others and feel good because they do so, few draw an artificial distinction between whether they are "really" acting in order to help others or to feel better themselves, because they accomplish both at the same time. As political philosopher Joseph Carens puts it, people do not normally "regard the good to others and the good to themselves as distinct and independent motives."[26] It seems far more appropriate simply to note this linkage rather than to use it to suggest in a reductionist fashion that one type of behavior is "really" another.

None of this suggests that ethics is a matter of biology. That some behavior has a genetic base does nothing to establish that the behavior is ethically right. Homicide may have a genetic base as well. It would be more appropriate to argue that genes that hardwire us for altruism (and also those that allow us to reason) make it possible to reflect on ethical truths it otherwise would be impossible for us to conceive. (There are almost certainly many truths that the human mind is simply incapable of understanding.) The philosopher Peter Singer compares the genetics of ethics with the genetics of mathematics:

> The capacity to count must have emerged at an early point in human development. . . . It is said that if four hunters go into a thicket and only three come out, the baboons will keep away, for they know that someone is still there. . . . If this report is true the ability to count has

practical value for them, and the baboons who can count a little may sometimes survive when less gifted baboons perish. The ability to count must have conferred a similar advantage on our own ancestors. . . . No doubt human beings are able to reason and count because in the evolutionary struggle for survival, a set of genes leading to these abilities was more likely to survive than a set of genes which did not; but once these abilities had emerged, the development of mathematics is explicable, not only in terms of genes, but also in terms of the inherent logic of the concepts of numbers.[27]

Thus, from a genetically based concern for others can develop ethical cognitions about the importance of concern for others that go beyond their genetic origins. Altruistic behavior that provides few rewards can then occur. "I wanted to go to the movies tonight, but I visited my sick grandmother because I believed I had an obligation to" is a sentence that expresses thoughts that should be perfectly plain to most of us. Ethical behavior can result from values that we have reasoned toward, not simply emotions that assault us.

How strong is our inclination to show concern for others? An intelligent, or even intelligible, version of the argument just stated would not, I think, deny the force of self-interest. Even utopian settlements have had a hard time motivating members consistently to sacrifice themselves for the group. "Rather than proving that people will automatically choose the benefits of an affective, communal form of life if only they have the opportunity to experience them, the record of most nineteenth-century communes seems to indicate otherwise," notes William Kelso.[28] Furthermore, social psychological experiments on altruism show that the higher the cost of helping, the less likely people will be to help. Despite the possibility of altruism, self-interest plays an overwhelming role in human affairs.

If the inclination to both self-interest and to concern for others coexist, how do people deal with these conflicting desires? One strategy when both inclinations are relevant is to make the choice that optimizes attainment of the individual's total utility. Thus, if we could help an old lady by walking her across the street at little cost to ourselves, we will. If we would need to go to the ends of the earth to bring a person a candy bar, we would not.

But another strategy also exists, involving sequential attention to goals. Rather than weighing conflicting goals in each decision, the individual might instead use different kinds of decisions to give expression to the different goals.[29] Instead of trying to mix self-interest and altruism into every decision, the individual might try to reserve certain decisions to self-interest and others to altruism. To the extent this is not completely possible, the individual could at least give the different inclinations pride of place in different kinds of situations. Just as there is a time to be born and a time to die, a time to cast away stones and a time to gather them together, so too there is, in this view, a time to care about oneself and also a time to care about others.

There are good reasons for people to follow such a strategy. Psychologically, it is a way to avoid the costs of having to choose in each decision between desired, but conflicting, goals. Such a strategy might be regarded as fitting and not simply comfortable. One way of demonstrating that something is important is to insist on not mixing it together with the run of ordinary things with which it might otherwise be identified. This is, Durkheim noted long ago, the essence of sacredness.[30] People may thus wish to reserve a pride of place for concern for others in some sphere of decisions as a way of demonstrating that ethics is important. They might also do so if they were afraid that, despite a considered view of the importance of concern for others, temptation would lead to sacrificing such concern in individual cases for the lure of self-interest. Reserving a sphere for altruism can, to use the phrase of economist Thomas Schelling, be part of a strategy for "self-command." Like a decision by a person on a diet to keep ice cream out of the house, erecting a barrier against temptation allows people to act according to their more considered views.[31]

People might, then, choose different forums for the display of self-interest and for the display of concern for others. They would seek forums to display an altruism that does not get expressed often enough in their everyday lives in the marketplace. Such choices, I think, would not be random. Some forums are more fitting than others for the activities we undertake. We dance at parties, not in the classroom; we contemplate art in museums, not in garbage dumps; we make love in our homes, not on the street. So, too, can there be fitting forums for self-interested behavior and for ethical behavior that shows concern for others.

This brings us back to public spirit and the policy-making process. In arguing for the export of the self-interest assumption from the marketplace to public behavior, James Buchanan notes that otherwise

man must be assumed to shift his psychological and moral gears when he moves from the realm of organized market activity to that of organized political activity. . . . [One must demonstrate there] to be something in the nature of market organization, as such, that brings out the selfish motives in man, and something in the political organization, as such, which in turn, suppresses these motives and brings out the more "noble" ones.[32]

That is exactly what the alternate view of the wellsprings of political behavior maintains. It is that there are features of public life that make it an appropriate forum for public spirit —in other words, for concern for others in the realm of our behavior around the processes of government. These features have already been discussed.[33] In making collective decisions we are making decisions not just for ourselves but also for others. In making decisions democratically, we require the co-operation and consent of others to get them made. It should, furthermore, be noted that if people seek fitting forums to display concern for others that they do not get the same chance to display in the marketplace, then one of the *roles* of government—and one standard against which we would judge the policy-making process—is the extent to which government is able to serve as a fitting forum for displaying concern for others.

Once we see that the same human beings may seek to give pride of place to self-interest in economic contexts and public spirit in political ones, much seemingly inconsistent behavior becomes easier to comprehend. Some find it surprising that, since we buy and sell television sets, clothing, or cars without a second thought, we should find the idea of buying and selling votes repugnant. (In a renowned and highly ironic passage, economist James Tobin has noted laconically that "any good second-year graduate student in economics could write a short examination paper proving that voluntary transactions in votes would increase the welfare of the sellers as well as the buyers."[34] The repugnance relates to views of what is fitting in different contexts. Similarly, in a fascinating early example of empirical social science research, the sociologist Robert Merton investigated a marathon war bond appeal in 1943 by the popular radio personality Kate Smith. Examining the content of Smith's appeals, Merton noticed that she stated nothing about war bonds as a sound investment. Merton also found that a majority of respondents in the survey he conducted opposed offering prizes to people who bought war bonds.[35] In a sense, the approach by Smith, and the reactions of citizens, might seem odd. Surely advertisers trying to persuade people to purchase ordinary products find it advantageous to appeal to ways the products help the purchasers personally. And few people object in a market context to receiving greater rewards for behaving desirably. People's views of war bonds and of behavior in the marketplace are "inconsistent" only if we fail to recognize that people give priority to different motivations in different spheres.

It might be noted that the more people seek to behave differently in different realms, the less possible it is for the policy-making process to serve as a school for teaching ethical behavior in everyday life, because people might not apply the lessons from one realm to another. Fortunately, pride of place is one thing and watertight separation another. The separation of private and public, self-interested and public spirited, is not complete; just as self-interest seeps into public behavior, so too can concern for others appear in private behavior. Furthermore, there are many spheres of everyday life that have no clear self-interested or altruistic orientations, where lessons learned in one sphere may be applied to others. There is room for learning in one realm to be applied in other realms. In this alternate view, self-interest by no means disappears from public life. It is far too powerful a motivating force in human behavior for that. But public spirit has a pride of place that translates into an important role in the policy-making process. When self-interested participants express their arguments in terms not of their own personal interests but rather as good public policy, this is more than the compliment that vice pays to virtue. The requirement to express arguments in such terms limits the extent of what self-interested advocates can demand. It also constitutes acceptance of a criterion against which their arguments are to be judged that makes it easier to reject them.

In this alternate view, to return to examples cited at the beginning of this chapter, rollbacks in federal regulation, which advocates of the dominance of self-interest in the policy-making process see mostly as a result of heightened business lobbying, are seen instead as predominantly a result of a victory for the idea that such regulation had become excessive, not just from the point of view of business concerned, but excessive—period. In this alternate view, for protectionism to be strong, those who advocate it from a self-interested point of view need to convince others that their cause is just in order to succeed. And the limits of their ability to persuade others on grounds of justice set limits for what they ask for in the first place. And in this alternate view, problems with the performance of government organizations occur despite the role of public spirit in motivating people who work in the public sector. Solutions to the problems of inadequate performance should tap the resource that such public spirit constitutes, something that argues against privatization.

I have already stated where I stand in this debate on the wellsprings of public behavior. In the next two chapters I specifically argue my case.

11

Evaluating the
Political Process

This chapter argues for the unconventional proposition that
the political process in the United States works reasonably
well and hence merits the participation of people seeking a
good society. The key issue I examine is the prevalence of
public spirit. Public spirit, of course, is a state of mind, and
states of mind are notoriously difficult to pin down. I "test"
for the presence of public spirit in three ways. First, the best
operational test of the importance of public spirit in the political process, I think, is the ability of ideas to overcome interests in determining the content of political choices. If self-
interested behavior, whether of popular majorities or of
interest groups, would have dictated one kind of outcome,
and general ideas about good public policy another, then the
extent to which political choices reflect the ideas rather than
the interests constitutes a strong test of the importance of
public spirit. Second, I look at individual political behavior, to
see the extent to which the stands that citizens take in the

political process are explained by their self-interest or by general ideas they have about right and wrong. Finally, I spend some effort examining directly the question of public spirit in the motivations of professional participants in the political process such as politicians and government officials.

Twenty years ago the conclusion that the political process worked reasonably well was under attack in the scholarly community most insistently from the embittered Left. Critics of pluralism painted a dark portrait of a power elite and of domination over the system by the wealthy. Today, it is under attack most insistently from the crusading Right. Theorists of "public choice" find politics wanting compared with the market. This chapter constitutes a defense from the impassioned center.

My argument is not only unfashionable in conclusion but also, as my discussion of Madisonianism and pluralism should have made clear, untypical in form. In general, those who have evaluated the American political process against a standard of the presence of public spirit have found it wanting, while those who have been sanguine about the process have not evaluated it against a public spirit standard. By contrast, I evaluate it against a standard of the presence of public spirit, and I am still rather sanguine about it.

At the same time, my conclusion that the political process works reasonably well is a close call. I argue that a good part of the edifice is held up by norms that prescribe public spirit in politics. Those norms work against powerful forces of self-interest in human nature, and they can be very fragile. The danger exists that a cynical description of a political world based on self-interest can itself serve to undermine these norms and thus become a self-fulfilling prophecy.

In this chapter I examine the relationship between public spirit and the substantive results of the political process, and I also pay attention to the role of public spirit in evaluating the process against the standards of promoting our dignity and helping mold our character.

The Evidence: Does Self-Interest Dominate Political Choices?

Does self-interest in fact turn out to dominate the results of the political process? It is no trick to come up with countless specific examples of situations where political choices have been crucially determined by participants furthering quite narrow selfish interests. Everyone has a favorite story of the highway that got built because a powerful member of Congress wanted it in his district or of a tax loophole an interest group sneaked through with few in Congress knowing anything about it. Certainly there is no lack of straightforwardly self-interested behavior in the political process.

As a general rule, however, the more important a policy is, the less important is the role of self-interest in determining that policy. Self-interest does a great job explaining the location of a new federal building in Missoula. When all is said and done, it falls down with regard to the major policy upheavals of the past decades.

Self-interest cannot account, except through the grossest of contortions, for the vast increases in spending for the poor that occurred in the 1960s and early 1970s. The poor were not an electoral majority, nor were they well organized into interest groups. (Public choice theorists sometimes point to the power of interest groups representing providers of services to the poor. The hypothesis that an invincible lobby of social workers overwhelmed a defenseless political system is, to put it diplomatically, idiosyncratic.) What about the growth of health, safety, and environmental regulations during the late 1960s and early 1970s? These programs were adopted against the wishes of well-organized producers. They were intended for the benefit of poorly organized consumers and environmentalists. (Much of the organization of environmentalists into interest groups *followed* environmental legislation, rather than preceding it.)

In addition, biases in the political process that public choice advocates believe produce a government that is too big can hardly explain the *growth* of government in the 1960s and 1970s unless one can successfully argue that the size of any bias increased during the period when the growth took place. Otherwise, the bias should have already produced larger government in the earlier period.[1] Furthermore, as noted earlier in the chapter on Congress, the big increases in government spending since the 1950s have not been in grants to localities, which provide particularistic constituency benefits, but in various general transfer programs that do not allow members to demonstrate they have gotten something special for the district.[2]

The self-interest model of politics does equally poorly in accounting for rollbacks in government programs during the late 1970s and 1980s. In the late 1970s, the greatest victories for industry deregulation were won in exactly those industries, such as trucking and airlines, where well-organized producers benefited from regulation and the consumers who would benefit from deregulation were largely unorganized. By contrast, little occurred in areas such as environmental policy where well-organized producers supported deregulation.[3] In other words, the pattern of deregulation was exactly the *opposite* of that predicted by the self-interest model.

It is, furthermore, hard to see any one-to-one correspondence between the economic difficulties the country faced during the 1970s and the program of reduced government intervention adopted to deal with these problems. Economic difficulties in the 1930s had produced a growth in the role of government in managing the economy, not a rollback. Economic distress itself neither made government grow nor shrink. What made it grow or shrink was the force of ideas linking the problems everyone perceived with solutions that government could adopt. Furthermore, well-entrenched interest groups fought to retain each government program President Reagan sought to cut. Often, only the diffuse interest of citizens in general stood on the other side. And the adoption of Reagan's tax reform proposals in 1986 represents a dramatic victory of ideas over interests on the latter's home turf.

The story of government growth in the 1960s and of its limitation in the 1980s, then, are both stories of the power of ideas. They reinforce quite powerfully the message presented in chapter 2 that persuasiveness is the most underrated political resource.

The self-interest theories not only have a difficult time explaining most of what has been important in American politics over the past twenty years. They also give, at best, an incomplete feel for the process itself. To be sure, the political process is hardly a model of deliberation and learning, where all participants are open to reasoned persuasion based on an agreed standard of seeking good public policy. If nothing else, this image has a disembodied, bloodless quality far removed from the sweaty contact sport of political contention. But the view of how the process works that grows out of the self-interest model is a parody.

For starters, the model runs up against an embarrassing bit of evidence from the real world, namely, that lots of people vote.[4] The so-called paradox of voting has been noted by public choice theorists going back to Anthony Downs. The "paradox" is that public choice theorists do not expect individuals motivated only by self-interest to go to the polls, because their chance of having any impact on an election outcome is so minute that the expected value to them of their vote is less than the cost to them of deciding for whom to vote and of going to the polls.[5]

That public choice advocates regard the fact that people vote to be paradoxical reminds one of Walter Heller's definition of an economist as somebody who, when he sees that something works in practice, wonders whether it will also work in theory. William Riker and Peter Ordeshook, two public choice scholars, suggest that voting is rational because citizens receive rewards from "compliance with the ethic of voting" or "affirming allegiance to the political system."[6] These "rewards," however, are for behaving in ways inconsistent with the model of self-interest. Political philosopher Brian Barry has calculated that scores on a "citizen duty" scale far better predict the likelihood of voting than do people's expectations about how close the election would be.[7] The solution to the "paradox" of voting is public spirit.

The naive observer expecting in politics public-spirited deliberation unsullied by parochial perspectives and even by some dirty trickery would hardly be prepared for Washington. But neither would the hardboiled, street-wise cynic or his public-choice counterpart in academia. The theory of self-interest gives no sense of the importance for political success of the skill at making a good argument, of having the facts on one's side, of being able to present an appealing public vision, or of having a reputation for seriousness and commitment. Yet all this clearly appears in descriptions of the process by close observers.[8]

The view that self-interest is key to understanding how the political process works is also belied by the influence of the media. On superficial examination, the influence of the media might be seen as consistent with the view that people in government are out only for adulation or reelection, because the way officials are treated in the media certainly has an impact on their attaining either goal. It is necessary to remember, however, that what generates good (or bad) attention in the media is generally whether people have sought to do the right thing or whether instead they acted selfishly. If neither people in government themselves, nor the voters who select elected officials, thought that it was important to try to do the right thing in politics, media brickbats would be a matter of indifference to their intended victims. Sticks and stones could break their bones, but names would never hurt them. The great influence of the media suggests that failure to show public spirit *can* indeed hurt these people, in their own eyes and in the eyes of others. Alternately, media influence can be treated as a constant and the way the media cover politics as a variable. Seen this way, the choice of topics for muckraking and exposé reflects the role that public spirit plays in the system. In a political system where self-interest were the acceptable norm, what is presented as scandal would not be so.

The unrealistic feel for the process that we get from the self-interest model applies even to Congress, the political institution generally regarded as resembling most closely the political process as described by the theorists of self-interest. David Mayhew, in *Congress: The Electoral Connection,* writes that "the congressmen's lack of interest in impact has as a corollary a lack of interest in research. To assign committee staffs or the Congressional Research Service to do research on the nonparticularistic effects of legislation . . . would be to misallocate resources. Hence, generally speaking, congressmen do not so assign them."[9] Given the gargantuan production of policy research of just the sort Professor Mayhew believes "generally speaking" does not occur by the General Accounting Office, Congressional Budget Office, Office of Technology Assessment, Congressional Research Service, and the staffs of every major committee, not to speak of the reams of studies advocates prepare for members of Congress, it is tempting to ask just what the evidence is for Mayhew's contention. (The answer appears in Mayhew's footnote on his argument—the evidence is a single quote from Senator Mike Monroney of Oklahoma about misuse of the Congressional Research Service.)[10] Mayhew's conclusion about lack of interest in research follows logically from the earlier conclusion about a congressman's lack of interest in accomplishing anything for which individual credit could not be claimed. That conclusion in turn followed logically from Mayhew's starting assumption of a single-minded interest in reelection. It is the starting points of public choice theorists that must be questioned. Regarding Fiorina's view that congressmen pass legislation to create bureaucratic problems they can then solve for their constituents, about the most charitable thing that can be said is that he provides no evidence that anyone has ever thought this way.[11]

The Political Behavior of Citizens

What best explains the voting behavior of individual citizens? The classic view in the early empirical voting studies, such as *The American Voter,* was that voting behavior is guided mostly by self-interest. This view was developed in works appearing during the 1970s on the link between economic conditions and election results. With modern techniques of social science, these studies confirmed something politicians knew intuitively, namely, that incumbents do well in times of economic prosperity and badly during economic distress.[12]

In what has probably been the most interesting body of empirical political science research of the last decade, extensive evidence has now been developed questioning this view.[13] The connection between economic conditions and overall electoral results is indeed very clear. What researchers have now done is to move from the aggregate level of overall economic conditions and overall electoral results to the level of individual economic conditions and individual voting decisions. When they do so, the results are surprising. If voters vote their personal pocketbooks, we would expect those who have themselves become better off because of improved economic circumstances to favor the incumbents. Those not personally sharing in the prosperity would not be expected to display such a tendency. Likewise, in times of economic distress we would expect the individual victims of bad times to punish the incumbents. However, series of tests by Donald Kinder and Roderick Kiewiet using individual-level survey data have devastatingly shattered this hypothesis. Respondents' answers to a question about whether their personal financial situation has improved, worsened, or stayed the same over the previous year show essentially *no* connection to changes in voting behavior. By contrast, though, there are substantial correlations between a voter's views of economic conditions in society *as a whole* and the individual's voting behavior. This relationship holds even when the possible effects of personal economic situation on judgments of overall economic conditions are controlled for. The observed connection at the aggregate level between the economy and the electoral success of incumbents results not from self-interested rewards or punishments from voters who have personally done well or badly. The connection comes instead from judgments by voters about whether the economy *as a whole* is doing well, independent of how the voter is doing *personally*. [14]

A conceptually similar body of research has been conducted by social psychologist David Sears and his colleagues, who have investigated how well personal self-interest in a political issue accounts for attitudes on the issues. Thus, for example, these scholars have examined the extent to which attitudes on busing among whites can be explained by whether one's own family has been affected by a busing plan, or the extent to which attitudes toward the war in Vietnam were influenced by whether one had family or close friends fighting there.[15] The findings are dramatic. Regarding attitudes on Vietnam, having a relative or close friend actually fighting in Vietnam had far less effect on views of what American policy should be than the respondent's self-anchoring on a liberal-conservative scale or his or her attitudes toward communism. In multiple regression equations where various possible sources of political attitudes appeared as independent variables, liberal or conservative ideology better predicted a respondent's views on government national health insurance or guaranteed jobs programs than whether the respondent himself was covered by health insurance or had recently been unemployed. In other words, conservatives who themselves had no health insurance protection were less likely to favor national health insurance than liberals who had coverage of their own. As part of a study on business and American foreign policy, Bruce Russett and Elizabeth Hanson did a survey of the attitudes of corporate executives on foreign policy issues. They found that respondents' views on domestic liberal-conservative issues such as civil rights were better predictors of their foreign policy views than whether their company had defense contracts or investments overseas.

In fact, the connection between the self-interest economic variables and foreign policy views was quite small.[16]

These data taken as a whole suggest quite strongly that general ideas about what kinds of policies are right play an important role in influencing the attitudes of individual citizens on many political issues. These ideas can also form a context in which citizens interpret and evaluate their personal experience —having, for example, a relative fighting in Vietnam did not itself determine attitudes on American policy there except for a context of general ideas that served to make that personal involvement a source of pride or dissatisfaction.[17]

One possible response to these data would be to suggest that politics is not crucially important for most people and that, therefore, it is easy to display public spirit in our political attitudes because it does not cost much. On issues that *really* are important to people, including political issues, we might, according to this view, expect self-interest to hold sway. The political philosopher Russell Hardin presents an intriguing, somewhat different version of this argument. Hardin argues that we can expect a high proportion of altruistic behavior in public contexts because of the kind of free-rider problem that Mancur Olson discusses for collective action in general. Since political action is hardly ever in an individual's self-interest (because costs outweigh expected benefits), those political actions that do end up getting performed are disproportionately altruistic. However, there is a larger number of nonevents—of political actions that are never performed—that would have been self-interested.[18]

This argument is not incorrect, but I think it is somewhat off the point. The evidence is overwhelming that most people are not keenly interested in politics. Significant numbers of citizens have weakly held opinions, or no opinions at all, on many political issues. The point is not that people are saints, willing to sacrifice all for the sake of others. Having political opinions based on general views about what public policies would be right may indeed often be a low-cost form of altruism, although the cost in taxes may not be insignificant, at least in the case of those whose views lead them to support government programs that cost money. Nor are most people philosophers or professional policy analysts. Views can be based on general conceptions of right and wrong without being particularly sophisticated. Nonetheless, in a world of many political issues and of an overall modest level of interest in politics, we can expect to find a strong reservoir of political input based on general ideas of what policy would be right. Such input is likely to be an important factor in the process.

Similarly, it should not be surprising that the ideas about what constitutes good public policy individuals find persuasive will be influenced by their upbringing, their social class, and their religious, ethnic, or regional identity. These kinds of influences can produce a "where you stand depends on where you sit" situation similar to that described earlier for government officials supporting the values behind their agencies' programs.[19] Just because an individual's stands are influenced by their circumstances does not mean public spirit is absent. Such people may sincerely believe that the face of the issue they see is the one that embodies good public policy. But "where you stand depends on where you sit" also partakes of self-interest, both because our perspective is strongly biased by our personal experience and because, in general, the policy we advocate will end up helping the group, class, or organization to which we belong.

I also agree that in situations where people have substantial personal interests at stake, interests that can be perceived fairly clearly without the interpretation that general ideas of right and wrong provide, and where some clear government policy will affect those interests, the role of self-interest in the political behavior of individuals is likely to increase. One example is tax policy. Others are decisions regarding particularized government-provided benefits, such as those involving public works construction. Thus, Russett and Hanson, in their study of the foreign policy views of business executives, discovered that defense contractors were far more likely to favor high levels of defense spending than executives in general, although, as reported above, being a defense contractor had rather little influence on overall foreign policy views.[20] Behavior is also more likely to be self-interested when a policy alternative under consideration will make us demonstrably worse off compared with our current situation.

People in either of the situations promoting self-interest are more likely to organize into interest groups because of their strong concern with a certain issue. Interest groups such as the Synthetic Organic Chemicals Manufacturing Association, the National Association of Dredging Contractors, the Society of American Travel Writers, or the National Association of Scissors and Shears Manufacturers, which are everywhere in Washington, are hardly brought into existence by public spirit. Their behavior, however, can be held in check by public-spirited norms in the system, which, as noted earlier, can affect the way interest groups present their demands, and the nature of the demands they make on the political system. (These norms might even affect the way interest group members and representatives genuinely feel, although that is more difficult to gainsay.) Certainly, the political behavior of many interest groups constitutes the most important exception to the conclusion that public spirit is important in accounting for the stands that citizens take in the political process.

Public Spirit and the Motivations of Politicians and Government Officials

Professional participants in the political process receive rewards, and bear costs, far more significant than those of individual citizens, most of whose participation in politics is quite casual. For example, on the rewards side politicians get their names in the newspapers and on television. They may frequently be the objects of deference and adulation. And those professional participants in the political process who possess some formal authority can experience the feeling of power that derives from the ability to establish public policies with the force of law. At the same time, politicians also work very long hours, much of it on the road away from their families, for salaries that are relatively low for work with the responsibilities and time demands their jobs have. Given the diversity of rewards and punishments, the motivations of professional participants in government are doubtless more complex than a simple dichotomy between public spirit and advancement of personal economic or power interests. Furthermore, motivations vary. Harold Lasswell probably got the study of the motivations of politicians off to a poor start when he argued that political man above all seeks power. The approach of James David Barber in *The Lawmakers,* or of Richard Fenno in *Congressmen in Committees,* based on typologies of different kinds of politicians with different predominant motivations, is more promising.[21]

For many professional participants in government, probably more in the past than now, politics is a fairly conventional job. Many enter politics for the mix of reasons people go into any jobs. A number of studies of professional politicians have found, for example, that politicians tend to come from families of politically active people—not unlike the situation where the children of plumbers tend to become plumbers.[22]

What are the distinctive advantages that might draw people to government? It is hard to see the lust for power, in a general sense, as a *distinctive* advantage of a career in government. Business leaders, within their own firms, doubtless have occasion to exercise greater power, with fewer checks against its exercise, than do participants in the American political process. "The search for the jugular of power," notes Robert Lane, "may very likely lead to the world of finance, journalism, or industry instead of politics."[23] This doesn't mean that nobody who is power hungry will go into politics, only that there is no reason to expect a disproportionate number of such people to do so.

There remain two motivations that are, I think, relatively distinctive to government. One (more for elected officials than for civil servants) is the desire for attention and adulation. Anyone who has dealt with politicians knows how important media attention, for example, can be to them. People can gain similar attention by careers in the entertainment industry, but aptitudes for the two worlds may be of limited transferability (the career of President Reagan to the contrary notwithstanding). A second motivation is the desire to participate in formulation of good public policy. This is something that, for reasons obvious enough to border on tautology, only participation in the public sector can provide. People who go into politics for this reason may be seen as "seeking power," but of a special sort —influence over government choices.

The desire for adulation and attention does not work against public spirit but in the same direction. People who are driven by personal self-interest are not likely to get far in the estimation of others, who have no particular reason to value the self-interest of another person. But the person who seeks the admiration of others to an unusual degree is both dependent on them and aware of their importance. Although such admiration can be achieved by advocating the demands of a narrow group, not by seeking what is right for society as a whole, this tendency is countered by the interest of the national media in exposing such behavior.

The sparse literature on the topic of why people enter careers in government is not very enlightening, both because authors need to rely on the self-reports of respondents and because many authors tend to psychoanalyze their subjects. However, the literature at least suggests that public spirit is an important reason many people go into politics. The largest group in James David Barber's sample of Connecticut legislators fits into the category he calls "lawmakers," who derive satisfaction from producing good legislation. The self-reports of top federal appointed officials about why they went into government heavily emphasize the unique vantage point government service gives for making the world a better place.[24] In a 1984 survey of senior civil service managers in the federal government, respondents were given a list and asked, "To what extent are the following reasons to continue working for the government?" Only 18 percent said that their salary was a strong reason for staying (or more of a reason to stay than to leave), and only 10 percent claimed that their promotional opportunities were a strong reason to stay. Seventy-six percent, however, responded that "opportunity to have an impact on public affairs" was a reason to stay.[25] A study comparing the importance of pay as a motivator for different kinds of managers concludes that "managers in industrial organizations place the most importance on pay; people who work in government agencies place less emphasis on pay; and people who work in hospitals and social service organizations place the least emphasis on pay."[26] Dean Mann and Jameson Doig report that recruiters trying to persuade people to take jobs as assistant secretaries, many of whom would be serving at considerable financial sacrifice, make heavy use of arguments about serving one's country. Likewise, they report that the ability to influence policy in the direction of one's policy views was a strong reason for candidates offered these positions to accept them.[27]

Vocational guidance tests provide an unconventional source of insight here. These tests help young people determine what careers might be appropriate for them, through a battery of questions to reveal interests and inclinations. The most highly regarded of such tests does not include "politician" as a possible occupation, but it does include "public administrator." It is interesting to note that the cluster of occupations in which public administration is included, based on similar responses to the battery of questions, also includes the occupations of rehabilitation counselor, YMCA general secretary, social worker, and minister.[28]

Public Spirit as a Norm for Political Behavior

Why do we observe so much public spirit given the thundering force of self-interest? The answer must be that government is seen as an appropriate forum for the display of the concern for others that many people wish to show.

Such a situation has its roots in the basic features of the process of government. However, public spirit is not sustained simply by an agglomeration of individual decisions to regard public spirit as the appropriate motivation for political action. Development of a social *norm* of concern for others is crucial. Norms are devices that help us enormously in organizing and assigning meaning to our lives. It would be an incredible and unsustainable burden on the human mind to decide each time we confront a situation how to interpret and respond to it. Norms simplify our lives by framing situations in certain ways. And such framing often strongly influences our responses. As Erving Goffman writes, "What is play for the golfer is work for the caddy."[29] In a series of justifiably renowned experiments, social psychologists Amos Tversky and Daniel Kahneman have demonstrated that people make different decisions in dealing with problems that are in fact identical but that are framed in different ways.[30]

The effects of norms on promoting altruism are illustrated in experimental research. In one experiment, subjects told in advance to empathize with somebody asking for help ended up helping more.[31] In another, bystanders were considerably more likely to intervene to help someone in distress if they knew that others were aware of their actions.[32]

Since behavior is often contagious, norms can have a cascading effect. The norms influence the behavior of some directly, and then the behavior of still others is influenced as people imitate behavior they have seen. There is extensive experimental evidence that the more people observe altruistic behavior around them, the more likely they are to behave altruistically themselves. In one experiment amusingly titled "A Shill for Charity," the presence of other people enthusiastically giving donations at a Volunteers of America table considerably increased donations from the public.[33] In other experiments, students were more likely to volunteer for an experiment if they saw other students volunteer; and motorists were more likely to stop to help somebody fix a flat tire if they had just driven past an experimenter's confederate who was fixing a flat tire.[34]

The norm of public spirit can influence the behavior of the uncommitted or the unreflective, and change the behavior of the self-interested from what it otherwise would have been. It can also, because there are few saints on earth, sustain the behavior of those inclined to be public-spirited. The behavior of all of us arises from a complex set of motivations not completely understood even by ourselves. The norm of public spirit does not assure public-spirited behavior, but it loads the dice.

In their very influential experimental research on individual behavior in group decision-making situations, Morris Fiorina and Charles Plott fail to show an appreciation for the role of public-spirited norms in politics. In their experiment, subjects had to make a group decision about where to locate a point on a continuum. Each subject was assigned a preferred location, and Fiorina and Plott found in analyzing the results of the process that subjects' behavior was self-interested and not altruistic.[35] The authors, however, steadfastly refused to suggest to the subjects any norms about how they should behave, despite the subjects' evident desires.

Subjects regularly asked, "What are we supposed to do?" ("Get what's best for ourselves?" "Do what's fair?", etc.) We shrugged off such questions with a poker-faced, "whatever you want."[36]

It is exactly such normlessness that does *not* characterize politics. Norms encouraging public spirit in politics are sustained by the kinds of institutional features discussed in earlier chapters

—ranging from the robes that Supreme Court justices wear to the requirement that government agencies present statements of reasons for their actions. They are also sustained by educational institutions and by the verbal or written signals of what is expected that people hear in their everyday lives.

The Effects of the Political Process on our Dignity and our Character

As noted earlier, there is a connection not only between the presence of public spirit and the ability of the political process to produce good public policy. There is also a connection between public spirit and the ability of the political process to provide recognition and mold character. A positive evaluation of the level of public spirit in the political process thus also suggests a positive evaluation of the ability of the political process in these regards. I have a few observations about how well the policymaking process serves to signal recognition. If public spirit is high, then public recognition of individual dignity can be an important function that the process of government fulfills for people. And people do appear to value the statements of recognition that government gives, beyond the instrumental value such statements may have in terms of the substantive results of the political process.

Giving every citizen the right to vote allows everyone to influence the substantive policies that come out of government. But beyond that, it also makes the statement that everyone has a basic dignity that is respected equally. Appointing blacks or women to high government positions aids nobody directly but the appointees. But such appointments display a recognition by government of the worth of the groups involved. This is sometimes disparagingly referred to as "symbolic politics." How does it help a woman caught in a typing pool to have Sandra

Day O'Connor as a Supreme Court justice? In a widely cited book, Murray Edelman presents the argument that, in effect, the wealthy get the material benefits out of politics, while the poor must make do with symbols.[37] I have no quarrel with the expression "symbolic politics." But I do quarrel with the disparagement. People do not live by bread alone. The statement that our democratic institutions make about the dignity we all share appears to be powerful enough to serve as the basis for the view of government that sees our democracy as an important source of pride. The Irish exulted in their rise to political prominence in the cities of nineteenth-century America, as much for the recognition such rise implied as for any concrete benefits in terms of jobs or favors. And blacks and women regard black and women Supreme Court justices as important for the same reason. The wealthy seek statements of social recognition, just as others do. The recognition of dignity is one of government's most noble roles, and it is often through symbols that such recognition is shown.

Conclusions and Sources of Concern

Nothing in this chapter should be taken to imply that there is no self-interested behavior in government. There is, obviously, lots of it—a testimony to the power of self-interest. My examination suggests, however, that concern for others has a pride of place in public behavior it does not have in the marketplace.

Nor need self-interest disappear from the political process for the system generally to produce good public policy. For one thing, I do not disagree with the argument, as far as it goes, that self-interested participants provide a good source of information about the impacts of alternative policy proposals. For another, as long as the level of public spirit among those with the formal authority to make political choices remains reasonably high, self-interested participants will need to have their arguments judged by others whose perspective is broader. And, of course, checks and balances and pluralism remain as a back-up protection.

Perhaps the largest area for concern is the large role that interest groups play in influencing the results of the political process. Pluralists correctly note that the simple statement that interest groups have disproportionate influence does not by itself mean the process works badly, because those with intense interests *should* have disproportionate impact. At the same time, my criticism of pluralism in chapter 9 suggests that we cannot count on an institutional weighing of self-interested forces to tend by itself to produce good public policy. The problem is that interest groups are the strongest self-interested force in the process, even if their behavior is held in check by public-spirited norms in the system.

There are, secondly, reasons for concern, or at least ambivalence, about the ways participants in the process may use power —including the power that comes from strategic skill—to influence the results of the process. Advocates typically fight hard for what they believe in, and frequently they are tempted to believe that the ends justify the means. The use of strategic skills may make it more difficult for other views to be articulated and considered—by getting participants to see only one face of the issue or by making the rules most favorable to the advocates' views. There is unfortunately no reason to expect that this will be less the case for advocates motivated by public spirit than those motivated by self-interest.

At the same time, I think we should want people to be passionate about their beliefs. People should not be indifferent about whether what they believe to be right comes to pass or not. So I do not think we would want to remedy the evils of advocacy by eliminating the passion that gives rise to them. While some uses of power can and should be prohibited through decisions about institutional design, too much interference may constitute a cure worse than the disease. Presumably, advocates emphasize a certain face of an issue because they believe that face is the most important. And it is often difficult to discern a correct answer to the question of which decision-making procedure is most appropriate independent of what substantive result the choice favors. (How does one determine, for example, whether a bill on handicapped access to public transportation "should" go to a transportation or welfare committee?)

There are, I think, two cures for the problems that strategic skill and other forms of power create, beyond the standard ones offered by Madisonianism and pluralism. One is a solution in the spirit (though not the letter) of Madisonianism, in that it doesn't transform motives but reduces their ability to be effective. Liars generally are ineffective in ongoing political processes because nobody trusts them. They can get away with lies once but not repeatedly. Similarly, power breeds resentment, and eventually victims gang up against musclemen—and even against manipulators. The rise of interest groups over the past decades has, for example, produced a popular counterreaction against interest groups such that to label a political candidate a "tool of special interests" is a potent electoral argument against him. These kinds of counterreactions are based on human psychology rather than institutional design. I feel more comfortable with Madisonian remedies to the evils of an "ends justify the means" mentality because I do not believe that public spirit itself inoculates against it.

Institutional design should also help reduce the misuse of power and not simply check it. Because political success in a democracy is easier the more we can genuinely put ourselves in others' shoes serves to broaden our perspectives about what policies might be right. It can also serve to take the rough edges off the means we are willing to use to achieve our ends. Fortunately, there are even rewards for genuine empathy. When the ability to empathize is feigned, it is seen as another example of manipulation and is resented accordingly. One may justly demand of advocates that they demonstrate genuine respect for other participants in the process and that they open themselves up to the possibility of persuasion. The less these characteristics are present in advocates, the more we have cause for alarm about the role of advocacy skills in the political process.

A final area for concern is the tendency in our political system to use what I in an earlier work called "adversarial" rather than "accommodationist" political institutions.[38] By adversarial institutions I mean those modeled on an adversarial judicial proceeding. Those with different views participate in the process by presenting their best possible case. An independent judge or judges, impartial and separate from the parties, is then given formal authority to make the decision, without involvement of the parties. By accommodationist institutions I mean those where the various parties sit down together with government representatives to work out a solution as acceptable to all of them as possible. While the rules for making decisions may give no formal authority to nongovernment participants in the process, informally the intention is to get as many as possible of those involved to agree.

Our general tendency in the United States is to adopt forms modeled on the adversary trial when institutional choices are consciously made. Thus we have developed adversary trial forms in the administrative process and in congressional committee hearings, and there has been a push toward creation of similar institutions for political choice within the White House. In all these cases, the United States has developed institutions that far more closely resemble adversary trials than those developed outside this country. In Europe, the tendency has been to get political parties and interest groups together to work out political choices, in ongoing institutional settings that encourage agreement.

Accommodationist institutions, more than adversarial ones, encourage public spirit among advocates. When people have ongoing small-group ties, they tend to develop an increased liking of and respect for one another. The process humanizes adversaries and hence contributes to the concern for others that underlies public spirit. It also encourages the ability to put ourselves into others' shoes.

Both adversarial and accommodationist institutions allow the jostling of different views about the values at stake and the consequences of alternate policies. But adversarial institutions put too much of the burden on a separate, limited group of "judges" to draw the best conclusion about what would be right. Participants are encouraged to stick to their guns and leave it to others to do the learning that results from exposure to diverse views.

By doing little to encourage agreement among those with different views, adversary institutions run a greater risk of leaving a residue of discontent and even anger in their wake. This is especially the case when participants believe that the "judges" making the decisions were not really neutral—as members of Congress, presidents, and bureaucrats in fact rarely are. Such a residue of discontent is significant, both for the perception of the political process and for the inclination to cooperate in the production process following political choice.

My own judgment is that the level of public spirit remains high enough in our political system so that it both encourages the choice of good public policy and produces positive effects on us as people. This is a matter of feel and judgment, I concede. I certainly believe that the call is close enough so that we need to be vigilant about the level of civic virtue in our society. The norms that sustain public spirit need to be defended from assault.

12

Evaluating the Operating Performance of Government Organizations

Government performs better than its reputation, but not well enough. That is the double message of this chapter. Government organizations take millions of young children every year and teach them to read. ("If you can read this," to quote a bumper sticker, "thank a teacher.") A government organization gets millions of old people a pension check every month. Government organizations enforce environmental laws, and the air gets cleaner. The wilder tales of government waste and incompetence generally turn out to be grossly exaggerated upon closer examination. Furthermore, just as new government programs can fail, so too can new products from private firms fail because of the inability to create organizational capacity to make them succeed. (The bugs can't be gotten out of a new computer in time, or the marketing people prove to be inept at trying to sell to a different type of customer than they are used to.) At the same time, systematic sources of underperformance built into the institutional design of government organizations make the production process in government more difficult than it otherwise would be.

Government performs better than its reputation. For example, few beliefs are more deeply embedded in popular consciousness than that government wastes money. In surveys asking the public how many cents of each tax dollar the federal government wastes, the median response is a whopping forty-eight cents.[1] And, as noted in the Introduction, the view that government is very wasteful has grown apace over the last twenty years together with other measures of declining confidence.[2] The belief in enormous amounts of waste is a comforting one, for it allows the public to support almost every existing government program while calling for tax and spending cuts, through the belief that the budget can be cut dramatically without slashing programs, simply by eliminating waste.

Though comforting, this perception turns out to be dramatically exaggerated. One survey, for example, showed that on average the public thought that over $52 of every $100 in social security expenditures went to administrative costs. The real figure is $1.30.[3] And federal employment as a percentage of the total labor force actually *declined* between 1960 and 1980, despite public impressions of an ever-more-bloated federal bureaucracy.[4]

Perhaps the supreme monument to the perception that the operating performance of government is horrendous was the 1984 report of the "President's Private Sector Survey on Cost Control," generally known as the Grace Commission, after its head, J. Peter Grace, chief executive officer of W. R. Grace and

Company. The Grace Commission recruited over 2,000 corporate executives to scrutinize the government. Backed up by forty-eight volumes of reports and 2,478 recommendations for cutting waste, the commission concluded that a total of $424 *billion* in savings was obtainable over a three-year period simply by controlling waste, "without weakening America's needed defense build-up and without in any way harming necessary social welfare programs." These were stupendous numbers, enough almost to eliminate federal deficits.

Yet a closer look at the Grace Commission reveals an effort mired in fraudulent classification and hopelessly sloppy research. Most of the dollar savings the Grace Commission purported to uncover arose in fact from changes in substantive federal policies, rather than from elimination of what is properly called waste, that is, use of excessive inputs to produce a given output. For example, big dollar savings came from proposals such as reducing the rate of increased spending on Medicare to that of the annual increase in the GNP and cutting retirement benefits for federal employees. Furthermore, an examination of the "horror stories" about waste, in which the commission specialized, shows that their accounts are beset with problems ranging from oversimplification of the issues involved to elementary errors of arithmetic.[5]

The Grace Commission claimed, for example, that "In comparison to a private sector company, managing comparable building space, the General Services Administration employs 17 times as many people and spends almost 14 times as much on total management costs." This contention is wildly inaccurate because of two whopping errors in the Grace Commission numbers on the property management division of the large life insurance firm being compared with the General Services Administration. The commission's chart stated that the insurance company in question was managing 10,000 buildings, "comparable building space" to the General Services Administration. In fact, no insurance company has a portfolio anywhere near that large. It turns out that the insurance company with which the

Grace Commission was making the comparison owns not 10,000 buildings but *1,000*. So, rather than managing a comparable number of buildings, the figure for the private company is more like one-tenth as many. Furthermore, the Grace Commission stated that the insurance company employs a total of 300 professionals, 100 in central administration, and 200 under contract. It turns out, however, that the company in question does not employ 200 *individuals* under contract, but rather hires 200 property management *firms* to manage its buildings. These firms, in turn, may have many professionals working for them.

Repeating stories that since have become almost part of American political folklore, the Grace Commission also alleged that the Defense Department was overpaying for inexpensive spare parts, such as hammers or screws. ("The Pentagon has been buying screws, available in any hardware store for 3 cents, for $91 each.") One has reason to doubt these stories, even before further investigation, on strictly logical grounds. To suggest that defense contractors could routinely charge the government $91 for something that costs a few pennies is to suggest that the defense contracting business is the easiest avenue to unearned fortune since the invention of plunder. If there were such enormous profits to be made, we could predict that every entrepreneur in the land would hire a retired general and set up shop as a defense contractor.

In fact, it turns out that the Defense Department did not negligently allow itself to be hoodwinked. Most of these cases had a common explanation, involving an accounting quirk in pricing material purchased from contractors, that produced astronomical numbers with no substantive significance.

Anytime anybody buys something, the price includes not only the direct cost of the materials, machines, and labor to produce it, but also a share of the company's joint costs such as running the quality control or maintenance department. The alarming stories arose in situations where the government was ordering many different spare parts at one time. Simply as a matter of accounting convenience, contractors sometimes allocated the joint costs to the individual parts on an item basis rather than a value basis. Say that an order was for 10,000 parts, some of which had a direct cost of $25,000 each and others of 4¢ each. Then, instead of allocating the $1 million total joint costs so that the $25,000 part gets a lot and the 4¢ part a little, the computer printout allocated $100 to each part. This produced a charge to the government of $25,100 for the expensive part and $100.04 for the cheap one.

Although this produced horror stories, nothing horrible had occurred. The total joint costs represented real resources. If $100 did not get allocated to the 3¢ screw, the screw would no longer appear so outrageously expensive. But the $100 would not disappear; it would just get allocated somewhere else.

Other stories had a different explanation. Many parts the Defense Department procures are "common use items." That is, they are the same as commercially produced parts that might be used in a car as well as a tank. Others need to be custom designed for use in military equipment. Custom designing often produces an extremely high price per unit, because, unlike Chevrolets, much military equipment is produced in small quantities and thus requires only a few of the same spare part. The initial cost to design the part and make the machine die or molding to produce it can then be spread out over only a few units. (If it costs $3,000 to design and tool up a plastic cap, that will add only 1¢ onto the cost of the cap if 300,000 are produced, but $1,000 if only three are produced.)

Special design is sometimes necessary despite these cost-enhancing implications. But the economics of tooling up do suggest that common-use parts be used whenever possible. And the Defense Department does make efforts to get common-use items. Spare parts are frequently procured on a sole-source basis from the contractors for the original weapon. When the contractor submits designs for spare parts, a designation of which are common-use must be included. This list is reviewed by the Defense Department contracting officer, who is to make suggestions for common-use procurement when appropriate.

After the contractor proposes prices, the contracting officer requests an independent evaluation of the offer by Defense Department value engineers, who may question whether a newly designed part is sufficiently different from common-use items to justify special tooling up.

Contractors have something of an incentive to propose custom-designed parts. A custom-designed part is indeed that—a contractor does not just go out and buy a wrench for 12¢ and resell it for $9,609. The contractor, however, is still allowed to take the normal percentage profit, which is far greater for a $1,000 item than a $1 item. Cheating is presumably discouraged by the negative impact repeated discovery would have on the contractor's relationship with the Defense Department. But the department has an enormous review task—there are about 300,000 parts in an airplane—and sometimes an item that should have been classified as common-use ends up getting designed to order.

Other commission horror stories turned out to be exaggerated rather than just plain wrong. Of the commission-highlighted stories that I examined, the one that came closest to the truth was the contention that "the Justice Department just sits on the cash seized from criminals, not bothering to deposit the money in interest bearing accounts while cases are being adjudicated."

Even here, however, the story the Grace Commission told was oversimplified. Traditionally, cash seized from criminal suspects indeed was not deposited in interest-bearing accounts. "Not bothering," however, was not the reason. Attorneys prosecuting cases wanted the actual bills in hand to gain the dramatic impact on juries of displaying wads of ill-gotten lucre. Depositing the money would mean losing the ability to show it to juries: only a statement from a government bank account would be available. Furthermore, some jurisdictions require that actual bills be submitted as evidence.

Until quite recently, very little cash had been seized from criminal suspects at all. In the late 1970s, however, the Justice Department began actively to seize cash and physical assets (such as cars and boats), and to seek forfeiture of those assets, as a tactic against organized crime. Soon thereafter, the department realized that this vastly increased quantity of assets had created a management problem. The Justice Department had a policy of not questioning legitimate third-party liens on seized assets; if there was a $110,000 loan outstanding on a $150,000 boat, the government would not contest the bank's right to collect $110,000 from the sale of the boat. The problem was frequently that the boat had deteriorated so badly while in the government possession that when it was sold after having been forfeited, less than $110,000 was realized, and the government had to make up the difference. The local U.S. Attorney offices had no capability to manage seized assets while they awaited disposition (lawyers are experts at trying cases, not managing property), and no centralized management system had ever developed, because there were so few seized assets.

In 1981 the Justice Department appointed a task force to examine the management of seized assets, and the task force issued a report in 1982. The report recommended that the department establish a central organizational capability through the U.S. Marshall Service, to undertake this task for local U.S. Attorney offices. After agreement was obtained within the department (including from the U.S. Attorney offices), this new management responsibility of the U.S. Marshall service, which included as a small part of it putting seized cash into bank accounts, was established in 1984.

Popular impressions of enormous waste appear, then, to be exaggerated. What about impressions that government officials dealing with the public are surly or indifferent? Here there is evidence from surveys of people's actual encounters with government that presents a more nuanced picture than the stereotype.

According to a national survey conducted in 1973 (none more recent appears to exist), citizens generally report themselves "very satisfied" or "fairly well satisfied" in their personal encounters with service-providing government organizations ranging from social security offices through job-training programs and unemployment compensation bureaus.[6] Furthermore, by a margin of 61 percent to 28 percent the total sample answered affirmatively the question, "By and large, do you think most government offices do a good job?" By a margin of 68 percent to 25 percent, respondents agreed with the statement that "government workers are generally helpful."[7] In addition, those coming to work in Washington for the first time in high-level positions, often with business backgrounds, generally express pleasant surprise at the competence and diligence of those with whom they work.[8] And, of course, those who complain of a government that is overbearing in the interferences bureaucrats impose on citizens would hardly complain about *ineffectuality* in implementation (though they do complain about the decisions to adopt the policies in the first place).

The popular images of ineffectuality, indifference, and waste in government bear, then, only pale resemblance to reality. At the same time, government agencies do not rate a clean bill of health. In the 1973 survey, government came out somewhat below private business in the quality of service delivery. To be sure, when asked to rate government versus business along various dimensions of service, the largest single number of respondents—generally around half—saw no difference. Of those who did perceive a difference, however, around three times as many thought business did a better job.[9] If we compare average satisfaction levels in this survey for government services (69 percent) with those reported in a different study of consumer satisfaction with private service delivery, it can be seen that satisfaction with service delivery by government ranks neither at the top nor at the bottom. (See Table 12-1.) The perceptions, then, are of performance that is neither terrible nor perfect. And downright production failures are a serious enough problem in government so that it would be foolish, and false, to adopt anything like an uncritical view of the quality of the operational performance of government organizations.

Furthermore, government does not just provide services. It

TABLE 12-1.

*Percentage of Users Satisfied
(Always/Usually) With Selected
Private-Sector Service Encounters*

Auto repair	51%
Architects, home designers	60
Appliance repairs	62
Travel agencies	81
Medical doctors or nurses in office or home	82
Laundry or dry cleaning	84

SOURCE: Ralph L. Day and Muzaffar Bodur, "A Comprehensive Study of Satisfaction with Consumer Services," in *Consumer Satisfaction, Dissatisfaction, and Complaining Behavior*, ed. Ralph L. Day (Bloomington: Indiana University School of Business, 1977), pp. 67–68.

also regulates people's behavior and sometimes makes them act in ways they would prefer not to act. The same survey that showed relatively high levels of satisfaction in *service* encounters with government showed considerably lower satisfaction among citizens dealing with police, tax officials, traffic violations, and similar types of regulatory situations. Only 35 percent of respondents, on average, thought government officials handled those situations well.[10]

The chapters on the production stage of the policy-making process should have made clear that frequently problems with the performance of government organizations are inherent in the task and/or common to large organizations in general, but that at the same time there are important areas where the performance of American public organizations is systematically handicapped compared to that of private business firms and even many other governments. The chapter on the choices about the institutional design of the civil service also made clear that these choices are neither arbitrary nor capricious, but grow out of special features of operating government agencies in a political environment and of our attitudes toward government officials. I do not mean this as a criticism, much less a quixotic call to "get politics out of government." As long as government organizations remain involved in the political process—and the powerful reasons motivating that involvement have already been discussed—the strong admixture of politics into organizations also charged with production will be inevitable.

Is there anything, therefore, that can feasibly be done to improve the quality of the operating performance of governments? There are many small changes that would be helpful, and might be feasible, and a few bigger ones. One example of a small change would be to continue the tendency toward naming assistant secretaries from among career civil servants. This has the positive effect of obtaining top management that already knows the agency before coming on the job. It also increases incentives for good people to come into the civil service in the first place if civil servants know that an organization's top job is available to someone who has worked up through the organization. Assistant secretaries who were career civil servants are also likely to stay longer as assistant secretaries.

I argued earlier in the chapter on the bureaucracy in the political process that it made sense for high government officials to be politically attuned to the president's values, including officials even below the level of assistant secretary. But, as I noted there, such political attunement need not imply that appointees come from outside rather than inside the career civil service. Even when appointing civil servants, the president can still select someone who shares his values. It does, to be sure, decrease the opportunity for presidential rewards to campaign loyalists. But the president is likely to gain the benefits of more effective performance for the cost in lost patronage.

A bigger change would be to pay more attention to developing a culture of management in government organizations. Generally the best people who come into government are attracted by the prospect of participating in grand political choices, not by the grimy details of service delivery, cost savings, or other "mere" questions of operations. As Jeffrey Pressman and Aaron Wildavsky note in a widely cited passage:

The view from the top is exhilarating. Divorced from the problems of implementation, federal bureau heads, leaders of international agencies, and prime ministers in poor countries think great thoughts together. But they have trouble imagining the sequence of events that will bring their paths to fruition. Other men, they believe, will tread the path once they have so brightly lit the way.[11]

Many career government managers, promoted because they were good at jobs calling for individual accomplishment, are never informed that being a good manager is not the same as being a good individual achiever.

As a result, many government managers fail to conceptualize that their job is to get an *organization* to perform well, not simply to perform diligently themselves. Indeed, there is insufficient recognition within government organizations that managers are indeed managers. In his book *Managing the Public's Business*, Laurence Lynn, an academic who has had extensive experience in government, stated that improvements in governmental competence require that public managers "take time to manage."[12] This statement is noteworthy for what it suggests about current practice, for one would think it superfluous. That it is not superfluous creates problems for successful production. And to the extent that they don't think like managers, those with managerial responsibilities whose hands are tied by the institutional choices discussed in chapter 9 won't know what they're missing and hence will not be a vociferous force for institutional change.

A culture within government that public managers *are* indeed managers thus needs desperately to be fostered. Increased use of management training for newly appointed career managers can help. ("Large private companies," states corporate executive and former government official Frederick Malek, "invest from six to eight times as much as the average agency in career training.")[13] The growth of professional schools in public policy and management (if I may be permitted a bit of institutional chauvinism) can also contribute to the growth of a public-management professional culture. This would mirror the growth of self-consciousness about the management function that the business historian Alfred Chandler observed in the private sector during the first decades of the twentieth century.[14]

A culture of public management can be furthered by identification with specific professional management communities, such as maintenance managers or vehicle fleet managers. When I studied the sources of innovation in the operational management of government organizations, I found that frequently innovations occurred when government managers identified with professional communities and sought to introduce changes into their organizations so they could "keep up with the profession" and "follow the state of the art."[15]

The most difficult and intractable challenge is to do something about the incentives that bind people in government to detailed rules, clearances, and second-guesses. Perhaps the most important thing that could be done to improve the operating performance of government agencies is to increase the freedom and the individual responsibility of people working in them. People in government need more freedom to make decisions, to take more initiative, to innovate—and then to take responsibility for the results.[16] The results we look at should be balanced better between positive achievements and simple avoidance of scandal.

Is it possible to make this happen? The incentives that produce the fixation on wrongdoing, scandal, and horror stories on the part of elected officials and the media are understandable. My own view is that there are two archimedian points for changing the bureaucratic orientation. One is the development of output-oriented performance measures in government agencies and the evaluation of performance against those measures. The other is conscious efforts to develop further an organizational culture of public spirit in government agencies.

I believe that the output-based performance evaluation constitutes one archemedian point because it does not simply have the direct effects on improving performance that were discussed in the chapter on the production process.[17] It also strikes at the major underpinning of a bureaucratic orientation in government organizations, the pressure to avoid the downside rather than reach for the upside. You can't beat something with nothing. As sociologist Donald Warwick has noted in his study of the State Department, in the absence of other performance measures, adherence to rules provides some standard, however pitiful, of successful performance. "The official may not be sure of what he has produced or how well he has produced it, but he can be sure he did it in the right way."[18] Performance measures liberate people to gain job satisfaction from a feeling of accomplishment over something else than simply following rules.

In addition, output-based performance evaluation can reduce the incidence of some of the abuses that outside overseers worry about. For example, the best inhibitor of the problem of management cronyism or "politicization" is the need to have competent subordinates to get an organization's work done. In the spoils system regime of the nineteenth century, the jobs of agencies such as the Patent Office and the Department of Agriculture (an organization that then largely did scientific research) had a complex technical component. These tasks simply could not have been accomplished by unqualified spoilsmen, and these agencies introduced a merit system on their own initiative, without outside legislation or rules.[19] If managers can really be judged on the substantive performance of their units, then they will have an interest in making sure they have good people working for them. Concern with displaying positive achievement can thus inhibit bad behavior, without the need to focus specifically on rules to avoid misbehavior.

The development of output-oriented performance measures should thus be of the highest priority for government organizations. Institutionally, perhaps the next reform might be to see if an agency and a congressional oversight committee could agree in advance on performance measures to which the agencies would be held accountable.[20] It would be interesting to see whether agreement on such measures would modify the tendency by congressional committees to focus on scandal alone. It is also an open question whether the White House would permit such close collaboration between an agency and Congress. The other archimedian point, I believe, is managing the development of an organizational culture emphasizing public spirit; this too can directly improve the performance of government officials. If public spirit motivates people in government, a culture of public service within government organizations should be proudly proclaimed, not hushed up and hidden. Public organizations waste a valuable resource when they do nothing to build on the enthusiasm of people taking government work. Furthermore, a culture based on public spirit expresses a different view of government officials from the view on which the system of rules and clearances is based. A rules-based organizational design proclaims that the people who work for government are the problem. Left to their own devices they will be lazy or corrupt, so we must shackle them with rules to assure that they behave up to the high standards we expect of government. By contrast, animating government organizations with a culture of public spirit makes it easier for us to see the people working in government as these organization's most important resource, not their most important problem. The different view of government officials that a public-spirited culture conveys in turn itself encourages easing the system of rules and clearances, because it changes our image of those whom the rules and clearances were designed to control.

I am cautiously optimistic—perhaps the emphasis should be more on my caution than on my optimism—about the possibilities for change. Given the unfavorable environment in which the 1978 Civil Service Reform Act has had to function, and the general difficulty of changing large organizations, I am impressed by the extent of change that legislation has brought about. I am perhaps most impressed, as I indicated earlier, by the development of an ongoing interest in the operational performance of government organizations. An entrenched system of institutional choices has been cracked, and there is ferment in the air.

The crisis of confidence in the performance of government

can contribute to making better choices about the institutional design of government organizations more likely. The political task of advocates of continued reform is twofold. First, advocates must try to keep the focus on the face of this issue most favorable to their cause, namely the need to "make government work better." Second, advocates must remind civil servants that popular dissatisfaction with the way government works is the greatest long-term threat to their job security, their pay and working conditions, and, indeed, the viability of programs in which they believe. Outside pressure can thus be a force to encourage inside acquiescence to some changes that many civil servants might rather have avoided.

In many respects, the atmosphere is ripe for a reorientation of government organization away from excessive reliance on rules and clearances over to a greater reliance on individual judgment and initiative. Large corporations have frequently become dissatisfied in recent years with the negative effects their own systems of rules and clearances have on their ability to adapt in a world of increasing competition. The importance of an appropriate organizational culture has increasingly been recognized by private business as key to organizational success. As the educational level of the government work force grows and the tasks government faces become more complex, the use of standard operating procedures as a basis for organizational design becomes less appropriate. The public-spirited among those working in government should appreciate the improvements in performance that these kinds of changes can bring; the more educated and venturesome should realize that the opportunity to use greater judgment and more initiative can make their own jobs more interesting.

The challenge is to produce fewer bureaucrats. Government organizations and the people who work in them having nothing to lose but their chains. They have a world to win.

13

Conclusion: The Only Government We've Got

This book has presented an unfashionably sanguine view of how well the policy-making process in the United States works. Although my argument is unfashionable, is it really when one stops and thinks so surprising? Seen over the broad span of historic time and place, American society works pretty well. We have been spared secret police knocking at our doors; we have enjoyed extended economic prosperity; there has been no widespread starvation. We have absorbed multitudes of the wretched of the earth, succeeded in assuring most people a decent old age, and saved a surprising amount of the natural beauty on the American continent. Compared with our achievements, our problems and shortcomings seem trivial. Although we should not give government all the credit for this, we should not deny it *any* credit either.

Yet there remains the stubborn fact that cynicism about government and the policy-making process coexists with our justifiable pride. In this concluding chapter, we return to this theme of cynicism.

Why is there such a high level of dissatisfaction with government? Several reasons should become clear from the arguments that have been developed in earlier chapters of this book:

1. Even in the private sector, most new product introductions fail. Marketing professor Philip Kotler, in his book *Marketing Management,* reports on a study by a consulting firm that concludes:

Of every fifty-eight-odd ideas, about 12 pass the initial screening test, which shows them to be compatible with company objectives and resources. Of these, some seven remain after a thorough evaluation of their profit potential. About three survive the product-development stage, two survive the test-marketing stage, and only one is commercially successful.[1]

The private-sector equivalent of the policy-making process, then, is also laden with pitfalls on the road separating initial ideas from final real-world outcomes. And in government, where so many issues involve problems—such as hard-core poverty—that were too difficult for the private sector to solve, the difficulties are even greater. The difference in this regard between the private sector and government is that the rocky road of government policy making is exposed to full view. In business, it is mostly shrouded in secrecy.

2. The mathematics of simple probability are biased against successful policy making, something that may explain the kinds of results just noted. If successful policy making requires (hypothetically) fifteen discrete steps—involving political success, successful production, and a correct theory linking final government actions with real-world outcomes—then it is not enough to succeed at every step but one. A single failure is enough to doom the entire enterprise. Brilliant political skills do not help if the program adopted turns out to be impossible to

produce. Success at politics, and even at production, count for nothing if the final government actions obtained do not produce the real-world changes that were sought. I pointed this out earlier in my discussion of the implementation of new programs.[2] It applies with even more devastating results when the perspective is expanded to the policy-making process as a whole. "The cards in this world," Jeffrey Pressman and Aaron Wildavsky conclude, "are stacked against things happening. . . . The remarkable thing is that new programs work at all."[3] Another way of expressing the same thought is: we do unbelievably well, all things considered.

3. Policy-making success is relatively rare; most participants in the policy-making process experience more defeats than victories. At the same time, people tend to believe that their causes are just and that they deserve to be successful. The stage is thus set for the special resentment that arises when people believe that justice has been thwarted. They tend to blame the process itself for failures, because they wonder why a good idea would fail if not for the excessive influence of "selfish special interests," "recalcitrant bureaucrats," or other demonic—but powerful—inhabitants of the policy-making world. Power denial produces an unhealthy paranoia about the policy-making process.[4]

4. To the casual outside observer, "government" seems to be of a piece. Problems in one area tend to be seen from the outside as problems with "the government," not with a particular program alone. This makes achievement of the perception of governmental competence as difficult as the task faced by the Dutch boy putting his finger in the dike. Yesterday the scandal might have been with the failure to collect overdue student loans. But plug up that problem and another will emerge (defense contract fraud? ketchup classified as a vegetable for school lunch regulations?). The enormous conglomerate known as the government is bound to face a number of crises at any one time. When each problem is attributed to "government," as if it were one unit, the impression is almost bound to be pathetic.

5. In terms of dissatisfaction with the results of the political

process in particular, it must be kept in mind that politics would not occur unless there was at least some disagreement about what policy should be chosen. That sets limits on how many people can be satisfied with the substantive results of any particular decision, absent truly heroic institutions for consensus building. Such disagreement creates dissatisfaction with the final choice, no matter what it is. Resentment increases because the losers are coerced to go along with the winners, and coercion always creates resentment. This creates what Laurence Lynn has called "Murphy's Law of Politics": "Whatever you did, you should have done something else." Such dissatisfaction becomes especially hard to eliminate when little attention is paid in the design of our political institutions to the achievement of agreement among people with contending views.

6. The political process itself produces frustration. In designing our institutions, the founders made the decision to sacrifice governability for liberty. We approve that choice—except when we see how it does indeed sacrifice governability. People get frustrated over the difficulty of getting choices made in political institutions that have been designed to divide formal authority. At the same time, we fear the concentration of power that is required to make decisions flow more easily: a majority of Americans tell opinion pollsters that they prefer a situation where the president and the majority in Congress belong to different parties.[5]

7. Disgruntlement with the political process grows when adversaries use means other than persuasion to bring about political choices they support. People get upset not only because they have lost on the substantive issue. They also get upset because they believe that successful use of power, or successful political strategies, reward manipulation and hence send the wrong signals of social recognition. Yet we would also be upset over the feeble levels of political commitment implied by a world where people did not try hard to get their views accepted.

8. Dissatisfaction with the results of the production process occurs because we make operational management difficult in order to deal with the political environment in which govern-

ment organizations function. We then are dissatisfied with the government performance that results from an environment that makes good performance hard to obtain.

9. Finally, social science knowledge about the policies that come out of government and outcomes in the real-world lives of citizens is imperfect. There is uncertainty about the government policies—or if there are any possible policies—that can best deal with such intractable problems as decreasing recidivism among criminals, getting jobs for teenagers growing up in ghettoes, or stopping nations from making war against each other. Our lack of knowledge about the linkage between the final actions of government and real-world outcomes is an important source of the impression that government does not succeed at solving problems. But it's not that government is failing while some hypothetical others are doing better. It's rather that we are *all* failing.

Perhaps the most basic of the built-in sources of dissatisfaction with government is this: the policy-making process does not live up to the ideals that we have for it. Indeed, it cannot. In this sense, the "civics textbook" and the cynical views of government are not simply unresolved contradictory images in our mind. The one gives birth to the other. It is in significant measure *because* we hold the policy-making process to high standards of public spirit that we become cynical when we see selfishness, greed, or incompetence. Seymour Martin Lipset and William Schneider, in their fascinating work on declining trust in institutions, note that the institutions in which citizens have the lowest confidence are those that rank poorly, in the public's judgment, on ethical and moral practices.[6] In his work on the growth of political cynicism among children from the 1960s to the 1970s, F. Christopher Arterton found that the biggest changes in the attitudes of children came on questions regarding the ethical integrity of politicians. Thus, between 1962 and 1973 the percentage of fifth-graders who believed that candidates for public office are "less selfish than almost anyone" (or "than most people") declined dramatically from 54 percent to

20 percent. The percentage believing they were more honest dropped from 59 percent to 30 percent. By contrast, the percentage believing candidates were smarter declined only modestly.[7]

What has set in motion the increased salience of the cynical side of our views of government? Given that cynicism began to increase in the late 1960s and continued to grow during the 1970s, we should be on the lookout for changes in that period that could have precipitated it. Lipset and Schneider argue in their book *The Confidence Gap* that a good deal of what went on is explained by the poorer substantive performance of government, particularly as regards the war in Vietnam, Watergate, and economic growth. People lost confidence in government, they argue, because government began to perform more poorly. This argument helps explain the modest recovery in confidence in government during the Reagan years, at least through the Iran-contra affair, as the economy in particular began to look better.[8] If Lipset and Schneider are correct, the remedy for cynicism about the policy-making process is simply to improve the results of the process.

Lipset and Schneider's argument surely captures at least part of what changed in the 1960s and 1970s. But something else changed in the late 1960s, as the role of government in society increased. Government simply became more *prominent* in people's lives. And with that increased prominence came an increased consciousness of all the sources of frustration and resentment I have discussed.

The sources of public frustration should provide some guidance to those who wish to become active participants in the policy-making process. My advice concerns both the substantive results of the process and the conduct of the process itself. The roadmap of the policy-making process presented in the Introduction starts from policy ideas at the beginning and emerges at real-world outcomes at the end. This reflects the temporal ordering of the process: production does not begin until political choices have been made, and the real-world outcomes are hidden until after final governmental actions have occurred. This progression describes the way participants usually conceive of the process. Typically they think first of a policy idea, with some conception of what kinds of changes in the real world they wish, then they predict the obstacle course their idea will need to run, asking whether it is politically feasible or whether organizations can produce it, and whether the world will change in the hoped-for ways when the government behaves the way it should.

Perhaps, though, it makes more sense for participants to start off by laying out the real-world outcomes they strive for and working back from there. They would then consider what final government actions would most likely produce the real-world outcomes they seek, and they would evaluate the political and production processes to see what could reasonably be expected to come out of them, either left to their own devices or as a result of feasible interventions. Proposals would be developed only after policy makers went through this exercise.

Parts of this suggestion are less controversial than others. The realization is growing that it simply will not do to say about a proposal, "It's a great idea, but it won't work." If there is no conceivable way to produce something successfully, it makes no more sense to talk about it as being a good idea "except for" that fact than it does to speak that way about an idea for a perpetual motion machine. If an idea won't work, it can't be great. Policy ideas must be crafted so that they can be produced, and they must changed if that is not feasible.

The suggestion that policy ideas should be adapted so as to be politically feasible may smack of opportunism, leaving little room for doing battle for what is right even against hopeless odds. My own view is that there are occasions when one may decide to plant one's flag and fight for an idea that is politically hopeless. It is not that one always should trim one's sails in the political winds. The advice is more subtle than that. One may decide to proceed with a proposal whose political prospects are difficult. However, one needs to do so with open eyes, a clear strategy, and the realization that one might be passing up the opportunity to accomplish something as important in a different area. Furthermore, if a policy idea seems politically hopeless, this should at least suggest that one might reconsider one's own views to see if the massive opposition is perhaps justified. Even when the odds are not hopeless, listening to the views of others affords the possibility of political learning. In this sense, a regard for political feasibility before the strategist formulates policy ideas suggests an appreciation of politics as deliberation.

My second piece of advice to the participant in the policy-making process arises from my discussion of the sources of frustration with the process. The advice is never to forget to show—and to feel—respect for the other participants in the process. Manipulation breeds resentment and can be devastating to a manipulator's reputation and ability to be politically successful. Victims will end up ganging up on you. And the ability to understand genuinely the concerns of others is important in developing successful strategies. Beyond that, though, the abuse of power damages public perceptions of government as a whole. Economists tell us that individual participants in the process will try to get a free ride on the integrity of others, while behaving badly themselves, leading to underproduction of the "public good" called positive popular perception of government. That observation does an injustice to the many participants in the process who take their obligations seriously—and provides a cheap excuse to the dishonorable.

The policy-making process is filled with the possibilities for both virtuous and vicious cycles. The more the norm of concern for others reigns in the political process, the more people will come under its sway. This virtuous cycle produces both better political choices and better people. By contrast, self-interest in politics begets self-interest. The more it is believed that people in government are simply out for themselves, the more it will become true that this is the case.

There are also possibilities for both virtuous and vicious cycles in the production process. An important way the public sector attracts good people to work for government organizations is by appealing to the desire to show public spirit. Since it is unlikely that pay scales for top managers will ever become high enough to allow the public sector to motivate by appealing to the prospect of great personal wealth the way private firms do, this alternative will have to do. Thus, the more the public sector is seen to represent an arena where important work is being done, the better the people government organizations can attract to do that work. Furthermore, given the responsiveness of government organizations to the pressures around them, a movement for excellence in government management can increase the likelihood of achieving the goal simply by making the effort to press for it. But the more government organizations are vilified, the poorer the quality of people who will be attracted to them. In addition, we bind government officials to detailed rules and procedures because we distrust them. The rules and procedu.es then hinder them from doing a good job, thus fostering the performance problems that are one of the roots of the imposition of the rules in the first place. And anomalies produced by slavish application of the rules provide grist for the mills of the "horror story" peddlers who use the stories to promote further distrust and contempt for government officials, producing yet more rules and poorer performance.

In recent years the downward spiral of a vicious cycle in the policy-making process has been more apparent. Cynical descriptive conclusions about behavior in government threaten to undermine the norm prescribing public spirit. The cynicism of journalists—and even the writings of professors—can decrease public spirit simply by describing what they perceive as its absence. The cynics thus make prophecies that threaten to become self-fulfilling. That is one reason why my intention in this book has been to demonstrate the opposite. I believe that knowledge about how the process really works—including knowledge about the level of public spirit that still remains—can counteract the dissolution of norms that are necessary if the policy-making process is to work well.

Although the evidence here is spotty and needs to be interpreted with caution, there is some suggestion that a decline in the norm of public spirit with regard to government has been translated into a declining ethical climate in our everyday behavior outside government. Because people's behavior is always some mixture of long-term dispositions that serve to anchor them and short-term forces that tend to buffet them, we would expect any changes in a society's ethical climate to show up more strongly among young people, whose behavior is not yet securely anchored.[9] There exists a time series since 1964 in surveys conducted by the Institute for Social Research at the University of Michigan with the questions, "Would you say that most of the time people try to be helpful, or that they are mostly just looking out for themselves?" and "Do you think most people would try to take advantage of you if they got the chance, or would they try to be fair?" That time series displays some changes since 1964 among the youngest age cohort (ages 18–24). On the surveys between 1964 and 1968 the average percentage of the 18–24-year-olds who felt that people generally tried to be helpful (rather than mostly just looking out for themselves) was 51 percent. The average fell to 44 percent in the period between 1970 and 1976. On the question about taking advantage of others, the percentage disagreeing that most people will try to take advantage declined from 65 percent to 53 percent. For the oldest age cohort (and thus the one least influenced by the spirit of the times), there was no change during this period.[10] Similarly, in surveys conducted among 17-year-olds in 1971 and 1976 there was a decline from 74 percent to 67 percent in the percentage of respondents who said that they would report and describe to the police a stranger they saw slashing the tires of a car.[11] None of these changes is overwhelming. They point, however, in the same direction of a declining climate of ethical behavior in our everyday lives. These changes followed, with some lag, the growth of cynicism about government. If government is a school, it started doing more poorly at teaching the proper lessons.

Surely the policy-making process does not live up to the ideals we have for it. For that situation, it is easy to blame "them"—the selfish politicians or special interest groups. In fact, though, the enemy is us. We have established ideals for public spirit in the policy-making process. But imperfect humans that we are, we have trouble living up to the standards we have established. As government comes to loom larger for us, that failure becomes more apparent and more irritating.

To what extent does this diagnosis suggest a solution? Perhaps only in that it suggests both that we hold high the ideal *and* that we show a greater tolerance for imperfection in its realization. An intolerance to imperfection in the realization of our ideals becomes a threat to sustenance of the ideals themselves.

Key to the tolerance should be the insight that the short-comings in the policy-making process that produce cynicism are frequently built into any process for making collective decisions and producing them through large organizations. Indeed, some of the shortcomings are built into our own imperfections as human beings. Generally we accept the imperfections that are built into a competitive market system for the production of goods and services, such as the human costs of competition for the defeated, or the encouragement of selfishness. We do so to gain the benefits of efficient satisfaction of our economic wants. Similarly, imperfections in the policy-making process may be the price we must pay to get the benefits, visible and otherwise, we obtain from government. This is the only government we've got.

NOTES

Introduction

1. Gabriel A. Almond and Sidney Verba, *The Civic Culture,* abridged ed. (Boston: Little, Brown, 1965), pp. 64–65.

2. Cited in Seymour Martin Lipset and William Schneider, *The Confidence Gap* (New York: Free Press, 1983), p. 271.

3. Harvard C. Lehman and Paul A. Witty, "Further Study of the Social Status of Occupations," *Journal of Educational Sociology* 5 (1931): 109.

4. Mapheus Smith, "An Empirical Scale of Prestige Status of Occupations," *American Sociological Review* 8 (April 1943): 185–92.

5. See, generally, Robert E. Lane, "The Politics of Consensus in the Age of Affluence," *American Political Science Review* 59 (December 1965). These survey results are reported on p. 894.

6. Morris Janowitz and Deil Wright, "The Prestige of Public Employment: 1929 and 1954," *Public Administration Review* 31 (Winter 1956): 15–21.

7. M. Kent Jennings et al., "Trusted Leaders: Perceptions of Appointed Federal Officials," *Public Opinion Quarterly* 30 (October 1966): 372, 377.

8. These figures are reported in Lipset and Schneider, *Confidence Gap,* p. 17.

9. Frances FitzGerald, *America Revised: History Schoolbooks in the Twentieth Century* (Boston: Little, Brown, 1979), p. 140.

10. F. Christopher Arterton, "The Impact of Watergate on Children's Attitudes Towards Political Authority," *Political Science Quarterly* 89 (June 1974): 273, 278, 280.

11. Michael Lipsky, "Toward a Theory of Street-Level Bureaucracy," in *Theoretical Perspectives on Urban Politics,* ed. Willis Hawley and Michael Lipsky (Englewood Cliffs: Prentice-Hall, 1976); pp. 196–213.

12. Frank J. Goodnow, *Politics and Administration* (New York: Macmillan, 1900).

13. Quoted from Albert O. Hirschman, *Essays in Trespassing* (Cambridge: Cambridge University Press, 1981), p. 297.

Chapter 2

1. See p. 30.

2. On these points, see the brief discussion in Robert A. Dahl and Charles E. Lindblom, *Politics, Economics and Welfare* (Chicago: University of Chicago Press, 1953), p. 422. See also John Stuart Mill, *Considerations on Representative Government* (New York: Harper & Brothers, 1862), p. 79.

3. I owe this point to Richard Neustadt.

4. Note that what is seen as being "rational" is the selection of the choice that maximizes attainment of our values. Nothing is said about the rationality of the

values themselves. Thus, for instance, Hitler could be a rational maximizer as long as he chose alternatives that maximized attainment of his values.

5. On the first line of criticism, see Charles E. Lindblom, *The Intelligence of Democracy* (New York: Free Press, 1965). On the second, see Irving L. Janis and Leon Mann, *Decision Making: A Psychological Analysis of Conflict, Choice and Commitment* (New York: Free Press, 1977). The *Peanuts* quote comes from p. 3 of that book. On these issues in general, see Daniel Kahneman et al., eds: *Judgment Under Uncertainty: Heuristics and Biases* (Cambridge: Cambridge University Press, 1982).

6. Anthony Downs, *An Economic Theory of Democracy* (New York: Harper & Brothers, 1957), Ch. 7.

7. John D. Steinbruner, *The Cybernetic Theory of Decision* (Princeton: Princeton University Press, 1974), Ch. 7–8.

8. Jimmy Carter, *Keeping Faith: Memoirs of a President* (New York: Bantam Books, 1982), pp. 486–87.

9. On this subject, I have found the following works helpful: Dennis H. Wrong, *Power: Its Forms, Bases and Use* (Oxford: Basil Blackwell, 1979); Robert A. Dahl, *Modern Political Analysis*, 4th ed. (Englewood Cliffs: Prentice-Hall, 1984), Ch. 3–4; James Q. Wilson, *Political Organizations* (New York: Basic Books, 1973), Ch. 3; Amitai Etzioni, *A Comparative Analysis of Complex Organizations*, 2nd ed. (New York: Free Press, 1975); and Peter Blau, *Exchange and Power in Social Life* (New York: Wiley, 1964).

10. See, for example, Matthew A. Crenson, *The Un-Politics of Air Pollution: A Study of Non-Decisionmaking in the Cities* (Baltimore: Johns Hopkins University Press, 1971).

11. Etzioni, *Comparative Analysis,* pp. 5–6.

12. R. H. Tawney, *Equality* (London: Allen and Unwin, 1931), p. 229.

13. Sidney Verba and Gary R. Orren, *Equality in America: The View From The Top* (Cambridge: Harvard University Press, 1985), Ch. 9.

14. Richard E. Neustadt, *Presidential Power* (New York: Wiley, 1969), Ch. 3.

15. Kay Lehman Schlozman and John T. Tierney, *Organized Interests and American Democracy* (New York: Harper & Row, 1986), pp. 104–6.

16. Jeffrey M. Berry, *The Interest Group Society* (Boston: Little, Brown, 1984), p. 119.

17. Verba and Orren, *Equality in America*, p. 189.

18. This account, though not the specific examples, is based heavily on John W. Kingdon, *Agendas, Alternatives and Public Policies* (Boston: Little, Brown, 1984). The idea of "incubation" is Nelson Polsby's. *Political Innovation in America* (New Haven: Yale University Press, 1984).

19. Steven Kelman, *Improving Doctor Performance: A Study in the Use of Information and Organizational Change* (New York: Human Sciences Press, 1980), p. 169.

20. See the discussion in David A. Stockman, *The Triumph of Politics* (New York: Harper & Row, 1986), pp. 71–73.

21. Eric Redman, *The Dance of Legislation* (New York: Simon & Schuster, 1973).

Chapter 3

1. Randall B. Ripley, *Congress: Process and Policy,* 3rd ed. (New York: Norton, 1983), p. 3.

2. In multi-party systems without stable coalitions among parties, such as in The Netherlands, or during the French Fourth Republic, the power of parliament increases because the prime minister is not assured of a stable parliamen-

tary majority, but rather can be defeated on important votes, leading to resignation from office.

3. See, for example, Anthony King, "How to Strengthen Legislatures—Assuming We Want To," in *The Role of the Legislature in Western Democracies*, ed. Norman J. Ornstein (Washington: American Enterprise Institute, 1981), p. 89.

4. George G. Galloway, *History of the House of Representatives*, 2nd ed. (New York: Crowell, 1976), p. 6.

5. Wilfred E. Binkley, *President and Congress*, 3rd ed. (New York: Vintage Books, 1962), p. 49.

6. Ibid., p. 50.

7. See the chart in Nelson W. Polsby et al., "The Growth of the Seniority System in the House of Representatives," in *Congressional Behavior*, ed. Nelson W. Polsby (New York: Random House, 1971), p. 171.

8. See James L. Sundquist, *The Decline and Resurgence of Congress* (Washington: The Brookings Institution, 1961), pp. 377–81.

9. See Robert Katzmann, *Institutional Disability* (Washington: The Brookings Institution, 1986), Ch. 2–5.

10. On environmentalists, see Steven Kelman, *What Price Incentives: Economists and the Environment* (Boston: Auburn House, 1981), pp. 139–42 and on energy policy, Bruce I. Oppenheimer, "Congress and the New Obstructionism: Developing an Energy Program," in *Congress Reconsidered*, 2nd ed., ed. Lawrence C. Dodd and Bruce I. Oppenheimer (Washington: CQ Press, 1977), pp. 275–95.

11. In Britain only a certain proportion of private member bills are even considered by Parliament, the determinations of which ones being made by lot. See Gerhard Lowenberg and Samuel C. Patterson, *Comparing Legislatures* (Boston: Little, Brown, 1979), p. 249.

12. See the overview discussion in Joseph Cooper and David W. Brady, "Institutional Context and Leadership Style: The House from Cannon to Rayburn," *American Political Science Review* 75 (June 1981): 411–24.

13. On these issues in general, see the essays in Thomas E. Mann and Norman Ornstein, eds., *The New Congress* (Washington: American Enterprise Institute, 1981).

14. See the chart in Gary C. Jacobson, *The Politics of Congressional Elections* (Boston: Little, Brown, 1983), p. 133.

15. See Thomas E. Mann, *Unsafe at Any Margin* (Washington: American Enterprise Institute, 1978), p. 85.

16. Norman J. Ornstein, "The Open Congress Meets the President," in *The New American Political System*, ed. Anthony King (Washington: American Enterprise Institute, 1978), p. 203.

17. John F. Bibby, ed., *Congress Off the Record: The Candid Analyses of Seven Members* (Washington: American Enterprise Institute, 1983), p. 25.

18. Joshua Tropper and Philip B. Heymann, "Auto Safety" (Cambridge: Kennedy School of Government, 1977), p. 4.

19. See p. 39.

20. See James L. Sundquist, *Politics and Policy* (Washington: The Brookings Institution, 1969).

21. See the chart in Roger H. Davidson and Walter J. Oleszek, *Congress and Its Members* (Washington: Congressional Quarterly Press, 1981), p. 33, and Allen Schick, "Politics Through Law," in *Both Ends of the Avenue*, ed. Anthony King (Washington: American Enterprise Institute, 1983), p. 168.

22. Davidson and Oleszek, *Congress and Its Members*, p. 31.

23. Roger H. Davidson, "Subcommittee Government," in Mann and Ornstein, *New Congress*, pp. 112–13.

24. John Kingdon, *Congressmen's Voting Decisions* (New York: Harper & Row, 1973).

25. Abner J. Mikva and Patti B. Sarris, *The American Congress* (New York: Franklin Watts, 1983), p. 221.

26. Ripley, *Congress*, pp. 261–62.

27. Austin Ranney, "The Working Conditions of Members of Parliament and Congress," in Ornstein, *Role*, p. 70.

28. Davidson and Oleszek, *Congress and Its Members*, p. 235.

29. Ripley, *Congress*, p. 261.

30. Charles O. Jones, *Every Second Year* (Washington: The Brookings Institution, 1967), pp. 89–90.

31. Schick, "Politics Through Law," pp. 157–58.

32. Ibid., p. 162. See the discussion in Sundquist, *Decline*, pp. 99–103.

33. Occupational Safety and Health Act (PL 91-956), Section 6(b)5.

34. Sundquist, *Decline and Resurgence*, p. 35.

35. Leonard White, *The Jacksonians: A Study in Administrative History 1829–1961* (New York: Macmillan, 1954), p. 40; idem, *The Republican Era: A Study in Administrative History 1869–1901* (New York: Macmillan, 1954), pp. 28–29.

36. See White, *Jacksonians*, Ch. 8; idem, *Republican Era*, Ch. 4.

37. See p. 39.

38. Michael V. Malbin, *Unelected Representatives* (New York: Basic Books, 1967), p. 34.

39. Ibid., p. 34, and generally, Ch. 3.

40. See p. 37.

41. Samuel Huntington, "Congress Responds to the Twentieth Century," in *The Congress and America's Future*, 2nd ed., ed. David B. Truman (Englewood Cliffs: Prentice Hall, 1973), p. 15.

42. See, for example, Joseph P. Kalt, *The Economics and Politics of Oil Price Regulation* (Cambridge: MIT Press, 1981), Ch. 6; Joseph P. Kalt and Mark Zupan, "Capture and Ideology in the Economic Theory of Politics," *American Economic Review* 74 (June 1984): 279–300, James B. Kau and Paul H. Rubin, "Self-Interest, Ideology and Logrolling in Congressional Voting," *Journal of Law and Economics* 22 (October 1979): 365–84. See also Jerrold E. Schneider, *Ideological Coalitions in Congress* (Westport: Greenwood, 1979). For a different view, see Sam Peltzman, "Constituent Interest and Congressional Voting," *Journal of Law and Economics* 27 (April 1984): 187–210.

43. Kalt and Zupan, "Capture and Ideology." The disentanglement of constituency interests and of ideology is easier on issues such as oil price regulation, because the economic interests within oil-consuming and oil-producing areas are relatively homogeneous. The issue does become more complicated, and difficult to disentangle, in policy areas where economic interests within a constituency are more divided, and where a member may be elected by one *element* of the constituency. Thus, two states may have relatively similar per capita incomes, but in one state a Senator is elected predominantly through the votes of the wealthier people in the state and in the other the Senator is elected predominantly by the poorer people. The states would produce different kinds of Senators, even though "on average" the constituency characteristics looked similar. Once one begins to disaggregate a constituency to the member's own electoral coalition, the overlap between ideology and the interests of those constitutents who voted for the member in question becomes great, and it therefore becomes difficult to disentangle ideology and constituent influence on many votes because they both tend in the same direction and do not require the member to make a hard choice. This also suggests that the

ideology a person develops may initially be related to the person's economic interests, although that says nothing about the independent significance of ideology once developed. Nonetheless, Kalt and Zupan find that even when a series of constituency-related variables used to predict a member's ideology is included in an analysis, the ideological residual not predicted by those constituency-related variables still ends up having an impact on votes on the issues they examined. Sam Peltzman gets different results by using a stepwise regression equation, where he enters the constituency-related variables first and the ideology variables afterward. Given the collinearity between the variables, it is hardly surprising that this produces overwhelming effects for constituency and small ones for ideology. The effect, though, is an artifact of the procedure used.

44. Bernard Ashball, *The Senate Nobody Knows* (New York: Doubleday, 1978), and Elizabeth Drew, *Senator* (New York: Simon & Schuster, 1979).

45. Hanna Renichel Pitkin, *The Concept of Representation* (Berkeley: University of California Press, 1967), pp. 277–78.

46. Arthur Maass, *Congress and the Common Good* (New York: Basic Books, 1984).

47. Ashball, *Senate Nobody Knows*, p. 210.

48. Drew, *Senator*, p. 61.

49. Bibby, *Congress Off the Record*, p. 15.

50. Richard Fenno, *Congressmen in Committees* (Boston: Little, Brown, 1973).

51. R. Douglas Arnold, "The Local Roots of Domestic Policy," in Mann and Ornstein, *New Congress*, p. 263.

52. Donald E. Stokes, "Parties and the Nationalization of Electoral Forces," in *The American Party Systems*, ed. William N. Chambers and Walter Dean Burnham (New York: Oxford University Press, 1967), pp. 182–202. The study unfortunately goes only through 1960.

53. See Arnold, "Local Roots," pp. 281–83.

54. Ibid., p. 287.

55. This point is made by Ripley, *Congress*, p. 174.

56. Davidson and Oleszek, *Congress and Its Members*, p. 112.

Chapter 4

1. See George C. Edwards, III, *The Public Presidency* (New York: St. Martin's Press, 1983), p. 106.

2. Michael Nelson, "The Psychological Presidency," in *The Presidency and the Political System*, ed. Michael Nelson (Washington: CQ Press, 1984), p. 160.

3. Michael Nelson, "Evaluating the Presidency," in Nelson, *Presidency*, p. 17.

4. Graham Allison and Peter Szanton, *Remaking Foreign Policy: The Organizational Connection* (New York: Basic Books, 1976), p. 61.

5. John Kennedy, "Mid-Term Television Conversation on the Presidency," in *The Power of the Presidency: Concepts and Controversy*, 2nd ed., ed. Robert S. Hirschfield (Chicago: Aldine, 1973), pp. 141–42.

6. Quoted in Thomas E. Cronin, *The State of the Presidency*, 2nd ed. (Boston: Little, Brown, 1980), p. 122.

7. Quoted in ibid., p. 150.

8. See pp. 28–29.

9. Richard Neustadt, *Presidential Power*, 2nd ed. (New York: Wiley, 1980), p. xi.

10. Stephen Hess, *Organizing the Presidency* (Washington: The Brookings Institution, 1976), p. 15. See also the discussion in Anthony King, "A Mile and a Half is a Long Way," in *Both Ends of The Avenue,* ed. Anthony King (Washington: American Enterprise Institute, 1983), pp. 247–50.

11. Hugh Heclo and Lester Salamon, eds., *The Illusion of Presidential Government* (Boulder, Colo.: 1981), p. 1.

12. For a discussion, see Aaron Wildavsky, "The Two Presidencies," in *Perspectives on the Presidency,* ed. Aaron Wildavsky (Boston: Little, Brown, 1974), particularly pp. 448–53.

13. See Hirschfield, *Power of the Presidency,* pp. 53–65. Alexander Hamilton defended Washington's action, although my own view is that any fair reading of the debate suggests that, as a matter of constitutional interpretation, Hamilton got the worse of the argument. Having decided that there was nothing in existing treaties "incompatible with an adherence to neutrality," Hamilton argued that Washington had the right "as executor of the laws to proclaim the neutrality of the nation." That there was nothing *prohibiting* such an action does not, in a system of enumerated powers, imply that the action is authorized.

14. Stephen J. Wayne, *The Legislative Presidency* (New York: Harper & Row, 1978), p. 15. On the development of the president's role in the legislative process, see generally Ch. 1.

15. Ibid., p. 19.

16. See generally Paul Light, *The President's Agenda* (Baltimore: Johns Hopkins University Press, 1982), and John Kingdon, *Agendas, Alternatives and Public Policies* (Boston: Little, Brown, 1984), particularly Ch. 2–3.

17. See Neustadt, *Presidential Power,* Ch. 3–5.

18. Woodrow Wilson, "The President's Role in American Government," in Hirschfield, *Power of the Presidency,* p. 93.

19. Edwards, *Public Presidency,* p. 44. This phenomenon occurs more for foreign policy than domestic issues.

20. See William Safire, *Before the Fall* (New York: Doubleday, 1975).

21. John Hersey, *Aspects of the Presidency* (New Haven: Ticknor and Fields, 1980), p. 71 and generally Ch. 4.

22. Michael J. Malbin, "Rhetoric and Leadership: A Look Backward at the Carter Energy Plan," in King, *Both Ends,* pp. 212–45.

23. James W. Fesler, *Public Administration* (Englewood Cliffs: Prentice-Hall, 1980), p. 134.

24. Richard Rose, "British Government: The Job At the Top," in *Presidents and Prime Ministers,* ed. Richard Rose and Ezra Suleiman (Washington: American Enterprise Institute, 1981), p. 4, and Anthony King, "Executives," in *Handbook of Political Science,* v. 5, ed. Fred I. Greenstein and Nelson W. Polsby (Reading, Mass.: Addison-Wesley, 1975), p. 193.

25. Paul J. Quirk, "Presidential Competence," in Nelson, *Presidency,* pp. 141–52.

26. See Edward S. Corwin, *The President's Office and Powers,* 4th ed. (New York: New York University Press, 1951), p. 11 and Alexander Hamilton et al., *The Federalist Papers* (Number 70) (New York: Modern Library, 1937).

27. Cronin, *State of the Presidency,* 2nd ed., p. 11.

28. See pp. 105–107.

29. Cronin, *State of the Presidency,* 2nd ed., p. 224.

30. See Roger B. Porter, *Presidential Decision-Making: The Economic Policy Board* (Cambridge: Cambridge University Press, 1980), pp. 6–11.

31. Heclo, "Illusion," in Heclo and Salamon, *Illusion of Presidential Government,* p. 6.

32. Cronin, *State of the Presidency,* 1st ed., p. 118; Hess, *Organizing the Presidency,* p. 1.

33. Hess, *Organizing the Presidency,* p. 150. Until 1971, the Office of Management and Budget was called the Bureau of the Budget.

34. See Porter, *Presidential Decision-Making;* Alexander L. George, *Presidential Decisionmaking in Foreign Policy: The Effective Use of Information and Advice* (Boulder, Colo.: Westview Press, 1980); Allison and Szanton, *Remaking Foreign Policy;* John H. Kessel, *The Domestic Presidency: Decision-Making in the White House* (North Scituate: Mass., Duxbury Press, 1975); Richard T. Johnson, *Managing The White House* (New York: Harper & Row, 1974); and Chester A. Newland, "Executive Office Policy Apparatus: Enforcing the Reagan Agenda," in *The Reagan Presidency and the Governing of America,* ed. Lester A. Salamon and Michael Lund (Washington: The Urban Institute Press, 1985), pp. 135–68.

35. Kessel, *Domestic Presidency,* p. 29.

36. Hess, *Organizing the Presidency,* p. 164.

37. Nelson, "Evaluating," p. 7.

38. Wilson, *President's Role,* pp. 91–92.

39. Lyndon Johnson, "Comments on the Presidency," in Hirschfield, *Power of the Presidency,* p. 150.

40. Some observers have had such a quarrel, especially during the worry about an imperial presidency around the time of Presidents Johnson and Nixon.

41. Quoted from Hersey, *Aspects of the Presidency,* p. 6.

42. Quoted from ibid., p. 9.

43. Quoted in Cronin, *State of the Presidency,* 2nd ed., p. 111.

44. Ibid., p. 196.

45. Edwards, *Public Presidency,* p. 196.

46. The more partisan division there is over foreign affairs, the less this works, of course.

47. Ezra N. Suleiman, "Presidential Government in France," in Rose and Suleiman, *Presidents and Prime Ministers,* p. 133. See also the discussion for Britain in Rose, "British Government," p. 38, and for Germany in Renate Mayntz, "Executive Leadership in Germany," in Rose and Suleiman, *Presidents and Prime Ministers,* p. 146.

48. Fred I. Greenstein, *The Hidden-Hand Presidency: Eisenhower as Leader* (New York: Basic Books, 1982).

Chapter 5

1. Leonard D. White, *The Jeffersonians: A Study in Administrative History 1801–1829* (New York: Macmillan, 1951), p. 93.

2. Idem, *The Jacksonians: A Study in Administrative History 1829–1861* (New York: Macmillan, 1954), p. 146.

3. See Theda Skocpol, "Bringing the State Back In: Strategies of Analysis in Current Research," in *Bringing the State Back In,* ed. Peter Evans et al. (Cambridge: Cambridge University Press, 1985) and Eric Nordlinger, *On the Autonomy of the Democratic State* (Cambridge: Harvard University Press, 1981).

4. Nordlinger, *Autonomy of the Democratic State,* p. 205.

5. On these issues see, for example, Barrington Moore, Jr., *Social Origins of Dictatorship and Democracy* (Boston: Beacon Press, 1966).

6. Ole Westerberg, *Allmän förvaltningsrätt (Administrative Law)* (Stockholm: Nordiska Bokhandeln, 1973).

7. This section closely follows Steven Kelman, *Regulating America, Regulating Sweden: A Comparative Study of Occupational Safety and Health Policy* (Cambridge: MIT Press, 1981), pp. 10–12, 139–40.

8. See ibid., p. 11.

9. For discussions, see George Eads, "Harnessing Regulation: The Evolving Role of White House Oversight," *Regulation* 5 (May 1981): 19–26 and Antonin Scalia, "Regulatory Review and Management," *Regulation* 6 (January 1982): 19–21.

10. Eads, "Harnessing Regulation," p. 19

11. Louis L. Jaffe, *Judicial Control of Administrative Action*, abridged stud. ed. (Boston: Little, Brown, 1965), p. 595. See generally Ch. 14–16.

12. For a detailed discussion of the Swedish case, see Kelman, *Regulating America*, Ch. 1, 2, 4. For the situation in the rest of Western Europe, see Ronald Brickman et al., *Controlling Chemicals: The Politics of Regulation in Europe and the United States* (Ithaca: Cornell University Press, 1985).

13. See pp. 79–83.

14. Richard Rose, "The Political Status of Higher Civil Servants in Britain," in *Bureaucrats and Policy Making: A Comparative Overview*, ed. Ezra N. Suleiman (New York: Holmes and Meier, 1984), pp. 152–61. See generally the essays in this collection for a discussion of the role of high bureaucrats in preparing legislation in western Europe. On the situation in Japan, see Chalmers Johnson, "Japan: Who Governs?" *Journal of Japanese Studies* 2 (Autumn 1975): 21–28.

15. See the essays in the studies cited above. On the Swedish situation, see Kelman, *Regulating America*, pp. 170–74.

16. See pp. 55–57, 74–76.

17. See Thomas Cronin, *The State of the Presidency*, 1st ed. (Boston: Little, Brown, 1975), pp. 5, 55.

18. John W. Macey et al., *America's Unelected Government: Appointing the President's Team* (Cambridge: Ballinger, 1983), p. 38.

19. Dean E. Mann and Jameson W. Doig, *The Assistant Secretaries* (Washington: The Brookings Institution, 1965), p. 88.

20. Hugh Heclo, *A Government of Strangers* (Washington: The Brookings Institution, 1977), p. 67 and Mann and Doig, *Assistant Secretaries*, p. 24.

21. Mann and Doig, *Assistant Secretaries*, p. 27.

22. See Hugh Heclo, "Issue Networks and the Executive Establishment" in *The New American Political System*, ed. Anthony King (Washington: American Enterprise Institute, 1978), pp. 87–124.

23. This material closely follows Kelman, *Regulating America*, pp. 98–100.

24. John Quarles, *Cleaning Up America* (Boston: Houghton Mifflin, 1976), pp. 117–18.

25. Barry R. Weingast and Mark J. Moran, "Bureaucratic Discretion or Congressional Control?: Regulatory Policymaking by the Federal Trade Commission," *Journal of Political Economy* 91 (October 1983): 765–800.

26. They argue that the case mix at the commission changed toward "small-time," less politically controversial cases after the congressional committee changes in 1977. Yet cases take years to wend their way up to the level of the commissioners, at which point the commissioners are merely reacting to an

issue being brought before them. The politically sensitive decisions about bringing cases are made much earlier; for cases coming before the commission during 1976–79, those decisions were often made well before 1977. Second, starting around 1974 the commission began devoting a much larger proportion of its resources to politically controversial and significant rule-making proceedings. Each such proceeding took up significant staff effort, yet it would only count as a single case for Weingast and Moran's calculations. Thus, even if the proportion of resources being devoted to the "small-time" textile and Robinson-Patman cases that Weingast and Moran use as their examples was declining significantly, such cases would probably come to constitute a growing percentage of the *number* of cases, because one *rule making* replaced perhaps tens of *individual cases* that would otherwise have been brought.

27. See Kelman, *Regulating America*, Ch. 3.

28. See Francis E. Rourke, "Variations in Agency Power," in *Bureaucratic Power in National Politics*, 3rd ed., ed. Francis E. Rourke (Boston: Little, Brown, 1978), p. 225.

29. Mark V. Nadel and Francis E. Rourke, "Bureaucracies," in *Handbook of Political Science*, v. 5, ed. Fred I. Greenstein and Nelson W. Polsby (Reading, Mass.: Addison-Wesley, 1975), p. 380.

30. Graham T. Allison, *Essence of Decision: Explaining the Cuban Missile Crisis* (Boston: Little, Brown, 1971), p. 168.

31. On this issue, see Frederick C. Mosher, *Democracy and the Public Service* (New York: Oxford University Press, 1968), Ch. 4. For a further discussion of the influence of mission and recruitment, in the context of the production process, see pp. 152–155.

32. See Kelman, *Regulating America*, Ch. 3.

33. See James C. Miller, III, "On Cable-TV and 'Lobbying' Before the Agencies," *Regulation* 1 (July 1977): 4–5.

34. Paul J. Quirk, *Industry Influence in Federal Regulatory Agencies* (Princeton: Princeton University Press, 1981), Ch. 5.

35. John E. Chubb, *Interest Groups and the Bureaucracy: The Politics of Energy* (Stanford: Stanford University Press, 1983), especially Ch. 5.

36. See Joel D. Aberbach et al., *Bureaucrats and Politicians in Western Democracies* (Cambridge: Harvard University Press, 1981), p. 216.

37. Theodore J. Lowi, *The End of Liberalism* 2nd ed. (New York: Norton, 1979).

38. Aberbach et al., *Bureaucrats and Politicians*, pp. 91–98.

39. I find some of those developed by Aberbach and his colleagues not to be completely persuasive.

40. Richard E. Neustadt makes a somewhat similar argument in "White House and Whitehall," *The Public Interest* 2 (Winter 1966): 56–58.

Chapter 6

1. See R. Shep Melnick, *Regulation and the Courts: The Case of the Clean Air Act* (Washington: The Brookings Institution, 1983), Ch. 4.

2. Stephen L. Wasby, *The Supreme Court in the Federal Judicial System,* 2nd ed. (New York: Holt, Rinehart & Winston, 1984), p. 264.

3. Quoted from Henry J. Abraham, *The Judicial Process* 4th ed. (New York: Oxford University Press, 1980), p. 311.

4. Lawrence Baum, *The Supreme Court* 2nd ed. (Washington: CQ Press, 1985), pp. 171, 173.

5. See Louis L. Jaffe, *Judicial Control of Administrative Action* (Boston: Little, Brown, 1965).

6. Robert Scigliano, *The Supreme Court and the Presidency* (New York: Free Press, 1971), p. 11.

7. Wasby, *Supreme Court,* p. 81.

8. Baum, *Supreme Court,* p. 171.

9. Nobody has attempted the well-nigh insurmountable task of determining what proportion over time of the total of all statutory provisions has been invalidated.

10. Donald L. Horowitz, *The Courts and Social Policy* (Washington: The Brookings Institution, 1977), p. 5. See also Nathan Glazer, "Toward An Imperial Judiciary?" *The Public Interest* 41 (Fall 1975): 104–23.

11. See Wasby, *Supreme Court,* pp. 147–48.

12. See Abraham, *Judicial Process,* p. 255.

13. Melnick, *Regulation and the Courts,* p. 375.

14. Wasby, *Supreme Court,* p. 127.

15. Ibid., p. 133.

16. Ibid., p. 130.

17. Until 1910, two assistants were normally present, but when a leak of conference proceedings was suspected, they were excluded. See Abraham, *Judicial Process,* p. 230.

18. Robert G. McCloskey, *The American Supreme Court* (Chicago: University of Chicago Press, 1960), p. 32.

19. Quoted from Joseph Alsop and Turner Catledge, *The 168 Days,* in Scigliano, *Supreme Court and the Presidency,* p. 75.

20. See Ibid., pp. 76–77.

21. See Abraham, *Judicial Process,* pp. 251–53.

22. Ibid., p. 253.

23. Bob Woodward and Scott Armstrong, *The Brethren: Inside the Supreme Court* (New York: Simon & Schuster, 1979), pp. 79–80.

24. William O. Douglas, *The Court Years 1939–1975* (New York: Random House, 1980), pp. 167–68.

25. Quoted in Baum, *Supreme Court,* p. 127.

26. Douglas, *Court Years,* p. 4.

27. See Robert A. Dahl, "The Supreme Court's Role in National Policy-Making," in *American Court Systems: Readings in Judicial Process and Behavior* ed. Sheldon Goldman and Austin Sarat (San Francisco: W. H. Freeman, 1978), p. 617.

28. Scigliano, *Supreme Court and the Presidency,* pp. 95, 111.

29. Baum, *Supreme Court,* p. 60.

30. Ibid., p. 46.

31. Abraham, *Judicial Process,* pp. 351–52.

32. On the Andrew Johnson incident, see Walter F. Murphy, *Congress and the Court* (Chicago: University of Chicago Press, 1962), p. 35.

33. Ibid., pp. 245–46.

34. Douglas, *Court Years,* pp. 114–15.

35. Abraham, *Judicial Process,* p. 222.

36. Baum, *Supreme Court,* pp. 100, 128.

37. See Ibid., p. 23.

38. Ibid., pp. 160, 168.

39. Ibid., p. 2.

40. Martin Shapiro, "The Supreme Court: From Warren to Burger," in *The New American Political System,* ed. Anthony King (Washington: American Enterprise Institute, 1979), pp. 180–81.

41. Among the recent conceptual discussions of the general issue of judicial review by law professors are Alexander Bickel, *The Least Dangerous Branch* (Indianapolis: Bobbs-Merrill, 1962); John Hart Ely, *Democracy and Distrust* (Cambridge: Harvard University Press, 1980); and Michael J. Perry, *The Constitution, the Courts, and Human Rights* (New Haven: Yale University Press, 1982).

42. Quoted in Abraham, *Judicial Process,* p. 295.

43. Quoted in H. N. Hirsch, *The Enigma of Felix Frankfurter* (New York: Basic Books, 1981), p. 172.

44. McCloskey, *American Supreme Court,* p. 128.

45. Quoted in Bickel, *Least Dangerous Branch,* p. 90.

46. Ibid., p. 3 and Scigliano, *Supreme Court and the Presidency,* p. 25.

47. Vagueness is not, however, inconsistent with the doctrine of "judicial restraint," which argues that the Supreme Court should be very hesitant about ever striking down democratically adopted legislation.

48. McCloskey, *American Supreme Court,* pp. 26, 221.

49. Bickel, *Least Dangerous Branch,* p. 90.

50. Perry, *Constitution and Human Rights,* p. 114.

51. Abraham, *Judicial Process,* p. 146.

52. See, for example, Glendon Schubert, *The Judicial Mind* (Evanston: Northwestern University Press, 1965).

53. Scigliano, *Supreme Court and the Presidency,* p. 157.

Chapter 7

1. Max Weber, "Bureaucracy," in *From Max Weber: Essays in Sociology,* ed. H.H. Gerth and C. Wright Mills (New York: Oxford University Press, 1958), p. 214.

2. See Harvey Leibenstein, *Beyond Economic Man* (Cambridge: Harvard University Press, 1976), Ch. 1.

3. Jeffrey Pressman and Aaron Wildavsky, *Implementation* (Berkeley: University of California Press, 1973).

4. Ibid., p. xviii.

5. It may be noted that the advantages of specialization may be reaped by discrete marketplace exchange as well as by the establishment of organizations. Individual chemists hire individual lawyers when they need them, outside any organizational setting. Dupont has both chemists and lawyers working in the same organization. For a discussion of the conditions that promote establishment of organizations rather than use of marketplace exchange to achieve the advantages of specialization, see Oliver E. Williamson, *Markets and Hierarchies* (New York: Free Press, 1975), especially Ch. 2–3.

6. I have been very influenced in what follows by materials appearing in Henry Mintzberg, *The Structuring of Organizations* (Englewood Cliffs: Prentice Hall, 1979), idem, *The Nature of Managerial Work,* 2nd ed. (New York: Robert E. Krieger Publishing, 1980), idem, *Leadership* (New York: McGraw-Hill, 1979); and Jay Galbraith, *Designing Complex Organizations* (Reading, Mass.: Addison-Wesley, 1973).

7. See Steven Kelman, *Regulating America, Regulating Sweden: A Comparative Study of Occupational Safety and Health Policy* (Cambridge: MIT Press, 1981), pp. 180–82.

8. David C. Rikert, "McDonald's Corporation" (Cambridge: Harvard Business School, 1980).

9. Steven Kelman, "Revenue Recycling: An Implementation Plan" (Harvard University: Energy and Environmental Policy Center, Discussion Paper H83-01, 1983), pp. 69, 81–82.

10. This example comes from James D. Thompson, *Organizations in Action* (New York: McGraw-Hill, 1967), p. 22.

11. Steven Kelman, "Using Implementation Research to Address Implementation Problems: The Case of Energy Emergency Assistance," *Journal of Policy Analysis and Management* 4 (Fall 1984): 87.

12. This argument was first made by Alvin W. Gouldner, *Patterns of Industrial Bureaucracy* (New York: Free Press, 1954), Ch. 9.

13. Tana Pesso, "Local Welfare Offices: Managing the Intake Process," *Public Policy* 26 (Spring 1978): 10.

14. Frederick C. Mosher, *Democracy and the Public Service* (New York: Oxford University Press, 1982), p. 103.

15. Mintzberg, *Structuring of Organizations*, p. 5.

16. Karl Weick, "Educational Organizations as Loosely Coupled Systems," *Administrative Science Quarterly* 21 (March 1976): pp. 1–19.

17. See pp. 104–105.

18. Chester I. Barnard, *The Functions of the Executive* (Cambridge: Harvard University Press, 1938), p. 77.

19. Leibenstein, *Beyond Economic Man*, pp. 34–37.

20. Ibid., p. 98.

21. Barnard, *Functions of the Executive*, pp. 167–69.

22. On employment contracts as incomplete contracts, see Williamson, *Markets and Hierarchies*, Ch. 4.

23. See pp. 31–32.

24. Jonathan Brock, *Managing People in Public Agencies* (Boston: Little, Brown, 1984), p. 79.

25. Quoted in ibid., p. 81.

26. Andrew Weiss, "Simple Truths About Japanese Manufacturing," *Harvard Business Review* 62 (July 1984): 122.

27. Terrence E. Deal and Allen A. Kennedy, *Corporate Cultures* (Reading, Mass.: Addison-Wesley, 1982).

28. James Q. Wilson, *Varieties of Police Behavior* (Cambridge: Harvard University Press, 1968), Ch. 5–6.

29. George Strauss and Leonard R. Sayles, *Personnel,* 4th ed. (Englewood Cliffs: Prentice Hall, 1980), p. 251.

30. Herbert Kaufman, *The Forest Ranger* (Baltimore: Johns Hopkins University Press, 1960), pp. 175–97.

31. Deal and Kennedy, *Corporate Cultures,* p. 107.

32. James Q. Wilson, *The Investigators* (New York: Basic Books, 1978).

33. Thomas D. Powers, *The Man Who Kept the Secrets: Richard Helms and the CIA* (New York: Knopf, 1979).

34. Harvey M. Sapolsky, *The Polaris System Development* (Cambridge: Harvard University Press, 1972), p. 46. See also pp. 18, 44–45.

35. This theme was discussed earlier in connection with political decisions made by agencies. See p. 106.

36. See Wilson, *Investigators*, pp. 13–14; Barnard, *Functions of the Executive*, p. 87; and Phillip Selznick, *Leadership in Administration* (Evanston, Ill.: Row, Peterson, 1951).

37. Occupational Safety and Health Act (P.L. 91-596), Section 2(b).

38. Age Discrimination in Employment Act (P.L. 90-202), Section 2(b).

39. Interestingly, private organizations frequently establish statements of mission as well. AT&T traditionally saw its mission as providing service for everyone, no matter where they lived; Sears defined its mission as providing "quality at a good price," selling to middle-income people who were price-conscious but did not want the bottom of the line either. See Deal and Kennedy, *Corporate Cultures*, p. 23.

40. Sapolsky, *Polaris System*, p. 46.

41. John Dilluo, "Can Prisons Be Improved?" (Ph.D. diss., Harvard University, 1986).

42. On the issues to be discussed in the rest of this section, an excellent source is Strauss and Sayles, *Personnel*.

43. See F. J. Roethlisberger and W. J. Dickson, *Management and The Worker* (Cambridge: Harvard University Press, 1939); Frederick Herzberg, "One More Time: How Do You Motivate Employees?" *Harvard Business Review* 46 (January 1968); and Rensis Likert, *New Patterns of Management* (New York: McGraw-Hill, 1961).

44. Edward E. Lawler, III, *Pay and Organizational Effectiveness* (New York: McGraw-Hill, 1971).

45. Brock, *Managing People*, pp. 20–22.

46. Paul E. Mott, *The Characteristics of Effective Organizations* (New York: Harper & Row, 1972), p. 71.

47. Quoted in Dorothy L. Robyn, "Capturing Lessons Learned" (Cambridge: stencil, 1985), p. 4.

48. Bruce Buchanan, II, "Government Managers, Business Executives, and Organizational Committment, '*Public Administration Review*, 34 (July 1974), pp. 341–42.

49. Neal Gross et al., *Implementing Organizational Innovations* (New York: Basic Books, 1971), pp. 10–15.

50. Pressman and Wildavsky, *Implementation*, p. 107.

51. See Steven Kelman, *Improving Doctor Performance: A Study in the Use of Information and Organizational Change* (New York: Human Sciences Press, 1980), pp. 58–59.

52. See Richard E. Neustadt and Harvey Fineberg, *The Epidemic That Never Was* (New York: Vintage, 1983), especially Ch. 12.

53. See Kelman, "Revenue Recycling."

54. See, for example, Warren Bennis, *Changing Organizations* (New York: McGraw-Hill, 1966); Daniel Katz and Robert L. Kahn, *The Social Psychology of Organizations*, 2nd ed. (New York: Wiley, 1978), Ch. 19–20; Paul R. Lawrence, "How to Deal with Resistance to Change," in Harvard Business Review, *On Management* (New York: Harper & Row, 1976); John S. Morgan, *Managing Change* (New York: McGraw-Hill, 1972); and Leonard R. Sayles, *Leadership*, (New York: McGraw-Hill, 1979), Ch. 9.

55. Stephen B. Hitchner, "The Academic Calendar Problem" (Cambridge: Harvard University, Kennedy School of Government, 1977).

56. See Kelman, *Doctor Performance*, pp. 126–27.

57. See Kelman, "Using Implementation Research," p. 84.

58. Wilson, *Investigators,* pp. 84–85.

59. Suzanne Weaver, "The Antitrust Division" in *The Politics of Regulation,* ed. James Q. Wilson (New York: Basic Books, 1980).

60. For accounts, see Mark H. Moore, "The Fourth Platoon" (Cambridge: Harvard University, Kennedy School of Government, 1971) and Jerry E. Mechling, "A Successful Innovation: Manpower Scheduling," *Urban Analysis* 3 (1974).

61. Mechling, "Successful Innovation," p. 298.

62. See Stephen B. Hitchner et al., "Federal Trade Commission (B)" (Cambridge: Harvard University, Kennedy School of Government, 1976).

63. See Mark H. Moore et al., "Patrick Murphy and Police Corruption" (Cambridge: Harvard University, Kennedy School of Government, 1973).

64. Pesso, *Local Welfare Offices,* p. 309.

65. See pp. 169–170.

66. Harvey M. Sapolsky, "America's Socialized Medicine: The Allocation of Resources Within the Veteran's Health Care System," *Public Policy* 25 (Summer 1977): 359–82.

67. On the organizational culture of CIA covert operatives, compared with that of spies and analysts in the same organization, see Powers, *The Man Who.*

68. Ernest R. May et al., "Kennedy and the Bay of Pigs" (Cambridge: Harvard University, Kennedy School of Government, 1983).

Chapter 8

1. See pp. 111–112.

2. Philip Jarymiszynx et al., "Chief Executive Background and Firm Performance" in *The Uneasy Alliance: Managing the Productivity-Technology Dilemma,* ed. Kim B. Clark et al. (Boston: Harvard Business School Press, 1986), p. 127.

3. Ibid., p. 131.

4. Hugh Heclo, *A Government of Strangers,* (Washington: The Brookings Institution, 1977), pp. 103–4.

5. For a discussion of the operation of the "rule of three" in practice, see Jonathan Brock, *Managing People in Public Agencies* (Boston: Little, Brown, 1984), pp. 81–124.

6. The President's Reorganization Project, *Personnel Management Project,* v. 1 (Washington: stencil, 1977), p. 35.

7. These results are reported, for 1979, in Dennis L. Dresang, *Public Personnel Management and Public Policy* (Boston: Little, Brown, 1984), p. 247 and for 1983 in Merit Systems Protection Board, *Report on the Significant Actions of Personnel Management During 1982* (Washington: Merit Systems Protection Board, 1983), p. 81.

8. Merit Systems Protection Board, *Report,* p. 69.

9. E. S. Savas and Sigmund G. Ginsburg make the point in "The Civil Service: A Meritless System?" in *Classics of Public Personnel Policy,* ed. Frank J. Thompson (Oak Park, Ill.: Moore Publishing, 1979), pp. 218–19.

10. Andrew S. Grove, *High Output Management* (New York: Random House, 1983), pp. 17–18.

11. Robert N. Anthony and David W. Young, *Management Control in Non-Profit Organizations,* 3rd ed. (Homewood, Ill.: Richard D. Irwin, 1985), p. 474.

12. James Q. Wilson, *Varieties of Police Behavior* (Cambridge: Harvard University Press, 1968), pp. 97–98.

13. For a discussion, see B. Guy Peters, "Administrative Change and the Grace Commission," in *The Unfinished Agenda for Civil Service Reform,* ed. Charles H. Levine (Washington: The Brookings Institution, 1985), pp. 24–26.

14. Ibid., p. 24.

15. Gary P. Latham and Kenneth N. Wexley, *Increasing Productivity Through Performance Appraisal* (Reading, Mass.: Addison-Wesley, 1981), p. 3.

16. Edward E. Lawler, III, *Pay and Organizational Effectiveness* (New York: McGraw-Hill, 1961), p. 158.

17. The material in this section is based on F. F. Ridley, ed., *Government and Administration in Western Europe* (New York: St. Martin's Press, 1979); Bruce L. R. Smith, ed., *The Higher Civil Service in Europe and in Canada: Lessons for the United States* (Washington: The Brookings Institution, 1984); Ezra Suleiman, *Politics, Power and Bureaucracy in France* (Princeton: Princeton University Press, 1974); and Statens Arbetsgivarverk, *Författningar om statligt reglerade tjänster* (*Regulations on Government Employment*) (Stockholm: Liber Förlag, 1984).

18. Suleiman, *Politics in France,* p. 144.

19. Leonard D. White, *The Jeffersonians: A Study in Administrative History 1801– 1829* (New York: Macmillan, 1951), p. 8.

20. See Leonard D. White, *The Jacksonians: A Study in Administrative History 1801–1861* (New York: Macmillan, 1954), pp. 300–301.

21. Quoted in ibid., p. 319.

22. See, generally, Leonard D. White, *The Republican Era: A Study in Administrative History 1869–1901* (New York: Macmillan, 1958).

23. See Congressional Research Service, *History of Civil Service Merit Systems of the United States and Selected Foreign Countries* (Washington: Government Printing Office, 1976), pp. 3, 182–87.

24. White, *Republican Era,* p. 341.

25. Ibid., p. 341.

26. Ibid., p. 344

27. Ibid, pp. 353–55.

28. See, generally, White, *Jacksonians,* Ch. 20.

29. James Q. Wilson, *Varieties of Police Behavior,* pp. 96–97.

30. Wallace S. Sayre, "The Triumphs of Techniques Over Purpose," reprinted in Thompson, ed., *Public Personnel Policy,* pp. 30–35.

31. See Committee on Post Office and Civil Service, *Civil Service Reform* (U.S. House of Representatives, 95th Congress, 2nd Session, Serial No. 93–95), for example, pp. 7, 160, 170, and a number of other locations.

32. For the changes in the various stages of the civil service reform process, see *Personnel Management Project,* and Committee on Post Office and Civil Service, *Civil Service Reform Act of 1978* (House Report No. 95-14003, 9th Congress, 2nd Session). I am also grateful to Alan K. Campbell for help in sorting out the changes.

33. U.S. Merit Systems Protection Board, *The 1984 Report on the Senior Executive Service* (Washington: Merit Systems Protection Board, 1984), p. 32 and U.S. General Accounting Office, *An Assessment of SES Performance Appraisal Systems,* GGD-84-16 (Washington: General Accounting Office, 1984), p. 24.

34. General Accounting Office, *Assessment,* p. 26.

35. Anne H. Hastings and Larry S. Beyna, "Managing for Improved Performance: Evaluating the Civil Service Reform Act" in *Performance and Credibility: Developing Excellence in Public and Nonprofit Organizations,* ed. Joseph S. Wholey et al. (Lexington, Mass.: Heath, 1986), p. 176.

36. Edie N. Goldenberg, "The Permanent Government in an Era of Retrenchment and Redirection," in *The Reagan Presidency and the Governing of America,* ed. Lester M. Salamon and Michael S. Lund (Washington: The Urban Institute Press, 1985), p. 400.

37. See Edie N. Goldenberg, "The Grace Commission and Civil Service Reform: Seeking a Common Understanding," in Levine, ed., *Unfinished Agenda,* p. 76. For survey results on perceived biases in the award of bonuses, see General Accounting Office, "Testimony of the Comptroller General on the Impact of the Senior Executive Service," GGD-84-32 (Washington: General Accounting Office, 1983), p. 304.

38. See Hastings and Beyna, *Improved Performance,* p. 178.

39. See General Accounting Office, "Testimony," p. 5.

40. See Office of Personnel Management, "Performance Management System," *Federal Register* 48 (October 25, 1983), pp. 49472–92.

41. See, for example, Robert Joyce, *Performance Incentives Work: The Navy's Performance Contingent Reward System* (Washington: Office of Personnel Management, 1981).

42. See Office of Performance Management, "Status of the Evaluation of the Navy Personnel Management Demonstration Project" (Washington: Office of Personnel Management, stencil, 1984).

Chapter 9

1. William K. Muir, Jr., *Legislature: California's School for Politics* (Berkeley: University of California Press, 1982).

2. Alexander Hamilton et al., *The Federalist* (New York: Modern Library, 1937), p. 337.

3. See Robert A. Dahl, *A Preface to Democratic Theory* (Chicago: University of Chicago Press, 1956).

4. See ibid., p. 104.

5. James Buchanan and Gordon Tullock, *The Calculus of Consent* (Ann Arbor: University of Michigan Press, 1962), p. 138.

6. See Edward L. Deci, *Intrinsic Motivation* (New York: Plenum Press, 1975).

7. See, for example, Dennis H. Robertson, *Economic Commentaries* (London: Staples Press, 1956). A good discussion of these issues appears in Albert O. Hirschman, "Against Parsimony," *Economics and Philosophy,* 1 (April 1985): 16–19.

8. Cited in Robert N. Bellah et al., *Habits of the Heart* (Berkeley: University of California Press, 1985), pp. 253–54.

9. Alexis de Tocqueville, *Democracy in America,* v. 1 (New York: Vintage Books, 1945), p. 334.

10. Robert K. Merton, *Social Theory and Social Structure,* rev., enlarged ed. (New York: Free Press, 1957), pp. 50–64.

11. For arguments of this sort, see Aaron Wildavsky, *The Politics of the Budgetary Process,* 4th ed. (Boston: Little, Brown, 1984), pp. 156–71; Edward C. Banfield, *Political Influence* (New York: Free Press, 1961), Ch. 12; and Charles E. Lindblom, *The Intelligence of Democracy* (New York: Free Press, 1965).

12. Wildavsky, *Budgetary Process,* p. 66.

13. See William Kornhauser, *The Politics of Mass Society* (Glencoe: Free Press,

1959). I am indebted to Eugene Bardach for bringing a version of this point forcefully to my attention.

14. Nathan Glazer, "Interests and Passions," *The Public Interest* no. 81 (Fall 1985): 27.

Chapter 10

1. Karl Marx and Frederick Engels, *The German Ideology* (New York: International Publishers, 1947), p. 39.

2. Gabriel Kolko, *The Triumph of Conservatism* (New York: Free Press, 1963).

3. See Frances Fox Piven and Richard Cloward, *Regulating the Poor* (New York: Pantheon, 1971).

4. Gordon Tulluck, "What Is To Be Done?" in *Budgets and Bureaucrats: The Sources of Government Growth,* ed. Thomas E. Borcherding (Durham: Duke University Press, 1977), p. 285. See also Winston C. Bush and Arthur T. Denzau, "The Behavior of Bureaucrats and Public Sector Growth," in ibid.; and James M. Buchanan, *The Limits of Liberty: Between Anarchy and Leviathan* (Chicago: University of Chicago Press, 1975), p. 160.

5. William A. Niskanen, Jr., *Bureaucracy and Representative Government* (Chicago: Aldine, 1971), pp. 38–39.

6. David R. Mayhew, *Congress: The Electoral Connection* (New Haven: Yale University Press, 1974) and Morris P. Fiorina, *Congress: Keystone of the Washington Establishment* (New Haven: Yale University Press, 1977).

7. E. S. Savas, *Privatizing the Public Sector: How to Shrink Government* (Chatham, N.J.: Chatham House Publishers, 1982), pp. 134–35.

8. James Buchanan and Gordon Tullock, *The Calculus of Consent* (Ann Arbor: University of Michigan Press, 1962), p. 20.

9. Gordon Tullock, "Public Choice in Practice," in *Collective Decision Making,* ed. Clifford S. Russell (Baltimore: Johns Hopkins University Press, 1979), pp. 31, 33.

10. Anthony Downs, *An Economic Theory of Democracy* (New York: Harper & Brothers, 1957), and Buchanan and Tullock, *The Calculus of Consent.*

11. Downs, *Economic Theory of Democracy,* pp. 27–28.

12. Buchanan and Tullock, *The Calculus of Consent,* p. 20.

13. Gordon Tullock, *The Vote Motive* (London: The Institute for Economic Affairs, 1976), p. 5.

14. James M. Buchanan, "Politics, Policy, and the Pigovian Margins," in *Theory of Public Choice,* ed. James M. Buchanan and Robert D. Tollison (Ann Arbor: University of Michigan Press, 1972), p. 174.

15. Buchanan and Tullock, *The Calculus of Consent,* pp. 135–140.

16. Mancur Olson, *The Logic of Collective Action* (Cambridge: Harvard University Press, 1965).

17. George J. Stigler, "The Theory of Economic Regulation," *Bell Journal of Economics and Management Science* 2 (1971): 3–21.

18. An interesting example is Brian Barry, *Political Argument* (New York: The Humanities Press, 1976), pp. 250–56. Another is Richard A. Musgrave, "Leviathan Cometh: or Does He?" in *Tax and Expenditure Limitations,* ed. Helen F. Ladd and T. Nicholaus Tideman (Washington: The Urban Institute Press, 1981).

19. See Jane Allyn Piliavin et al., *Emergency Intervention* (New York: Academic Press, 1981), p. 47 and generally, Ch. 3.

20. Martin L. Hoffman, "The Development of Empathy," in *Altruism and Helping Behavior,* ed. J. Philippe Rushton and Richard M. Sorrentino (Hillsdale, N.J.: Lawrence Erlbaum Associates, 1981), p. 44.

21. See Piliavin et al., *Emergency Intervention,* p. 164 and, generally, Ch. 7.

22. See Ibid., p. 45.

23. See Edward O. Wilson, *Sociobiology,* abr. ed. (Cambridge: Harvard University Press, 1980), Ch. 5, and Donald T. Campbell, "On the Genetics of Altruism and the Counter-Hedonic Components in Human Culture," *Journal of Social Issues* 27 (1972): 27.

24. See Philip B. Heymann, "The Two Worlds of Public Choice" (Cambridge: unpublished manuscript, 1986).

25. Hoffman, "Development of Empathy," p. 55.

26. Joseph A. Carens, *Equality, Moral Incentives and the Market* (Chicago: University of Chicago Press, 1981), p. 123.

27. Peter Singer, *The Expanding Circle: Ethics and Sociobiology* (New York: Farrar, Straus & Giroux, 1981), pp. 89–90.

28. William A. Kelso, *American Democratic Theory* (Westport, Ct.: Greenwood Press, 1978), p. 183.

29. For a discussion in another context, see pp. 25–27.

30. Emile Durkheim, *The Elementary Forms of Religious Life* (New York: Macmillan, 1915).

31. Thomas C. Schelling, "The Intimate Struggle for Self-Command," *The Public Interest* 60 (Summer 1980).

32. James M. Buchanan, "Politics, Policy," p. 177.

33. See pp. 21–23.

34. James Tobin, "On Limiting the Domain of Inequality," *Journal of Law and Economics* 13 (October 1970): 269.

35. Robert K. Merton, *Mass Persuasion: The Social Psychology of a War Bond Drive* (New York: Harper & Brothers, 1946).

Chapter 11

1. Richard A. Musgrave, "Leviathan Cometh: or Does He?" in *Tax and Expenditure Limitations,* ed. Helen F. Ladd and T. Nicholaus Tideman (Washington: The Urban Institute Press, 1981), pp. 77–81. (The argument is similar to the one economists make against the notion that oligopoly pricing or large corporate profits explain inflation: inflation is an increase of prices, and unless one can demonstrate that oligopolization has increased during the period of inflation, any effect of oligopolies on the price level will have already occurred previously.)

2. See R. Douglas Arnold, "The Local Roots of Domestic Policy," in *The New Congress,* ed. Thomas E. Mann and Norman Ornstein (Washington: American Enterprise Institute, 1981), pp. 281–83.

3. See Martha Derthick and Paul J. Quirk, *The Politics of Deregulation* (Washington: The Brookings Institution, 1985).

4. In other democratic countries, to a greater extent than in the United States, to be sure.

5. See Anthony Downs, *An Economic Theory of Democracy* (New York: Harper & Brothers, 1957), pp. 265–73.

6. William H. Riker and Peter C. Ordeshook, "A Theory of the Calculus of Voting," *American Political Science Review* 62 (March 1968): 25–42.

7. Brian Barry, *Sociologists, Economists and Democracy* (Chicago: University of Chicago Press, 1978), pp. 17–18.

8. See p. 65.

9. David Mayhew, *Congress: The Electoral Connection* (New Haven: Yale University Press, 1974), pp. 124–25.

10. Ibid., p. 125.

11. Morris P. Fiorina, *Congress: Keystone of the Washington Establishment* (New Haven: Yale University Press, 1977). Economists often posit theories that do not require conscious awareness in order to guide an actor's behavior. Businessmen, for example, need not be familiar with marginal productivity wage determination for the theory of marginal productivity to explain wages. But in such cases, this is so because market pressures bearing on individuals require behavior corresponding to the theory, even absent conscious understanding. This does not apply to Fiorina's theory, because there are no impersonal pressures to produce the behavior he hypothesizes. If nobody in Washington was smart enough to hatch Professor Fiorina's conspiracy, it never got hatched, period.

12. Gerald H. Kramer, "Short-Term Fluctuations in U.S. Voting Behavior, 1896–1964," *American Political Science Review* 65 (March 1971): 131–43, and Samuel I. Popkin et al., "What Have You Done For Me Lately? Toward An Investment Theory of Voting," *American Political Science Review* 70 (September 1976): 779–805.

13. A prescient early discussion of this issue, which emphasized ethnic variations in voting behavior driven by public spirit, is James Q. Wilson, "Public-Regardingness as a Value Premise in Voting Behavior," *American Political Science Review* 58 (December 1964): 876–87.

14. Donald R. Kinder and D. Roderick Kiewiet, "Economic Discontent and Political Behavior: The Role of Personal Grievances and Collective Economic Judgments in Congressional Voting," *American Journal of Political Science* 23 (August 1979): 495–527. See also Donald R. Kinder, "Presidents, Prosperity and Public Opinion," *Public Opinion Quarterly* 45 (Spring 1981): 1–21.

15. David O. Sears et al., "Whites' Opposition of Busing: Self-Interest or Symbolic Politics?" *American Political Science Review* 73 (June 1979): 369–84; Richard R. Lau et al., "Self-Interest and Civilians' Attitudes Toward the Vietnam War," *Public Opinion Quarterly* 42 (Winter 1978): 464–83; and David O. Sears et al., "Self-Interest vs. Symbolic Politics in Policy Attitudes and Presidential Voting," *American Political Science Review* 74 (September 1980); 670–84.

16. Bruce M. Russett and Elizabeth C. Hanson, *Interest and Ideology: The Foreign Policy Beliefs of American Business* (San Francisco: W. H. Freeman, 1975), pp. 123–24.

17. A word is in order about some alternate ways to account for these phenomena, which appear prominently in the political science literature reporting the findings. Sears, reflecting his own background in social psychological research on socialization, presents the alternative to the self-interest explanation. He criticizes what he calls a "symbolic politics" explanation. Rather than seeing views as driven by ideas about what kinds of policies are right, he suggests they may largely be noncognitive affective responses based on early childhood socialization. Sears recognizes that this view is neither supported nor disconfirmed by the data he has available, and he presents it as a speculation. It is not possible to know exactly how much of this is going on, but a number

of observations are in order. First, the childhood socialization view would hardly account for the parallel data by Kinder and his colleagues on views of the performance of the economy and voting behavior, since views of economic performance clearly change over time, in response to actual performance, and have a minor symbolic component. Furthermore, Sears's data show that "sophisticated" respondents (those with high degrees of political knowledge and interest) are more influenced in their attitudes by nonself-interest factors. If these nonself-interest factors reflected childhood socialization rather than cognitions about what policies were right, we would expect the opposite effect, because it is the less sophisticated who are more likely atavistically to stick with childhood indoctrination. Finally, the political socialization literature suggests that considerable attitude change does take place in the late adolescent and early adult years, when people are clearly capable of independent thought. In one panel study involving 17-year-olds and their parents, interviewed in 1965 and again in 1972, the correlation between party identification over time for the young people was .40, considerably less than the .69 correlation for their parents, indicating that greater changes in party identification had occurred among them over the period. In addition, views on issues are far less stable as between parent and children than is party identification. A second issue discussed in the political science literature on this question is the influence of self-reliant ideologies on dampening the connection between self-interest and political attitudes. The unemployed may not be likely to favor government jobs programs because they believe that they, not the government, have the responsibility for coping with their problems. I do not have any quarrel with this suggestion, which is backed by a fair amount of empirical data, but I would note, first, that such self-reliance is an example of a general idea (and not a selfish one) about what policies government should follow, and, second, that we still need to account for the behavior of those citizens, unemployed or not, who *do* favor government intervention.

18. Russell Hardin, *Collective Action* (Washington: Resources for the Future, 1982), p. 124.

19. See p. 105.

20. Russett and Hanson, *Interest and Ideology*, p. 117.

21. See Harold D. Lasswell, *Psychopathology and Politics* (Chicago: University of Chicago Press, 1977), James David Barber, *The Lawmakers: Recruitment and Adaptation of Legislative Life* (New Haven: Yale University Press, 1965), and Richard F. Fenno, *Congressmen in Committees* (Boston: Little, Brown, 1973).

22. For a study emphasizing this finding, see Robert H. Salisbury, "The Urban Party Organization Member," *Public Opinio Quarterly* 29 (Winter 1965–66): 550–64. See also Barber, *The Lawmakers.*

23. Robert E. Lane, *Political Man: Why and How People Get Involved in Politics* (New York: Free Press, 1959), p. 127.

24. See W. Lloyd Warner et al., *The American Federal Executive* (New Haven: Yale University Press, 1963), Ch. 13.

25. U. S. Merit Systems Protection Board, *The 1984 Report on the Senior Executive Service* (Washington: Merit Systems Protection Board, 1984), p. 15.

26. Edward E. Lawler, III, *Pay and Organizational Effectiveness: A Psychological View* (New York: McGraw-Hill, 1971), pp. 55–56. Lawler notes that at least some of this may be attributable to a reduction of cognitive dissonance that occurs after coming to the job, rather than to motivations that lead one to the job in the first place.

27. Dean E. Mann and James W. Doig, *The Assistant Secretaries* (Washington: The Brookings Institution, 1965), pp. 162–64.

28. See David P. Campbell, *Handbook for the Strong Vocational Interest Blank* (Stanford: Stanford University Press, 1971). To determine what answers incline a student toward given occupations, the test is first administered to a "sample of successful, satisfied men performing (an) occupation in a typical manner." The more a student's answers resemble those of people already in the jobs, the more inclined they are seen as being for the job. (Ibid., p. 25.)

29. Erving Goffman, *Frame Analysis: An Essay on the Organization of Experience* (Cambridge: Harvard University Press, 1974), p. 8.

30. Amos Tversky and Daniel Kahneman, "The Framing of Decisions and the Psychology of Choice," *Science,* 211 (January 30, 1981), pp. 453–58.

31. See Jane Allyn Piliavin et al., *Emergency Intervention* (New York: Academic Press, 1981), pp. 139–40.

32. See Ervin Staub, *Positive Social Behavior and Morality,* v. 1 (New York: Academic Press, 1978), p. 78.

33. Jacqueline R. Macaulay, "A Shill for Charity," in *Altruism and Helping Behavior,* in ed. J. Macaulay and L. Berkowitz (New York: Academic Press, 1970), p. 43. See also Ervin Staub, *Positive Social Behavior,* pp. 198–220.

34. See Dennis L. Krebs, "Altruism: An Examination of the Concepts and a Review of the Literature," *Psychological Bulletin* 73 (1970), pp. 268, 272.

35. Morris P. Fiorina and Charles R. Plott, "Committee Decisions Under Majority Rule: an Experimental Study," *American Political Science Review* 72 (June 1978), pp. 575–98.

36. Ibid., p. 578.

37. Murray Edelman, *The Symbolic Uses of Politics* (Urbana: University of Illinois Press, 1964).

38. Steven Kelman, *Regulating America, Regulating Sweden: A Comparative Study of Occupational Safety and Health Policy* (Cambridge: MIT Press, 1981), Ch. 4.

Chapter 12

1. Seymour Martin Lipset and William Schneider, *The Confidence Gap* (New York: Free Press, 1983), p. 345.

2. See pp. 4–5.

3. H. Brinton Milward and Hal G. Rainey, "Don't Blame the Bureaucracy!" *Journal of Public Policy* 3 (May 1983): 150.

4. See B. Guy Peters, "Administrative Change and the Grace Commission," in *The Unfinished Agenda for Civil Service Reform,* ed. Charles H. Levine (Washington: The Brookings Institution, 1985), p. 25.

5. I examined ten such horror stories highlighted by the Grace Commission itself in a press release accompanying the issuance of their report. See "The Grace Commission: How Much Waste in Government?" *The Public Interest* no. 78 (Winter 1985). The examples given are taken from that article.

6. Daniel Katz et al., *Bureaucratic Encounters: A Pilot Study in the Evaluation of Government Services* (Ann Arbor: Institute for Social Research, 1975), p. 64.

7. Ibid., pp. 118, 135.

8. See, for example, Robert J. Samuelson, "Regan Seeks His Rightful Place Among the Economic Policy Makers," *National Journal* 13 (March 28, 1981), p.

534. Asked about his biggest surprise in coming to Washington, Donald Regan, who had been chief of Merrill Lynch, responded, "The long hours people work for so little money . . . at the top levels of government. Our people are in here by 7:30 in the morning, certainly by 8. When I left last night at twenty of eight, there were still people around here working, which is a 13-hour day."

9. Katz et al., *Bureaucratic Encounters*, p. 102.

10. Ibid., p. 133.

11. Jeffrey L. Pressman and Aaron B. Wildavsky, *Implementation* (Berkeley: University of California Press, 1973), pp. 126–27.

12. Laurence E. Lynn, Jr., *Managing the Public's Business* (New York: Basic Books, 1981), p. 181.

13. Frederick V. Malek, *Washington's Hidden Tragedy: The Failure to Make Government Work* (New York: Free Press, 1978), p. 106.

14. Alfred D. Chandler, Jr., *Strategy and Structure: Chapters in the History of the American Industrial Enterprise* (Cambridge: MIT Press, 1962).

15. Kelman, "Grace Commission," especially pp. 70–71, 76–77. Of course, the dangers of identification with outside professional communities, both in the political and implementation processes, should be kept in mind as well. See pp. 105–107, 154.

16. I should add three caveats. One is that political choices will continue to need to be directed toward the top of the organization. A second is that the coercive authority attached to decisions made during the production process, as well as demands for equity in treatment of citizens, will probably always require the relatively greater use of rules in government. A third is that people in the private sector who take risks receive far greater rewards should they succeed than are possible in the public sector. They also face far greater dangers (of bankruptcy or of being fired) if they fail. Since rewards will be less for success in the public sector, it is appropriate that penalties for failure be kept less extreme as well.

17. See above, pp. 169–70, 199–202.

18. Donald P. Warwick, *A Theory of Public Bureaucracy* (Cambridge: Harvard University Press, 1975), p. 85.

19. Leonard D. White, *The Republican Era: A Study in Administrative History 1869–1901* (New York: Macmillan, 1958), pp. 221, 256.

20. This idea originated with my colleague Hale Champion.

Chapter 13

1. Philip Kotler, *Marketing Management,* 3rd ed. (Englewood Cliffs: Prentice Hall, 1976), pp. 198–99.

2. See pp. 162–163.

3. Jeffrey L. Pressman and Aaron B. Wildavsky, *Implementation* (Berkeley: University of California Press, 1973), pp. 107–8.

4. See pp. 36–37.

5. For one example of such a poll, see the Harris survey reported in *Business Week* (Oct. 8, 1984), p. 64.

6. Seymour Martin Lipset and William Schneider, *The Confidence Gap* (New York: Free Press, 1983).

7. F. Christopher Arterton, "The Impact of Watergate on Children's Attitudes Towards Political Authority," *Political Science Quarterly* 89 (June 1974): 278.

8. See Lipset and Schneider, *Confidence Gap,* Ch. 12 and Seymour Martin Lipset, "Feeling Better: Measuring the Nation's Confidence," *Public Opinion* 8 (April 1985): 6–9.

9. This is of course analogous to the observation from the literature of voting behavior that younger voters are more influenced by short-term electoral forces than are older voters, whose partisan allegiance is more stable.

10. These percentages are calculated from tables appearing in Philip E. Converse et al., *American Social Attitudes Data Sourcebook 1947–1978* (Cambridge: Harvard University Press, 1980), pp. 31, 33.

11. Morris Janowitz, *The Reconstruction of Patriotism: Education for Civic Consciousness* (Chicago: University of Chicago Press, 1983), p. 153.

INDEX